PORTUGUESE STUDIES

Volume 37 Number 1
2021

Brazil in the Midst of Neoliberal Turmoil:
Devastation and Resistance

Guest Editor
Márcio Seligmann-Silva

Founding Editor
Helder Macedo

Editors
Jane-Marie Collins
Catarina Fouto
Tori Holmes
Paulo de Medeiros
Paul Melo e Castro
Hilary Owen
Emanuelle Santos
Claire Williams

Editorial Assistant
Richard Correll

Production Editor
Graham Nelson

MODERN HUMANITIES RESEARCH ASSOCIATION

PORTUGUESE STUDIES

A peer-reviewed biannual multi-disciplinary journal devoted to research on the cultures, literatures, history and societies of the Lusophone world

International Advisory Board

David Brookshaw
João de Pina Cabral
Ivo José de Castro
Thomas F. Earle
John Gledson
Anna Klobucka

Maria Manuel Lisboa
Kenneth Maxwell
Laura de Mello e Souza
Maria Irene Ramalho
Silviano Santiago

Portuguese Studies and other journals published by the MHRA may be ordered from Turpin Distribution (http://ebiz.turpin-distribution.com/).

The **Modern Humanities Research Association** was founded in Cambridge in 1918 and has become an international organization with members in all parts of the world. It is a registered charity number 1064670, and a company limited by guarantee, registered in England number 3446016. Its main object is to encourage advanced study and research in modern and medieval European languages, literatures, and cultures by its publication of journals, book series, and its Style Guide. Further information about the activities of the Association and individual membership may be obtained from the Membership Secretary, email membership@mhra.org.uk, or from the website at: **www.mhra.org.uk**

Disclaimer: Statements of fact and opinion in the content of *Portuguese Studies* are those of the respective authors and contributors and not of the journal editors or of the Modern Humanities Research Association (MHRA). MHRA makes no representation, express or implied, in respect of the accuracy of the material in this journal and cannot accept any legal responsibility or liability for any errors or omissions that may be made.

Parts of this work may be reproduced as permitted under legal provisions for fair dealing (or fair use) for the purposes of research, private study, criticism, or review, or when a relevant collective licensing agreement is in place. All other reproduction requires the written permission of the copyright holder who may be contacted at rights@mhra.org.uk.

ISSN 0267–5315 (print)   ISSN 2222–4270 (online)
ISBN 978-1-78188-147-7

© 2021 The Modern Humanities Research Association
Salisbury House, Station Road, Cambridge CB1 2LA, United Kingdom

Portuguese Studies vol. 37 no. 1

Brazil in the Midst of Neoliberal Turmoil: Devastation and Resistance

CONTENTS

Introduction Márcio Seligmann-Silva	1
Overcoming the Legacy of the Military Dictatorship through the National Truth Commission in Brazil: An Ongoing Debate Janaína De Almeida Teles	5
Challenges to Democracy in the Twenty-first Century: The Current Situation of Brazil – New Variations of the Same Dilemmas Eduardo C. B. Bittar	32
Torture: Notes and Perspectives in a Context of Governmental Support for Gross Violations of Human Rights in Brazil Paulo Endo	47
Millennium Starts: Morphological and Seminal Embryos of Contemporary Brazilian Literature Roberto Vecchi	58
The Predicament of Contemporary Brazilian Fiction and its Spatiotemporal Modalities Karl Erik Schøllhammer	75
The Arts as a Space of Memory and Resistance to Denialist Policies in Brazil Today Márcio Seligmann-Silva	88
From 'Flocking for Rights' to the Politics of Death: Indigenous Struggle and Indigenous Policy in Brazil (1980–2020) Oiara Bonilla and Artionka Capiberibe	102
Reviews	120
Abstracts	135

NOTES FOR CONTRIBUTORS

Articles to be considered for publication may be on any subject within the field but must not exceed 7,500 words, and should be submitted in a form ready for publication in English, sent as an email attachment to the Editorial Assistant at portuguese@mhra.org.uk.

Contributions whose standard of English is inadequate will be returned. Any quotations in Portuguese must be accompanied by an English translation. Submissions in Portuguese may be considered, but full peer review and publication will be conditional on provision of a satisfactory translation by or on behalf of the author. The Editorial Assistant may undertake translations on request for a reasonable charge.

Text and references should conform precisely to the conventions of the *MHRA Style Guide*, 3rd edn, 2013 (978-1-78188-009-8), £9.50, $19.00, €12.00, obtainable in print or online version from www.style.mhra.org.uk. All articles are subject to independent, anonymous peer review by experts in the field; authors receive written feedback on the editors' decision and guidance on any revisions required. *Portuguese Studies* regrets it must charge contributors for the cost of corrections in proof deemed excessive.

It is a condition of publication in this journal that authors of articles and reviews assign copyright, including electronic copyright, to the MHRA. Inter alia, this allows the General Editor to deal efficiently and consistently with requests from third parties for permission to reproduce material. The journal has been published simultaneously in printed and electronic form since January 2001. Permission, without fee, for authors to use their own material in other publications, after a reasonable period of time has elapsed, is not normally withheld. Authors may make closed-access deposit of accepted manuscripts in their academic institution's digital repository upon acceptance. Full open access to the accepted manuscript is permitted no sooner than 12 months following publication of the Contribution by the MHRA. Contributions may also be republished on authors' personal websites without seeking further permission from the Association, but no earlier than 12 months after publication by the MHRA.

Books for review should be sent to: Reviews Editor, *Portuguese Studies*, Dr Emanuelle Santos, Ashley Building, Department of Modern Languages, University of Birmingham, Edgbaston, Birmingham B15 2TT, email e.santos@bham.ac.uk.

Introduction

Márcio Seligmann-Silva

> Let us exploit our full critical and creative capacity
> to make colourful parachutes.
> Ailton Krenak, 2019

This dossier features seven contributions that compose a current portrait of Brazil from the viewpoint of the difficult construction of its democracy in the twenty-first century. The works cover different areas such as law, psychoanalysis, literary and image studies, human rights and the pressing indigenous issue. The proposal to present this multidisciplinary outline is founded on the idea that such transdisciplinarity alone is up to the task of minimally representing the complexity of twenty-first-century Brazil. The contemporary challenges, given that these lines are written in complete isolation due to the Covid-19 pandemic, extend beyond the frameworks of subject areas of knowledge and require interdisciplinary transcendence and dialogue. This dossier trusts in the critical and creative capacity of academic production and its strength in the face of new challenges that present themselves as seemingly insurmountable.

Starting out with the contribution from the historian Janaína Teles, we have a detailed view of a key moment in the struggle for the right to memory, justice and truth in relation to the past of Brazil's military dictatorship of 1964–85. The article stresses the role played by the relatives of dead and missing politicians in the attempt to set up a National Truth Commission, ultimately created in 2011 but with severe limitations, considering the country's needs. This chapter in the history of our democracy explains why Brazil still lags behind its Latin American neighbours when it comes to building spaces for expressing and hearing the testimonies of the dictatorship's victims, to constructing authentic justice aimed at investigating crimes against humanity, to creating spaces of memory and landmarks that guarantee the establishment of ethics and politics based on human rights. The 'logic of reconciliation' that guided the transition to democracy after 1985 enabled the constitution of a veritable legal and memory blockade, extending the state of exception beyond 1964–85. This obstruction of the work of justice and memory is largely responsible for the election in 2018 of a government that denies the crimes perpetrated by the dictatorship regime. Such denialism also underpins modern-day torture, as we see in the article in this dossier written by the psychoanalyst Paulo Endo.

The contribution from Eduardo Bittar, of the Law School of the University of São Paulo, focuses precisely on the current debility of Brazilian democracy. He stresses the precariousness of our political practice stemming from unconditional privileges granted to the economic sector, as a consequence of which 'instrumental reason is placed above anything else'. Such instrumental reasoning, which is perfectly consistent with neoliberalism, has been linked to a neoconservative agenda based on a series of 'retro-topias', as Bittar calls them, aiming at 'the preservation of family, of religious values, of order and of progress'. This movement culminates today in the militarization of politics, the persecution of political opponents, the criminalization of politics, the moralization of public debate and an attempt to reduce the state's role in the economy to a bare minimum, aiming at unprecedented privatization. Bittar concludes with a series of suggestions that, if followed, should assist in redirecting Brazilian politics towards the construction of an authentic democracy.

Paulo Endo analyses the meaning for our current political context of the election of a president who openly defends the torture now taking place in prisons, an issue that is not given the attention it deserves on the political agenda. If I stated above that the failure to address the crimes against humanity committed during the civil-military dictatorship of 1964–85 means a continuation of the state of exception in the field of memory and justice, Endo's article reveals that such a state persists also in Brazilian prisons, but now aimed mainly at the poor, marginalized and black population. The author also stresses the importance of the 'domestic enemy' ideology that underlies Brazilian politics nowadays and 'justifies' the use of force by the state. As it was during the dictatorship period, so it is again today with the current government, which relies on a policy of mass incarceration, police violence, arming of the population and criminalization of the poor.

Roberto Vecchi and Karl Erik Schøllhammer focus their articles on contemporary Brazilian novels. Vecchi interprets works by Luiz Ruffato, Rubens Figueiredo and Sérgio Capparelli, while Schøllhammer covers novels by Chico Buarque de Holanda, Milton Hatoum, Itamar Vieira Junior, Ana Paula Maia, Joca Reiners Terron and also Luiz Ruffato. Vecchi shows how the works by his three chosen authors offer a comprehensive portrait of the geography of cities, correlating the fraying urban landscape with the political meltdown but also pointing to new zones of intensity that enable new responses to the challenge of recreating communal life. Literature emerges as a dystopian and utopian space, capable of imagining other community relations beyond the aporias that obstruct politics today. Schøllhammer's article, in turn, unveils a change in novels produced in recent years, following President Dilma's impeachment, which eluded the predictions emanating from literature in the early twenty-first century, inspired by budding optimism. The future no longer emerges as the time for solving problems and fulfilling promises. Quite the contrary, works like Itamar Vieira Junior's novel emphasize the continuity of colonial violence. Post-colonialism is still a utopia in Brazil. Likewise, Ana Paula Maia presents a world bogged down in the Anthropocene, where the most literal translation of the neoliberal textbook is the passage from the commodification of nature to its destruction. The authors and novels analysed in these two articles reveal literature's singular capacity to resist the attempted imposition of an authoritarian interpretation of history by big politics (or the politics of big business).

My own contribution focuses precisely on the above-cited authoritarian politics aimed at the control of literary, artistic and historical narratives, a control ever more present throughout 2019 and 2020. The article addresses the rise to power of a neoliberal, moralizing faction which, since the 2016 impeachment, has led to increasingly explicit and violent censorship of artistic expressions in Brazil. The article also features the other side of this movement, analysing to what extent the strength and originality of a new artistic scene that emerged over the early twenty-first century is precisely what triggered such an authoritarian and violent response against the arts and artists by an elite that feels alien to complex contemporary culture and the achievements in gender and racial freedom up to 2016. Examples include the new Brazilian Afro-descendant art and the trend — belated, it's true, but interacting strongly with the present — to inscribe the 1964–85 dictatorship period, especially by a new generation of artists.

Lastly, the contribution from the anthropologists Oiara Bonilla and Artionka Capiberibe takes its cue from our current state of pandemic, which makes even more explicit the genocidal project of the current government regarding minorities, especially the indigenous population. Covid-19 spreads in indigenous villages without the State taking the necessary precautions to ensure that the virus is isolated within the population and that those communities affected by the pandemic are cared for. In the case of the Yanomami in Roraima, they are additionally impacted by the invasion of more than 20,000 prospectors, who have generally enjoyed at least tacit support from the government. We can never speak of democracy in Brazil until this genocide has been suspended in favour of a genuine policy for the demarcation of and respect for indigenous lands. Capiberibe and Bonilla describe the dark decade of 2010–20, marked by major hydro-power projects, militarization of indigenous defence agencies and radical intensification of war in rural areas, with an exponential growth of agribusiness and invasion of indigenous reserves. On the other hand, they also highlight the birth of powerful resistance among indigenous peoples, with leaders whose voices resonate internationally, such as Davi Kopenawa and Ailton Krenak, besides indigenous women who are also organizing the resistance against this terrible genocidal wave.

A government with necropolitics at its heart is obviously unable to deal appropriately with the Covid-19 pandemic. Politicians and entrepreneurs linked to President Bolsonaro are against social distancing measures and claim that it is natural that a number of people should die. A government steeped in necropolitics would certainly find it natural to produce more deaths, especially when one observes that this epidemic affects more lethally the most impoverished strata, black and indigenous populations despised by the politicians currently in power and with poor access to hospitals and scarce ICU beds. Fortunately, we have inspirational individuals who help us reflect about times like these. I conclude by quoting a few passages from Ailton Krenak's small and powerful essay, *Ideas to Postpone the End of the World*, written in 2019 and drawn from a vast experience of 500 years of struggle and resistance. First I recall how perspective can change the way we view our problems and how to address them:

> In 2018, when we were on the verge of being assailed by a new situation in Brazil, I was asked: 'How are the natives going to cope with this?' I answered: 'The indigenous population has been resisting for five hundred years, I'm worried about the whites, how they are going to get out of this.' We have resisted by expanding our subjectivity, by not accepting this idea that we are all the same. There are still approximately 250 ethnic groups in Brazil that want to be different from each other, who speak over 150 languages and dialects.[1]

Secondly, I recall how indigenous peoples acknowledge aspects of our subjectivity that we repress in the West and that could open many doors to us:

> For some people, the idea of dreaming is akin to giving up on reality, to renouncing the practical meaning of life. However, there are also those who would see no meaning in life if it were not informed by dreams in which they can seek the spaces, the cure, the inspiration and even the resolution to practical issues they cannot discern, whose choices they cannot make outside dreams, but which are open there as possibilities. I felt quite at ease with myself this afternoon, when more than one of the colleagues who spoke here referred to dreaming not as an oneiric experience, but as a field related to background, to worldview, to the tradition of different peoples for whom dreaming is a pathway to learning, to self-knowledge about life, and the use of that knowledge in their interaction with the world and with other people. [...] Let us exploit our full critical and creative capacity to make colourful parachutes. Let us think of space not as a confined place, but as the cosmos where we can skydive with colourful parachutes. Where are the parachutes launched from? [...] From the place where visions and dreams are possible. From another place we can inhabit besides this harsh land: the place of dream.[2]

May our dreams, as well as their metamorphoses into works of art and literature, our colourful parachutes, be also viewed as this field of development and creation of new worldviews, as pathways to learning. May we be allowed this modest utopia.

---

[1] Ailton Krenak, *Ideias para adiar o fim do mundo* (São Paulo: Companhia das Letras, 2019), p. 31; my translation.
[2] Idem, pp. 30, 52–53, 65.

Overcoming the Legacy of the Military Dictatorship through the National Truth Commission in Brazil: An Ongoing Debate

Janaína de Almeida Teles

Universidade do Estado de Minas Gerais

The traumatic legacies of Latin American dictatorships and the variety of ways of dealing with this past have been the object of analysis by academics such as historians and social scientists as well as activists, due not only to the current political and social setbacks the region has been undergoing, but also to the return of a certain 'historical negationism' related to the denial of the authoritarian wave experienced in the region since the 1960s. In Brazil, the creation of the National Truth Commission (2012–14) — known in Portuguese by its acronym 'CNV', from *Comissão Nacional da Verdade* — thus represented a window of opportunity to reinterpret the scope of repression in the country and its repercussions, as well as the dictatorial legacy. Nowadays, analysts are further investigating the experience of the CNV in Brazil to fully understand the depth of its impact.

This article aims at analysing the extent to which this demand for the creation and development of a CNV has resulted in practical transformations. It considers this moment as particularly opportune for the understanding of facts of historical importance in Brazil. The specifics of the Brazilian case will be investigated throughout this article, giving special attention to the mechanisms that blocked testimonies, sent messages of denial of violations, and trivialized conflicts, and the dynamics of institutional debate. Those mechanisms prevented, for a long period, Brazil's traumatic memories from being widely expressed in the public space, both in its legal form and in other ways, which contrasts with the experience of other countries in Latin America's Southern Cone.

Aiming to contribute to the understanding of this historical process, this text seeks to outline a reflective panorama on the creation of the CNV, highlighting the role of the political stakeholders involved in it, with special attention to the family members of people who died or disappeared due to political persecution and violence. This article analyses the debate involved in the installation of the CNV, both in civil society and in the legislative powers, to address the contributions and constitutive limits of this process, which decisively influenced the results of its work. It is worth mentioning that this text is part of a broader study under development on the CNV and the repercussions of its activities and investigations.

Disputes and Controversies over the Establishment of the National Truth Commission in Brazil

The democratic transition in Brazil happened without evident ruptures with its dictatorial past. The lack of legal accountability of State agents who committed crimes against humanity during the dictatorship resulted in the construction of a distorted official version of the recent past, preserved, to a large extent, by the democratic governments that followed the promulgation of the Brazilian Constitution of 1988 — the so-called 'Citizen Constitution'. Throughout this process, discourses supposedly anchored in a 'logic of reconciliation' prevailed, as it was believed that the demand for justice would interfere with governability. Indeed, the Brazilian transition process back into democracy, characterized in many ways by its military control, left its mark both on the constitution and, later, in the guiding principles of the CNV.

From this point of view, it is worth noting that the creation of a commission responsible for investigating the crimes committed by the dictatorial regime was a longstanding demand from human rights organizations and movements in Brazil.[1] As of 2007, the political pressure exercised by the organized civil society, social movements and others, all pushing for the adoption of measures necessary for its creation, grew in intensity. This demand was discussed in more depth during the seminar 'South American Debate on Truth and Responsibility in Crimes Against Human Rights', held in May 2007. This event was hosted by the Public Prosecutor's Office of São Paulo, with the support of the International Center for Transitional Justice (ICTJ), a US-based organization, and the Brazilian Special Secretariat for Human Rights (SEDH). The seminar was attended by specialists in international law and transitional justice, as well as lawyers, historians and activists, who, at the end, presented a proposal to create the CNV, as recorded in the 'Letter of São Paulo'.[2]

Around this time, it had become quite clear to the families and to human rights activists that the Special Commission on Political Deaths and Disappearances (*Comissão Especial de Mortos e Desaparecidos Políticos*, CEMDP) would not

---

[1] We can trace this demand back to 1975, when relatives of members of the 'Authentics', a group of politicians and congressmen from MDB (Brazilian Democratic Movement) openly against the Brazilian dictatorial regime, organized a campaign in favour of the creation of a Parliamentary Inquiry Committee to discuss the violent acts of the Military Dictatorship within the National Congress cf. Janaína de Almeida Teles, 'Democratic Transition and Conciliation: Human Rights and the Legacy of the Brazilian Dictatorship', in *The Brazilian Truth Commission: Local, National and Global Perspectives*, ed. by Nina Schneider (London: Berghahn Books, 2018), pp. 86–108 (pp. 92–94).

[2] The author participated in this debate as a mediator at one of the event's round-tables. More information about the event is available at: <http://www.mpf.mp.br/sp/sala-de-imprensa/noticias-sp/mpf-divulga-a-carta-de-sao-paulo>.

carry on with the investigation and the search for the missing remains of the political victims of the dictatorial period. As a matter of fact, in October 2003, an inter-ministerial commission with members drawn from the Ministries of Justice, Defence, Human Rights and the Chief of Staff was created, with the participation of the Attorney General of Brazil. It was formed as a response to the judgement issued by Federal Court Judge Solange Salgado referring to the 'Araguaia Guerrilla War'.[3] The judgement ordered the opening of the military archives and records and requested the Brazilian Federal Government to take all the necessary measures to find those who had disappeared in the region of Araguaia and whose remains had not been located. The government of President Luiz Inácio 'Lula' da Silva appealed the decision through the Federal Attorney General's Office. After that, a new commission that could deal with the issues concerning Judge Solange Salgado's ruling was established, assisted by representatives from the Navy, the Army and the Brazilian Air Force, but it produced no concrete results.[4]

The appeal was signed by the country's Attorney General and presented to the Regional Federal Court (*Tribunal Regional Federal*, TRF) of the 1st Region, in Brasília. It acknowledged the rights of the families to locate the remains of their missing members as well as the obligation of the Federal Government to guarantee the families such a right. However, according to the text, Judge Salgado was believed to have gone beyond the requests of the family members, themselves the authors of the filed action in 1982, whose sole objective was supposedly to know where the missing victims were. That meant the military files would not be made available to the justice system or to the families. Luis Francisco Carvalho Filho, a lawyer who was the president of the CEMDP, severely reproached this decision, which he deemed '[...] technically unintelligible and politically disappointing'.[5]

In this context, the relationship between the two institutions — the inter-ministerial commission and the CEMDP — was marked by mistrust and great tension. A significant part of the members of the latter saw the creation of the inter-ministerial commission as an attempt to undermine the work that was being carried out by them. Some of the members even considered resigning

---

[3] Guerrilla movement organized by the Communist Party of Brazil (PCdoB), between 1972 and 1974, which counted on the participation of 73 members, spread across a territory of over 30,000km² in the southeastern part of Pará. The movement was known for the long training and preparation given to its members. Their activities started in 1964, when three groups of guerrilla members were sent to China to receive military training. The repression of the guerrillas was characterized by the brutal violence used by the Brazilian Armed Forces against this group as well as against the local populations. To date, the remains of only two individuals involved with the group have been identified. Janaína de Almeida Teles, 'The Araguaia Guerrilla War (1972–1974): Armed Resistance to the Brazilian Dictatorship', *Latin American Perspectives*, 44.5 (July 2017), 30–52.
[4] Vera Rotta, 'Governo institui três comissões relativas aos mortos e desaparecidos políticos', *Carta Maior*, 21 Feb. 2006. Available online at <https://www.cartamaior.com.br/?/Editoria/Direitos-Humanos/Governo-instituiu-tres-comissoes-relativas-aos-mortos-e-desaparecidos-politicos/5/9442> [accessed 9 Feb. 2020].
[5] Ibid.

from their positions within the commission in a collective move, but, in 2005, only Suzana K. Lisbôa actually resigned from her post as a representative of the family members of the dead and missing persons. According to her testimony:

> [...] Lula's government undermined the Special Commission and did not fulfil its promise to open the archives of the military dictatorship. We had very little opportunity of challenging institutions and it was taken away from us. There was no way to stay. The government [...] did not help in the clarification of the deaths and disappearances, that is, how they died, where they were buried and the authorship of these crimes. And it took no steps to punish those responsible for those acts. Furthermore, it did not clarify the episode that took place at the Salvador Air Base, where documents from the military period were burned, something that must have occurred in several other places [...]. Family members scheduled two meetings with President Lula, which were cancelled at the last minute. [...] The thing is that the CEMDP did not have any support to locate the remains of the missing people. [...] The State killed these people and, so far, it has been up to the victims' relatives to provide evidence of where they might have been buried.[6]

In this context, family members divided themselves into two groups: those who advocated for the need to remain active and stick with the CEMDP and those who preferred to leave it in order to give visibility to the protest against the governmental measures that aimed to hinder the delivery of Judge Salgado's judgement. From this conflict, two ideas arose: a proposal to create a Truth Commission and the public campaign for 'Unarchiving Brazil' (*Desarquivando o Brasil*), which prepared a draft bill to be presented to the Congress, later used as the basis for the text of the Access to Information Law (*Lei de Acesso à Informação*, LAI), presented by the Federal Government to the Brazilian National Congress in 2011.[7]

Shortly before, Brazil had been in a process of holding several local human rights conferences that would feed content to and create the agenda for the 11th National Human Rights Conference, to take place in Brasília, in December 2008. In one of its preliminary stages, during the debates promoted by the 1st City of Belo Horizonte Human Rights Conference,[8] held in 2008, a movement called '*Tortura Nunca Mais*' [Torture: Never Again] from Minas Gerais advocated for the creation of institutional spaces to debate at the national conference the issues of 'Memory, Truth and Justice'. These issues had, up to that point, been absent from the agenda for the state's debates proposed by the

---

[6] Suzana Keniger Lisbôa, interview given to the author (São Paulo, 23 July 2005).
[7] According to Almeida in the *Dossiê Ditadura: Mortos e Desaparecidos políticos no Brasil (1964–1985)*, ed. by Criméia A. S. Almeida, Janaína de A. Teles, Maria Amélia de A. Teles and Suzana K. Lisbôa (São Paulo: Imprensa Oficial, 2009), pp. 43–46. As well the *Dossiê Ditadura*, the author coordinated the campaign '*Desarquivando o Brasil*' (2005).
[8] This event occurred in preparation for the 3rd State of Minas Gerais Human Rights Conference (Alessandra G. Soares, 'Atores e ideias na constituição do direito à memória e à verdade: análise da mudança política no PNDH' (unpublished doctoral thesis, Universidade Federal de São Carlos, 2016), pp. 99–100).

Secretariat of Human Rights of the Presidency of the Republic.[9] In this context, Heloísa Greco (a member of 'Tortura Nunca Mais' group, from the state of Minas Gerais) also started to advocate for the creation of a National Truth and Justice Commission.

In December 2008, family members of the victims of state violence participated in the round-table on 'Memory, Truth and Justice', an event offered by the 11th National Human Rights Conference of Brazil, in Brasília. And that was precisely when the discussions about a National Truth and Justice Commission started to gain ground, according to the testimony of Maria Amélia de A. Teles:

> During the debates, Victória Grabois [another relative of a missing person] and I, we reiterated our defence of the proposal to create a National Truth and Justice Commission, as we understood that the commission should organize the information obtained through its investigation with the aim of, in the end, using the evidence acquired to take them to the courts for prosecution. We considered that symbolic reparation was part of the justice to which we were entitled, which meant recognizing the memory of the dead and missing and their families and also creating reference centres to develop research projects about Brazilian History and to foster a culture of human rights. Another member of the board, Paulo Abrão, disagreed, arguing that we could not include the term 'justice', as this could lead to a crisis between branches of government as that had to be taken care of by the Brazilian Judiciary. There was resistance to the proposal, but the black movement voted in favour of our project and, thanks to this support, we were able to approve it. The plenary voted for its full approval.

Indeed, the demands of family members and human rights movements made their way into the resolutions issued by the 11th National Human Rights Conference, as can be seen in item 9, of section 7:

> To create the National Commission for Truth and Justice, composed in a plural form, with a majority of representation from social movements and with the participation of family members of victims of the dictatorship; with a public, transparent character and a fixed period for the beginning and end of its work; with full powers for the investigation of crimes against humanity and violation of human rights committed during the coordination for the military coup and following dictatorship, and must nominate and forward to the competent bodies for the punishment of those accused of these crimes and register and disclose all their official procedures to ensure the detailed clarification of tortures, deaths and disappearances [...].[10]

In consonance with the debates established at the 11th National Human

---

[9] SEDH/Presidência da República, *Caderno de Deliberações da XI Conferência Nacional dos Direitos Humanos* (Brasília, DF, 2008). This absence was also reported in the City Conference of Rio de Janeiro, as Maria Amélia de A. Teles told the author in an interview (São Paulo, 14 January 2020, personal archive.)
[10] SEDH/Presidência da República, *Caderno de Deliberações*, pp. 154–55.

Rights Conference, its final document also contemplated the proposals for the implementation of Truth Commissions about different periods of Brazilian history, including slavery and the systematic killings of the black population, native and indigenous peoples and the repression of rural workers in Brazil. This final document also included proposals to carry out investigations into how, throughout the military dictatorship, specific social segments and institutions such as businesses and their leaderships, union members, the military, blacks, politicians, the judiciary, the various churches in the country, among others were targeted and had their rights violated.[11]

Shortly thereafter, in April 2009, the CEMDP launched 'A Dossier from the Military Dictatorship in Brazil: political victims, assassinated and disappeared in Brazil (1964-1985)'. That dossier was an updated version of the research carried out by the CEMDP throughout the years, which also underlined the need for a National Truth Commission:

> [...] These Commissions are expected to be plural, independent and use procedures that resemble the ones used by the Brazilian Judiciary [...]. However, the public and transparent character of these extra-judicial symbolic reparation procedures is highlighted, where, generally, the testimony of witnesses and confessions of defendants are provided. In this way, the investigation and retrieval of the facts, even if not accompanied by punishment, occur in a much more profound way. In different parts of the world, the remembrance of the past has been inseparable from the struggles for justice. Thus, we emphasize the close and complementary relationship between memory and justice [...].[12]

The proposition was based on the realization that

> [...] the Special Commission for the Political Victims of the Dictatorship as well as the Amnesty Commission, both of an administrative nature, have limited powers of investigation to delve into the needed research about the repressive activity of the State during the military dictatorship [...].[13]

This could also be considered an inversion of the burden of proof, since it is up to the victims to present evidence of the crimes committed by the State. In addition to this unfavourable scenario, these commissions '[...] did not obtain support from the various civilian governments to implement this task'. Besides, their diligences and decisions, '[...] although considered of public interest, are not followed in a broad, open and systematic way by society'. Given this context, they concluded that these institutions could not be considered Truth and Responsibility Commissions.[14]

The family members believed that it was only through a rigorous investigation carried out within the scope of a Truth Commission that the process of factual

---

[11] Ibid., pp. 155–56.
[12] Almeida et al., eds, *Dossiê Ditadura*, p. 50.
[13] Ibid.
[14] Ibid.

retrieval would be successful. The efforts to investigate the facts would contribute to clarifying the stories, establishing the truth and individual responsibility, as well as generate factual knowledge based on the untold and non-official stories of that historical period. It would be possible to analyse the structures of illegal repression and the broader context in which human rights violations systematically occurred. Its main contribution would be to welcome the narratives of the victims and survivors of State repression, thus contributing to the strengthening of democracy and the rule of law in Brazil.

The efforts started with an assessment of the concrete possibilities of promoting institutional changes, emphasizing that all the other international experiences of establishing Truth Commissions were followed by the failure of State to comply with their recommendations. Nevertheless, commissions were seen as instruments capable of drawing the attention of public opinion and, more broadly, of the whole of society, to the potential of international human rights law in favour of significant political changes at the national level:

> The South African experience shows that even when there are significant institutional and legislative changes [...] the investigation of the facts may not be guaranteed. Despite these limitations, Truth Commissions are important instruments for the effective incorporation of international human rights law into national contexts. It created the obligation for States to guarantee the right to justice, in its broadest and most comprehensive conception, including the investigation of the facts, the identification and further sanctioning of those responsible for the violations, the reparation of those affected, the right to the truth and the reform of public institutions to ensure the effectiveness of human rights.[15]

This issue gained greater visibility on the political scene with the launch of the 3rd National Human Rights Program (*III Programa Nacional de Direitos Humanos* — a.k.a. PNDH-3), instituted by a presidential act in December 2009, which updated previous versions and incorporated resolutions from the 11th Conference discussed above. Its guideline 23, axis VI ('Right to Memory and to the Truth'), on 'Recognition of memory and truth as the Human Right of citizenship and the duty of the State', established as its main objective to seek 'the investigation and public clarification of human rights violations practised in the context of the political repression that occurred in Brazil [...] and to promote national reconciliation'.[16]

The final text had undergone changes, with expressions such as 'dictatorial repression', 'popular resistance to repression', 'criminal accountability for cases involving acts related to the 1964–1985 regime' having been removed from it, alongside other provisions related to the 'justice'/legal accountability side of the future commission. The government's political line that oriented such a

---

[15] Almeida et al., eds, *Dossiê Ditadura*, p. 46.
[16] SEDH/Presidência da República, *11ª Conferência Nacional dos Direitos Humanos. Democracia, desenvolvimento e direitos humanos: superando as desigualdades* (Brasília, DF, 2010), p. 173.

softening of the linguistic tone was leaning towards a vision which understood that reparation measures should be diluted over a wider historical period, with no references to the dictatorial period that Brazil had gone through. Human Rights violations that occurred during that period would not be characterized as crimes against humanity for the discussion of further legal action, nor should they be punished, according to this line of thought. The government was leaning towards a general idea that it would be better (or easier) for the public debate if vague formulations regarding the measures to be recommended and adopted were the focus of the debates.[17]

The government also suppressed, from axis VI of PNDH-3, the proposals related to the creation of Truth Commissions on black slavery, on the violence inflicted against native and indigenous peoples, and on the repression of rural workers, present in the Compilation of Deliberations of the 11th National Human Rights Conference of Brazil, as mentioned above.[18] In this way, social sectors that were repeatedly marginalized were excluded from the public debate, making a wide democratization process in Brazil unfeasible. Furthermore, the government also minimized the political and social impact of the CNV, emptying its potential in promoting effective institutional transformations, the culture of human rights, as well as weakening its 'listening capacity' related to the country's historical traumas.

Nevertheless, PNDH-3 presented in its guideline 24, axis VI (concerning the 'promotion of historical memory and the public construction of truth'), the proposal to create a Truth Commission regarding the crimes of the dictatorship of the 'Estado Novo' historical period (1937–45). This proposal, however, was simply ignored, as well as the texts that were part of guideline 25, which dealt with 'the modernization of legislation related to the promotion of the right to memory and the truth', that had a focus on 'suppressing [...] norms remaining from periods of exception that oppose international commitments and constitutional principles on Human Rights from the Brazilian legal system'.[19]

At the same time, the discussions about the case of the Araguaia Guerrilla War at the OAS's Inter-American Commission on Human Rights (IACHR) had a key role in influencing the establishment of the CNV in Brazil. In October 2008, in response to a request made by the Centre for Justice and International Law (CEJIL — a Human Rights NGO then responsible for presenting a petition from the families of Araguaia Guerrilla War's victims before the Inter-American human rights system), the IACHR held a thematic hearing to collect information on the implementation of transitional justice measures

---

[17] Renan H. Quinalha, 'Com quantos lados se faz uma verdade? Notas sobre a Comissão Nacional da Verdade e a "teoria dos dois demônios"', *Revista Jurídica da Presidência*, Brasília, 15.105 (Feb.–May 2013), 181–204.
[18] SEDH/Presidência da República, *Caderno de Deliberações*, p. 156; Idem, *11ª Conferência Nacional*, pp. 169–78.
[19] SEDH/Presidência da República, *11ª Conferência Nacional*, pp. 175–77.

in Brazil, entitled *The Amnesty Law as an Obstacle to Justice in Brazil*.[20] The hearing, which was attended by the Regional Attorney, Marlon Weichert, and by the then President of the Amnesty Commission of Brazil and Secretary of Justice of Brazil, Paulo Abrão, clarified that the solution to the Brazilian case was not to revoke the Amnesty Law but to force its reinterpretation by the country's Supreme Court of Justice so as to ensure the criminal accountability of state agents, in consonance with the international obligations of Human Rights before the conventional instruments of the Inter-American system. In the following month, the IACHR notified the Brazilian State of the measures Brazil should take to comply with measures it had ratified, and more broadly with human rights principles and law.[21]

Given the failure to comply satisfactorily with these measures, in March 2009 the IACHR decided to refer the case to the Inter-American Court of Human Rights, with serious repercussions in Brazil. In July of the same year, the family members of victims presented a memorandum in which they demanded that the Brazilian State comply with the fifteen measures previously issued by the IACHR. Among those measures were the creation of a National Truth Commission alongside the criminal prosecution of all the perpetrators and accomplices involved in the disappearance of individuals involved, or not, in the resistance in the Araguaia Guerrilla War episodes. In its November 2009 response, the State expressed that it understood it was not within the prerogatives of the court to judge the case, and asked them to declare themselves incapable of doing it. To support this thesis, the Brazilian State drew the court's attention to the fact that the human rights violations being discussed were not part of an ongoing situation. The Brazilian State further tried to argue the inadmissibility of the case as the petitioners showed lack of procedural interest, as domestic instances within the Brazilian judiciary were still judging the same requests, or, in legal terms, there was a 'non-exhaustion of domestic remedies'. According to the Brazilian State's position, the same case was still being discussed in the Brazilian Supreme Court, considered the most appropriate forum to deal with the situation at that moment.[22]

---

[20] In Brazil, in 1979, the government enacted an Amnesty Law with the objective of stopping the spread of the campaign for the 'broad, general and unrestricted amnesty' organized by civil society to contemplate all those politically persecuted. The law was considered 'reciprocal', equating the violence of torture practised by state agents with the violence of opponents of the dictatorship. It was also restricted and partial, although it allowed the return to Brazil of the majority of those that were sent into exile. Prisoners convicted of more complex crimes (especially those involving armed violence against individuals) were not amnestied, but their sentences were reduced after the reform of the National Security Law (LSN) in 1978, and they were released on parole. The hegemonic interpretation of the law still protects State agents, considering torture to be an act 'connected' to the alleged crimes committed by those who were politically persecuted too. See Janaína de Almeida Teles, 'Memórias dos cárceres da ditadura: os testemunhos e as lutas dos presos políticos no Brasil' (unpublished doctoral thesis, Universidade de São Paulo, 2011).
[21] Bruno B. Bernardi, 'O sistema interamericano de direitos humanos e justiça de transição: impactos no Brasil, Peru, Colômbia e México' (unpublished doctoral thesis, Universidade de São Paulo, 2015), pp. 452–53.
[22] Ibid., pp. 453–54.

Shortly after, in April 2010, the Brazilian Federal Supreme Court received and analysed the case filed by the Brazilian Bar Association that challenged the validity of the first article of the Amnesty Law (1979). This article judges all the crimes committed between 1961 and 1979 to be pardoned, including political and related crimes, regardless of who committed them and of the nature of the crimes, including crimes against humanity.

According to the claim of non-compliance with fundamental precept, there were no collusions, shared goals or purposes between the agents of the state, on the one hand, and the politically persecuted, on the other. Quite to the contrary. The repression against those called 'subversive' should be deemed 'ordinary crimes', with no connection whatsoever to 'political crimes', as they threatened the established order in the military dictatorship. In accordance with this argument, the conclusion was that amnesty was inapplicable to the torturers of the period. The case, however, was dismissed by seven votes against two, in accordance with the wishes of the rapporteur (proposer) of the lawsuit, Minister Eros Grau, who stressed that there could be no legal revision of a political agreement that resulted in the Amnesty Law because it was precisely the existence of such a pact that allowed Brazil to transition from the military dictatorship to democracy.

Interestingly, according to the testimony of President Lula's former Defence Minister, Nelson Jobim, he visited all Supreme Court Ministers before the trial and presented them with a study contrary to the Brazilian Bar Association case (ADPF 153 — Non-Compliance With Fundamental Precept 153), written by former Supreme Court Minister Sepulveda Pertence.[23] According to the testimony of renowned jurist Fabio K. Comparato, author of the Non-Compliance document, on the day the Supreme Court was going to deliberate on the case, one of the Supreme Court judges told him that on the night before that occasion a dinner had taken place. President Lula, all Supreme Court judges and a member of the Brazilian Armed Forces were present. There, judges were pressured to vote against an interpretation of the Amnesty Law which would allow its revision, thus guaranteeing torturers their amnesty.[24]

In December 2010, the Inter-American Court of Human Rights condemned the Brazilian State, deciding that the crimes against humanity committed by State agents during the military dictatorship should be investigated, admitted by the country's courts, and punished. The Inter-American Court judgement followed the path of previous similar cases that had been heard before, such as Barrios Altos in Peru and Almonacid Arellano in Chile. Hence, the Amnesty Law was found to be incompatible with the American Convention on Human Rights and should have no legal effect. The historic decision discredited the

---

[23] Rubens Valente, 'Em vídeo, Jobim detalha como atuou para impedir a revisão da Lei de Anistia', *Folha de São Paulo*, 27 August 2019.
[24] Fábio Konder Comparato, '"Nós nunca tivemos uma democracia": entrevista a Cecília Luedemann, Hamilton O. de Souza e Tatiana Merlino', *Caros Amigos*, ano XIV, no. 163 (Oct. 2010), 12–16. Available online at <https://issuu.com/carosamigos/docs/pdfs_ca_163leitores> [accessed 2 March 2020].

myth about the foundation of a 'new republic' in Brazil, supposedly celebrated with the Amnesty Law.[25]

Within its judgement, alongside the recommendation that the Brazilian State should establish a National Truth Commission, the court suggested Brazil should pass new legislation for an Information Law that would allow citizens to have access to, among other things, the State's official files and documents of the military dictatorship. Such recommendations played a determining role in the later creation of the CNV, as analysed below.

The Legislative Debate about the Implementation of a National Truth Commission

The debate in the Chamber of Deputies

One month after the decision of the Brazilian Supreme Court, President Lula presented a bill to the National Congress proposing the implementation of the Truth Commission, based on the text of the working group previously instituted to elaborate the proposal. A little earlier, in October 2009, the Centre for the Study of Violence from the University of São Paulo (Núcelo de Estudos sobre a Violência — NEV/USP) had held an 'International Conference on the Right to the Truth', in which the outline of the preliminary bill was defined.[26] Their action reflected the expectation that a condemnation of the Brazilian State before the Inter-American Court of Human Rights of the OAS in the case related to the Araguaia Guerrilla War was only a matter of time.

The legislative debate that preceded the approval of the Brazilian National Truth Commission Law[27] was marked by a series of disputes and controversies, but, above all, by the lack of participation of civil society representatives, especially family members of the victims and survivors. At the Chamber of Deputies, one of the two houses of the Brazilian Congress, the debate kicked off with the presentation of a request to treat the bill as an 'emergency motion', dispensing with many of the usual formalities, signed by the majority of political party leaders in September 2011. During the debates, a sense of pragmatism and immediacy prevailed in most of the representatives' public speeches and positioning. Former President Lula's typical 'national reconciliation' discourse was still a factor that played a role in the debate, as can be seen by the speech provided by the then President of the Chamber of Deputies, Congressperson Marco Maia, from the Worker's Party (*Partido dos Trabalhadores*, PT). He

---

[25] Bernardi, p. 462.
[26] Minister Paulo Vannuchi (SEDH/PR) and Paulo S. Pinheiro were chosen to attend the group. See more at <https://nev.prp.usp.br/wp-content/uploads/2015/01/down241.pdf> [accessed 12 January 2020]. You may also want to refer to Decree no. 10, from 13 January 2010.
[27] The present analysis focuses on contextualizing the political dispute referred to and its agents instead of historiography's theoretical debate on the uses of the past (Carolina S. Bauer, 'O debate legislativo sobre a criação da Comissão Nacional da Verdade e as múltiplas articulações e dimensões de temporalidade da ditadura civil-militar brasileira', *Revista Anos 90*, Porto Alegre, 22.42 (Dec. 2015), 115–52).

stressed the merit of the compromise reached by the Ministry of Defence, the Ministry of Justice and the Special Secretariat for Human Rights: to approve the proposal of the Truth Commission that was originally presented to the House, considering that it was eligible for voting.[28]

Another PT congressperson, Paulo Teixeira from São Paulo, an important articulator of the proposal in the Brazilian Congress, highlighted the reasons why the approval of the government's bill to establish a Truth Commission would represent an advance in the ongoing construction of the democratic experience in the country, to the extent that it constituted *a reconciliatory commission that has no legal powers*, such as in Argentina, Chile and South Africa, which aims of make the period known '[...] and *search for the disappeared*, [...] so that their families can bury them'.[29]

On the other hand, Representative Chico Alencar, from the Socialism and Liberty Party (*Partido Socialismo e Liberdade*, PSOL) from Rio de Janeiro, more aligned with the left wing than the PT, insisted on the need to overcome the limits of consensus politics,[30] to guarantee a more qualified debate about the bill, the amendments to be presented and its implications, although he agreed with the request to speed up the voting process, as this would imply 'a repudiation [...] of acts of torture whilst being able to label it as a practice of State Terrorism'.[31]

Nelson Marquezelli, from São Paulo, a representative of the Brazilian Labour Party (*Partido Trabalhista Brasileiro*, PTB), more aligned with the right wing, spoke out against the request for emergency treatment. However, he did so to echo the previously made remarks by then far-right Congressperson Jair Bolsonaro, a member of the Progressive Party (*Partido Progressista*, PP) from Rio de Janeiro, underlining that bringing to trial those responsible for committing crimes during the dictatorial period would represent an insult to the military institutions, something that was, for him, simply out of question. His speech proposed a distorted conception of history, as well as reiterating a political conception that is typical of the 'theory of the two demons'[32] when he affirmed that '*The amnesty* [...] *it is a healed wound*, it is already in our Constitution, it is set in stone. [...] It is not necessary to review an amnesty law of over thrity years, *agreed by both parties, then*.'[33]

---

[28] Câmara dos Deputados. Sessão: 225.1.54.0, 21 September 2011, p. 74. Available online at <http://www.camara.leg.br/internet/plenario/notas/extraord/2011/9/EN2109111830.pdf> [accessed 20 December 2019].

[29] Ibid., pp. 238–39 (my emphasis).

[30] Jacques Rancière, 'O dissenso', in *A crise da razão* (São Paulo: Companhia das Letras, 1996), pp. 367–82.

[31] Câmara dos Deputados. Sessão: 225.1.54.0, 21 September 2011, pp. 82 and 94.

[32] Expression used in Argentina that equates the violence used by the State to that exercised by guerrilla groups, exempting various social sectors from the responsibilities for their support for the military dictatorship. See the preface published in 2006 in the reissue of 'Nunca Más' (1984), a report by the National Commission on the Disappearance of People (Conadep), in which a self-criticism on the topic is presented, cf. Emílio Crenzel, *La historia política del Nunca Más: la memoria de las desapariciones en la Argentina* (Buenos Aires: Siglo XXI, 2008).

[33] Câmara dos Deputados. Sessão: 225.1.54.0, 21 September 2011, p. 101 (my emphasis).

Finally, a former guerrilla exiled in 1971, Alfredo Sirkis, a leading exponent of the Green Party (*Partido Verde*, PV) from Rio de Janeiro, asked to speak to justify his vote in favour of the request to give emergency treatment to the vote for the implementation of the National Truth Commission, suggesting compliance with the 'logic of reconciliation' and the 'theory of the two demons'. For him, the Truth Commission's aims were:

> [...] to guarantee the future of Brazil and not make some sort of attempt to rewrite history. Bearing in mind that *mistakes were made not only by those who took power, [...] but also [...] by those who, like me, resisted the dictatorship with weapons in our hands.* [...] It is not about — and I am against it — revising the Amnesty Law, but [...] the country needs to look at its recent history and understand how democracy [...] was destroyed as of 1964; how [...] human rights violations occurred.[34]

Right after his intervention, the motion to give emergency treatment was put to the vote and was approved with 351 votes in favour, 42 against and 11 abstentions.[35] The majority of the representatives present agreed not to delay the creation of the National Truth Commission any longer. However, the bill would be analysed on that same day, with no extra time available to think it through.

After the opinion of the bill's rapporteur was read, the then Congressperson Onyx Lorenzoni, a member of the conservative Democrats Party (*Democratas*, DEM) from the Rio Grande do Sul (and currently a minister in Bolsonaro's cabinet), asked to speak. He underlined the need to respect the modified text, as established by the negotiations made with the leaders of the political parties, anchored in a model of 'national reconciliation' that set the tone of the negotiations among representatives and the then Minister of Justice, José Eduardo Cardozo, the Minister of Human Rights, Maria do Rosário, and the representative of the Minister of Defence, former Araguaia guerrilla José Genoíno. According to Lorenzoni, the agreement was made in a such a way that the bill's rapporteur should fully comply with the amendments proposed by PSDB, the Democrats and other right-wing parties, with the voting session taking place soon after.[36]

The President of the Chamber of Deputies took the floor to emphasize that a modified version of the bill would be presented at the plenary and amendments would be accepted. A few representatives, such as Arolde de Oliveira (DEM-RJ), took the microphone to speak in favour of the coup-d'état of 1964, saying it was the coup that prevented the implementation of communism in Brazil, and that Brazilians supported the coup. In line with other conservative speakers of the Chamber, he invoked the 'theory of the two demons' again, when he claimed that '[...] this Truth Commission will have to deal with violations from both sides'.[37]

[34] Ibid., p. 105 (my emphasis).
[35] Ibid., p. 110.
[36] Ibid., p. 156.
[37] Ibid., pp. 166–67.

A PT representative from Maranhão, Domingos Dutra, in turn, reiterated that the bill did not have the purpose of 'seeking revenge', in the words of the supporters of the military dictatorship. It intended to bring to the surface the events that took place in the past and that were still not openly discussed, associating such debates with the promotion of democratic values. The deputy, however, made no reference to the fact that the government's proposal touched on the confrontation of historical political conflicts. In effect, the project established as an objective of the CNV the investigation of serious human rights violations committed between 1946 and 1988, covering both the democratic period (1946–64) and the dictatorial period (1964–88).[38] Hence, the proposal did not establish a clear distinction in relation to the dictatorial period, thus neglecting the factual retrieval, as well as the transmission of memories and experiences of the authoritarian period.

In the end, former prisoner and representative Ivan Valente (PSOL), from São Paulo, gave the floor to Luiza Erundina, historical militant of the Catholic left, then a representative of the Brazilian Socialist Party (*Partido Socialista Brasileiro*, PSB) from São Paulo, who analysed the bill, from the perspective of family members of political victims of the dictatorship, stressing, overall, their demand for transparency and justice:

> [...] It was expected that [the bill] would be the object of [...] deeper debate, [...] so that the proposal could be refined as its text [...] lacks an objective [...] which is to get justice. [...] There has to be a commitment that [...] whatever is found [about violations] is forwarded [...] to the competent judicial authorities so that the crimes that have been identified and investigated can be an object of legal action. [...] The family members [...] demand that no military personnel take part in [the commission], as they [...] will not have the necessary autonomy and independence. There must be [...] absolute transparency [...] in the sharing of the data and information collected [...]. We must have the responsibility of not [...] frustrating public opinion and, above all, the families of the victims of the military dictatorship.[39]

Next, following approval of the emergency procedure which ended the discussion about the bill and determined its immediate voting, the leader of the PT took the next step. In line with what was discussed among the party leaders, Deputy Candido Vaccarezza, from São Paulo, presented a proposal that incorporated two amendments, made by representatives from the opposition. The first one dealt with the criteria for defining who could *not* participate in the Truth Commission, that is, who was not 'in a position to act impartially whilst exercising the powers of the Commission'. Soon after, he presented the text of an amendment to article 4 of the original text, authored by the PSDB, allowing individuals that wanted to come forward to testify before the Truth Commission to 'shed light on the truth' to do so.[40]

---

[38] Comissão Nacional da Verdade/Presidência da República, *Relatório da Comissão Nacional da Verdade* (Brasília, DF, CNV/PR, 2014), p. 20. Hereafter CNV.
[39] Câmara dos Deputados. Sessão: 225.1.54.0, 21 September 2011, pp. 183–85.
[40] Ibid., pp. 193–97.

Finally, both amendments were approved by the Plenary of the Federal Chamber, along with a third, which determined that all documents and reports produced by the Commission should be sent to the Brazilian National Archive. Despite the fact that the PSOL leaders voted against the final version of the bill as agreed by other party leaders, the bill was approved. After that, Deputy Jair Bolsonaro — who since becoming President has praised Col. Carlos A. Brilhante Ustra, the man in charge of the main torture centre during the Brazilian dictatorial period, as a 'national hero'[41] — made a threatening statement insinuating that the left-wing congresspeople were not interested in shedding light on all the truth regarding a recent past, and called them cowards.[42]

Under the protests of several congresspeople, the session was ended by the President of the Federal Chamber. Next, the bill was sent to the Federal Senate.[43] Its progress will be analysed in the next section.

Senate vote to approve the bill

Before the Senate voted on the bill, the family members of the dead and disappeared once again insisted on the need to make some changes to the text in order to guarantee greater independence to the Truth Commission. Among the demands presented at the Public Hearing promoted by the Human Rights Commission of the Federal Senate, in October 2011, were: a) the extension of another two years for the commission's term of operation; b) a change in the investigation's timeframe, covering the period from 1964–88 instead of 1943–88; c) the disclosure of partial reports/updates with information about the developments and findings; d) an increase in the number of commissioners; e) the exclusion of Armed Forces staff as members of the commission; f) making the results of ongoing investigations public immediately, and not withholding them until the conclusion of proceedings; g) the replacement of the expression 'national reconciliation' with 'promoting the consolidation of democracy'; and, lastly, h) the exclusion of any reference to the Amnesty Law.[44]

On this occasion, the representative of the Family Commission, Suzana K. Lisbôa, pointed out the fact that, since the end of the dictatorship, the remains of only four victims out of hundreds had been identified. She demanded the Brazilian State commit to their identification and investigation: 'We want them

---

[41] See <https://www.france24.com/en/20190812-brazil-bolsonaro-praises-torturer-carlos-alberto-brilhante-ustra-national-hero-dictatorship>.
[42] Bolsonaro is statistically the Brazilian deputy who has made the most statements against the CNV in the National Congress between 2011 and 2014, either opposing its implementation or trying to disqualify its performance. See Antonio Teixeira de Barros, 'O debate parlamentar sobre a CNV no Congresso Nacional Brasileiro', *Revista Brasileira de Ciências Sociais*, 35.104 (2020), 1–27 (p. 9).
[43] The rapporteur approved amendments nos. 12 and 23, rejecting nos. 1–11 and nos. 13–22 (Câmara dos Deputados. Sessão: 225.1.54.0, 21 September 2011, pp. 206, 243).
[44] PT no Senado, 'Comissão da Verdade: sociedade civil cobra alterações', 18 Oct. 2011. Available online at <https://ptnosenado.org.br/comissao-da-verdade-sociedade-civil-cobra-alteracoes/> [accessed 10 January 2020].

to find us the bodies, to tell us where they are, how they were killed and who murdered them. We do want the guilty to be accountable'.[45] A few days later, on 26 October, the opinion of Aloysio Nunes Ferreira Filho, former guerrilla and Social Democrat senator from São Paulo, on bill no. 88/11 was dealt with as an emergency motion. The bill still did not meet the demands from family members, and reiterated the 'non-jurisdictional and non-persecutory nature of the Commission', which aimed at investigating serious human rights violations in order to guarantee that they were not repeated and to secure the democratic consolidation in the country.[46]

The senator defended his opinion stressing the fact that the proposal reinforced structuring constitutional norms, such as the prevalence of human rights. He justified the implementation of the CNV, and pointed out that the greater part of the abuses committed by the authoritarian regime installed in 1964 remained 'wrapped in mystery'. From this point of view, the work of the Commission should shed light on what was hidden, fostering the 'construction of collective memory', to be ratified by the approval of the Access to Information Law and the consequent improvement in the 'culture of institutional transparency'. Ferreira also highlighted the fact that, initially, the material compiled by the Truth Commission would be kept in secrecy, being made public only after their work was done.[47]

The rapporteur justified the timespan defined by the proposal (covering the period from 1946–88), considering that it referred to the period covered by the Amnesty Law (1979) and by article 4 of the Constitutional Amendment no. 26 (1985), ignoring that such normative references were prior to the 1988 Federal Constitution. For him however, '[...] the political authority of the Truth Commission would only be consolidated if [it] focus[ed] on the military regime'.[48]

Ferreira reaffirmed that the implementation of the judgement in the Inter-American Court of Human Rights, whether civil or criminal in nature, concerning the Araguaia Guerrilla War should be in the hands of the Judiciary. Notwithstanding this, he underlined an extract of the court decision in which it is stated that the activities and information compiled by the CNV '[...] do not replace the State obligation of establishing the truth and guaranteeing the judicial attribution of individual responsibility through penal judicial lawsuits'.[49]

Ferreira stressed the non-jurisdictional and non-persecutory nature of the Truth Commission. The senator reproduced and endorsed the controversial interpretation of the Brazilian Supreme Court on its Amnesty Law, by arguing that it would have benefited 'both sides'. He considered the legal

---

[45] Ibid.
[46] *Diário do Senado Federal*, no. 181 (2011), p. 44.218.
[47] Ibid., p. 44.221.
[48] Ibid., p. 44.219.
[49] Ibid., p. 44.222.

figure of 'related crimes' from the perspective of the alleged national pact that inaugurated the New Republic, disregarding the strict analysis of the text of the law and the jurisprudence on comparative law and international human rights law.[50] Furthermore, he reaffirmed the controversial interpretation that the amnesty had been incorporated into the constitutional text through the Constitutional Amendment no. 26 (1985).[51] The senator underlined, though, the undeniable 'duty' of public servants and military personnel to contribute to the Truth Commission.

The rapporteur's opinion also revealed a biased juridical approach towards the neutrality and the objectivity of the Truth Commission, which appear to be connected to the absence of family members and survivors of repression amongst its members. This bias reproduces traces of the prevailing legal culture in Brazil,[52] characterized by a certain 'legal provincialism',[53] in contrast with the recommendation of the Human Rights Commission of the United Nations, which establishes broad public consultation processes to choose the members of the Truth Commission.[54] Furthermore, the senator expressed his approach towards the CNV, appealing to its supposed neutrality and stating that the aim was 'to produce reports and documents so that the Commission would not produce the official truth'. It would work in such a way so as to '[...] provide facts and investigate them, so each and every one can look at facts and individually use their best judgement'.[55]

In the plenary session, several senators took the floor to praise the rapporteur's opinion, highlighting its balance and responsibility, as well as the role of the CNV in the democratic consolidation. The representative of the Democratic Labour Party (*Partido Democrático Trabalhista*, PDT) from Mato Grosso, Senator Pedro Taques, however, asked to speak in order to enquire about the agreement among the Senate's leaderships, which determined the approval of the Truth Commission bill with no debate and, moreover, about the naming of members of the military to the CNV, supported by the rapporteur.[56] Senator Sergio Souza, from the Democrats Party of Paraná, also took the

---

[50] Bernardi, p. 462. Deisy Ventura characterized the predominant conduct in the Supreme Court decision regarding the Non Compliance with a Fundamental Precept 153 (ADPF 153) as '*à la carte* positivism', which means to benefit from its own logic by conveniently hedging the strict application of the law text or international conventions, whenever suitable, to favour your own side (Deisy Ventura, 'A interpretação judicial da lei de Anistia brasileira e o Direito Internacional', *Revista Anistia Política e Justiça de Transição*, 4 (Brasília, DF: Ministério da Justiça, 2011), pp. 196–226 (pp. 205–11)).
[51] *Diário do Senado Federal*, no. 181 (2011), p. 44.229.
[52] Pádua Fernandes, 'As fontes de pesquisa sobre o Poder Judiciário no relatório da Comissão Nacional da Verdade: problemas teóricos e metodológicos', *Revista Arquivo do Estado*, São Paulo, ano 1, no. 2 (2016), 3–4.
[53] Ventura, p. 204.
[54] UN Commission on Human Rights, 'Conjunto de principios actualizado para la protección y la promoción de los derechos humanos mediante la lucha contra la impunidad', 8 February 2005. Available online at <http://www.derechos.org/nizkor/impu/impuppos.html> [accessed 15 November 2020].
[55] *Diário do Senado Federal*, no. 181 (2011), p. 44.230.
[56] Ibid., p. 44.234–35.

floor to question the leadership agreement to treat the voting on the bill as an emergency motion, stating that the Senate lost its status when such negotiations were approved.[57]

After a series of speeches in favour, Senator Randolfe Rodrigues, at the time representative of PSOL from Amapá, presented the suggestions made by family members during a session at the Senate's Human Rights Commission. Rodrigues suggested the senators should consider the need for a revision of the Amnesty Law alongside the Commission's efforts.[58] Nevertheless, he further suggested the withdrawing of amendments that took into account the proposals of the relatives of the fatal victims of the military dictatorship:

> [...] perhaps, we will not come to terms with [...] the Amnesty Law through the work of the National Truth Commission. [...] There is a bill that is currently being processed by the Senate's Foreign Affairs and National Defence Commission that proposes the revision of the Amnesty Law, because that law needs to be revised. [...] We would have amendments [which] contemplate the concerns raised by the family members. [...] however, with the voting happening at this moment, [...] with all the problems we may have regarding its approval, it could represent [...] one of the worst things that could happen to us now. The worst thing that can happen now [...] would be to see this bill return to the Chamber of Deputies. I want to believe it is the Government's understanding, shared with its supporters, that they need to put all necessary efforts for that bill to move forward [...].[59]

One day after the approval of the Access to Information Law, the bill to implement the National Truth Commission was unanimously approved, disregarding the demands of family members and civil society movements.[60] The launch of the Brazilian National Truth Commission took place over six months later, in a prestigious ceremony attended by all the former Brazilian presidents of the democratic period.[61] However, the Commission was the result of a legislative debate held behind closed doors and in a hurry, which had a predictable impact on the *modus operandi* of the Commission itself and on its scope. It worked in accordance with the Brazilian (re)democratization process, marked by 'military tutelage', which was, interestingly, a key element that has been present throughout Brazil's republican history, especially since the 1930s.[62]

---

[57] Ibid., p. 44.240.
[58] See bill 573/11 (Federal Chamber). See also bill 237/13 (Senate) and Non Compliance of a Fundamental Precept 320/14 (ADPF 320/14), from PSOL.
[59] *Diário do Senado Federal*, no. 181 (2011), p. 44.245.
[60] Ibid., p. 44.248.
[61] The Brazilian Federal Constitution. Law no. 12.528, from 18 November 2011. Available at: <http://www.planalto.gov.br/ccivil_03/_Ato2011-2014/2011/Lei/L12528.htm> [accessed 15 January 2020].
[62] José Murilo de Carvalho, *Forças Armadas e política no Brasil* (São Paulo: Todavia, 2019), pp. 23–24.

A Much Needed Assessment of the CNV

It took Brazil about twenty-four years to establish a Truth Commission to investigate the serious violations of human rights committed by the State during the military dictatorship. This contrasts with the experience of most countries where commissions were established immediately after the end of periods of authoritarian rule or of war. This time window has greatly hampered the retrieval of facts, especially those regarding the location of the bodies and remains of the victims of politically motivated violence.[63] The temporal distance also diluted the political and symbolic impact that the commission could have had on the victims' relatives, on survivors and, more broadly, on Brazilian society. This circumstance attenuated the role played by the commission in the constitution of a collective memory regarding state violence in the dictatorial period.

The Brazilian National Truth Commission was established with enormous limitations, as discussed above. From the beginning, it was caught up in political and methodological disputes that reflected the broad ideological spectrum of its members. Additionally, the commission had not constituted itself as an enabling environment that would allow the engagement of the society and the participation of civil society movements and organizations in the process. Moreover, those involved in the perpetration of the abusive crimes committed during the dictatorship feared the possible legal consequences of the commission's investigations. The Presidency of the Republic, for its part, did not issue an administrative act to regulate the internal procedures of the commission, which represented a delay on the commission's operating environment.[64] Contrary to the guidelines provided by the OAS in the Gomes Lund case (concerning the Araguaia Guerrilla War) regarding the establishment and operation of Truth Commissions, the CNV did not have budgetary independence, nor did it have enough members and time to establish a rigorous investigation of the abuses committed during a long-lasting dictatorship, ended many years before but with no evident dissolution.[65]

Civil society movements and organizations started to advocate for more transparent procedures. At the same time, they also pressured the commission to publicize its work through openly communicating its agenda of activities to the population and inviting citizens to join the debates. The commission then gradually started to publicize the results of its hearings and release partial development reports, thus increasing the impact of its work on public opinion,

---

[63] The CNV was only able to find the remains of Epaminondas Gomes de Oliveira (CNV, vol. I, pp. 614–21).
[64] Quinalha, 'Com quantos lados se faz uma verdade?'
[65] Decree 12.528, from 2011, which instituted the CNV, did not make it compulsory for its members to devote themselves exclusively to their work on the commission (Roberto Duailibi, 'O caseiro confessa envolvimento em morte do coronel Malhães', *Revista Época* (Rio de Janeiro), 29 April 2014; available online at <https://epoca.globo.com/tempo/noticia/2014/04/bcaseiro-confessa-envolvimentob-em-morte-do-coronel-malhaes.html> [accessed 9 January 2020]).

albeit belatedly. A Truth Commission sets out to 'seek the facts'. Its function is to point out which facts should be recognized by the State, as well as what level of responsibility should be attributed to them. For those who have suffered serious violations of their rights, the Commission creates the conditions to 'remove the possibility of continued denial' by perpetrators. Besides, a Truth Commission is committed '[...] directly and widely to the affected population whilst gathering information about their experiences'.[66]

However, the CNV systematically stopped complying with its role of shedding light on the memories silenced by the dictatorial period. As a matter of comparison, while the São Paulo State's Truth Commission promoted 941 public hearings, the National Commission was able to hold only 246 public hearings.[67] It is worth noting that it was precisely the disclosure of the reports on the abuses committed by the dictatorship which played a crucial role in the decay of this political system and in the construction of a collective memory of state repression at the time, which could be seen in Chile, Uruguay and Argentina, or in the struggle for justice, which could be seen in Argentina. In this respect, the National Truth Commission was flying in the face of a growing global appreciation of testimony, something observed since the end of World War II. The centrality of the individual's testimonies and their experiences gave survivors and relatives a new status. The consistency of the survivors' testimonies turned their stories into evidence to back up prosecution for crimes committed against humanity.

The final report of the CNV was frustrating, as it dealt with only 434 deaths.[68] The survey of the 8,350 indigenous people (an estimate that involves only ten indigenous groups) and the 1,192 rural workers murdered in the period was recorded in Annex II of the CNV Report. Furthermore, the Commission did not systematically catalogue torture cases, disregarding the estimate that in the first months after the 1964 coup alone between 30,000 and 50,000 people

---

[66] Priscilla Hayner, *Verdades Silenciadas: la Justicia Transicional y el reto de las Comisiones de la Verdad* (Barcelona: Institut Català Internacional per la Pau, 2014), pp. 21, 11–12.

[67] Cristina Buarque de Hollanda, 'Direitos Humanos e Democracia: a experiência das comissões da verdade no Brasil', *Revista Brasileira de Ciências Sociais*, 33.96 (2018), p. 10. CNV's former executive secretary claims that the commission compiled around 500 testimonies, both public and confidential (André S. Martins and Vivien Ishaq, 'O legado da Comissão Nacional da Verdade: dois anos depois da entrega do relatório o reconhecimento judicial do direito à verdade desafia a falta de justiça efetiva', in *As recomendações da Comissão Nacional da Verdade: balanços sobre a sua implementação dois anos depois*, ed. by Amy Jo Westhrop et al. (Rio de Janeiro: ISER, 2016), pp. 42–55 (p. 53). This reminds us of the Chilean experience, where a second commission named 'National Commission on Political Imprisonment and Torture' (referred to as Valech Commission I) had to be installed to address exclusively the issue of torture. A total of 35,868 people have given testimony before this commission, out of which 28,459 have been classified as victims (Oriana B. Ramírez, Daniela M. Santelices and Rodrigo Suárez Madariaga, 'Las comisiones de la verdad en la batalla de la memoria: usos y efectos disputados de la verdad extrajudicial en Chile', *Colombia Internacional*, 97 (2019), 27–55 (p. 42)).

[68] The author has estimated this number to be 455, taking into account the survey carried out in *Dossiê Ditadura* (2009), by the CNV (2014), by the State of São Paulo Commission of Truth (CEV/SP Rubens Paiva) and CVPUC/SP (2017).

were arrested.⁶⁹ The CNV underestimated the magnitude of the violence used by the military dictatorship, as well as its legacy and its repercussions, and this reflects the poor quality of citizenship exercised in Brazil. This approach differs from the very review carried out by the CNV, which presented a panorama of the political and institutional changes promoted by the military dictatorship, aiming at obtaining broad social control.⁷⁰

A key witness for the reconstruction of the atrocities committed by State Security Organs during the dictatorship was retired Lieutenant Colonel Paulo Malhães, who was responsible for extermination missions aimed at politically persecuted people. Such missions were performed at the 'Death House' (*Casa da Morte*), located in Petrópolis, in the state of Rio de Janeiro, at the headquarters of the Araguaia Guerrilla Movement, and in locations in other countries of the Southern Cone of Latin America.⁷¹ However, Malhães's testimony remained unfinished, as he was murdered soon after testifying before the CNV.⁷² This crime intimidated both the society and the eyewitnesses of the violence perpetrated by the authoritarian State.

The CNV overcame a number of obstacles in order to gain access to the documents of the Brazilian Armed Forces, especially those produced by the now defunct secret services of the three armed forces: the Army Information Centre, the Navy Information Centre and the Air Force Information Centre, all of which were declared to be officially destroyed.⁷³ Nonetheless, the Access to Information Law states that 'no access can be denied to information necessary to the judicial or administrative authority of fundamental rights' (Article 21). The aforementioned law also guarantees free access to files which hold collections of documents that show evidence of human rights violations carried out by public agents or those working for them. The law also penalizes the destruction of documents related to the violations cited above (ibid.). Once again, the Brazilian State disrespected the judgements handed down by the Inter-American Court of Human Rights in the cases of Gomes Lund and Vladimir Herzog, as no independent investigation was established to verify whether documents had been destroyed or not, nor were the people held accountable for these crimes ever charged. There was not even an attempt to recover the documents or part of them.

Yet, the pressure from civil society was not enough to guarantee the enforcement of the law. No civil or military authority was penalized for their disrespect towards the above-mentioned laws. In this regard, the official legal

---

⁶⁹ Maria Helena Moreira Alves, *Estado e oposição no Brasil (1964-1984)*, 2nd edn (Rio de Janeiro: Vozes, 2005), p. 72; Rodrigo Patto Sá Motta, *As universidades e o regime militar: cultura política brasileira e modernização autoritária* (Rio de Janeiro: Zahar, 2014), p. 26.
⁷⁰ Furthermore, CNV did not conclude the investigation on the circumstances of the cases, so as to establish direct or indirect accountability on the part of the State, or the persecution suffered from other social groups and movements (CNV, vol. II).
⁷¹ Almeida et al., eds, *Dossiê Ditadura*, pp. 465, 512.
⁷² *Carta Capital*, 25 April 2014.
⁷³ CNV, vol. I, pp. 63–64, 963.

apparatus remained ineffective. The Access to Information Law was issued just for show, particularly as regards the registers of the crimes committed by the State during the dictatorial period.

The CNV has identified a total of 377 public agents as the authors of serious violations of human rights,[74] having overcome many obstacles in order to record the testimonies of military officers. In addition, several public agents refused to attend or remained silent in their sessions. In this respect, there was little progress in clarifying the circumstances in which deaths and disappearances occurred, especially those regarding the Araguaia Guerrilla War. The commission advanced very little in the investigation of the repressive operations carried out in the final stage of the guerrilla movement, started in October 1973. Most of the guerrillas were arrested, tortured and executed during this action.[75] The CNV has provided little clarification on the authorship and the circumstances of the imprisonments and tortures suffered by the rural population, especially those 400 who lived nearby, who were seen as supporters or new recruits to the movement.[76]

In this respect, the CNV had little to add in what concerns the details of the missions and the operation of military bases located in the Araguaia region.[77] The chain of command of the Armed Forces related to the repression against the guerrilla, particularly in its final stage, has not yet been figured out. Only two officers' names are known, as the commander of the Marabá Post and the sub-coordinator of the North Region.[78] Such scarcity of names and information is revealing of how engaged military officers and Brazilian authorities are in erasing the history and the memories of the Araguaia Guerrilla War.

The CNV had some success in proving that the use of torture with the politically persecuted was the main method to fight people's insurgency — so much so that it had become a systematic administrative practice and a political institution of the authoritarian State. But it is noteworthy that torture cases were not systematically recorded.[79] The CNV has established a fundamental

---

[74] In 1972, Amnesty International disclosed the number of 472 torturers, whilst Brazil: Never Again (*Brasil: Nunca Mais*) reported 444 names in 1985 (Janaína de A. Teles, 'As denúncias de torturas e torturadores a partir dos cárceres políticos brasileiros', in *Interseções*, Rio de Janeiro, 16.1 (2014), 31–68). Besides, the number of agents who received a medal for bravery, called *Medalha do Pacificador com Palma*, is as high as 541 (Mariana Joffily and Maud Chirio, 'A repressão condecorada: a atribuição da Medalha do Pacificador a agentes do aparato de segurança (1964–1985)', *História Unisinos*, 18.3 (Sept.-Dec. 2014), 440–51 (p. 445)).

[75] According to data from the CNV, vol. I, pp. 719–21. As of 2014, CNV had access to 150 pages of information about the postings of military officers, which could have been systematically studied (Martins and Ishaq, 'O legado', pp. 10–11).

[76] Leoncencio Nossa, *Mata! o Major Curió e as guerrilhas no Araguaia* (São Paulo: Companhia das Letras, 2012), p. 132.

[77] CNV, vol. I, pp. 680–725.

[78] CNV, vol. III, pp. 1181–84, 1741–42. Chapter 16 features a draft of a chain of command in which key characters in the attack to the guerrilla are revealed, without, however, clarifying the organizational structure and its action in the several stages of the repression (CNV, vol. I, pp. 688–89, 860–63, 885–92, 910).

[79] Marlon A. Weichert, 'O Relatório da Comissão da Verdade: conquistas e desafios', *Projeto História*, São Paulo, 50 (Aug. 2014), 86–137 (pp. 119–20).

investigation on the sexual violence perpetrated by the public agents during the Brazilian dictatorship, as well as on the places where it was practised.[80] However, the commission did not obtain a thorough and detailed list of the torture practices, as such investigation would demand a great number of testimonies from victims of torture, thus constructing 'the capacity to listen' regarding Brazil's traumatic, uncomfortable and neglected past.

It should be noted that, for the first time in the democratic period, the burden of proof regarding the crimes committed by public agents during the military dictatorship fell on the State. In effect, both in the CEMDP and in the Amnesty Commission it fell to the victims of human rights violations to collect proof of the State's criminal actions.

Another contribution given by the CNV concerns the acknowledgment of institutional responsibility by the Armed Forces for the serious violations of human rights committed by the State during the dictatorship. The CNV has shed light on the protagonism of the Armed Forces in the crimes of torture, summary execution, enforced disappearances and the concealment of bodies. The guidance to execute such tasks came from the president's cabinet and military ministers, thus dismissing the idea that these practices stemmed from 'excesses', alien to the standard of conduct of the above-mentioned Brazilian institutions and authorities.[81]

The CNV also conducted a fundamental investigation on the complicity of national and multinational companies in both the planning and the execution of 1964's military coup d'état as well as their decisive role in the construction of a conservative development project, favouring multinational capital in association with national. In fact, the commission made great progress in the search for information on the collaboration of businesspeople with the dictatorial State and its repressive apparatus during the dictatorship. The persecution suffered by the trade union movement and its members, which were among the main targets of the coup d'état, has also been underlined by the commission, but by comparison there was not much advance in the investigation on the repression against this group.[82]

The CNV reported clues and some evidence regarding the decisive role played by the Army Information Centre (CIE) in the repression carried out in the South America's Southern Cone,[83] although the investigations on 'Operation Condor' offered disappointing results. Nevertheless, the commission identified

---

[80] According to data from the CNV, chapter 10. CNV has disclosed relevant information about the places where torture was carried out in the country, having collected information about 230 centres for torture and extermination (CNV, chapter 15, p. 830).

[81] CNV, vol. I, pp. 844–46.

[82] Oddly enough, this investigation was published in Annex II of the CNV Report. Furthermore, some professional groups — such as teachers — were not included in the death toll. It is also worth noting, however, that cases up to 1988 were taken into account (CNV, vol. II, chapters 2 and 8, pp. 79–80).

[83] The people in charge of the Division of Operations were approached in a very incipient way (CNV, vol. I, pp. 224, 260). Little has been investigated about hints of their participation in the Araguaia Guerrilla War and in the Southern Cone (CNV, vol. I, p. 1685).

the chain of command and the accountability of the Foreign Affairs Minister, as well as of the Head of the Overseas Information Centre (CIEx) and also of the Army Attachés in operations carried out in the region. Although incipient, such investigations shed light on information exchange and the collaboration between the diplomatic representatives and the State Security organs from Brazil and also from other countries in the Southern Cone.

In this regard, the CNV obtained unpublished documents on the collaborative repression in the Southern Cone, prior to 'Operation Condor', regarding the cases of disappeared Brazilians and Argentinians who went missing in 1973, both in Rio de Janeiro and in Buenos Aires.[84] These documents attest how intense the information exchange was among Brazil, Uruguay, Chile and Argentina and allows for new research possibilities. In addition, the investigation carried out by the CNV also supported the data of a 2009 investigation on Maria Regina Marcondes Pinto and Edgardo E. Espinoza — the latter, one of the leaders of the Chilean Revolutionary Left Movement (*Movimiento de Izquierda Revolucionaria*, MIR) — in which it is revealed that they were murdered in Buenos Aires, not in Chile as it was believed, in 1976.[85] However, the CNV made little progress in investigating the attacks against the democratic governments in Chile promoted by the Brazilian dictatorship, especially Allende's.[86] Furthermore, Colonel Malhães's testimony, as well as the documents found in his residence, confirmed some details concerning 'Operation Gringo', with respect to an insider in the Montoneros group and the disappearance of its leaders between 1978 and 1980.[87]

It is noteworthy that the CNV acknowledged CIE's protagonism in the repression of the Araguaia Guerrilla War, as well as that of the Jungle Warfare Training Centre (*Centro de Instrução de Guerra na Selva*, CIGS), in Manaus, state of Amazonas.[88] General Ausserresse, who played an active role in the repression to the Algerian War of Independence (1954–62), trained Latin American military officers in this place between 1973 and 1975. Although it did not obtain many details in the survey about these facts, the CNV found signs of deep international alliances in fighting the armed struggle in Brazil and in

---

[84] Almeida et al., eds, *Dossiê Ditadura*, pp. 489–92.
[85] *Dossiê Ditadura*, pp. 647–49. Please note, however, that in chapter 6 of the Report, regarding 'Operation Condor', there is a mention of a CIA document stating that Espinoza had been sent to Chile. Judicial inquiries corroborate the outcome by the Argentine Forensic Anthropology Team (EAAF), published in *Dossiê Ditadura*.
[86] Roberto Simon, *O Brasil contra a Democracia: A Ditadura, o Golpe no Chile e a Guerra Fria na América do Sul* (São Paulo: Companhia das Letras, 2021); CNV, vol. I, pp. 191, 193–94, pp. 1302–12, 1346–60.
[87] According to CNV, vol. I, chapter 6, pp. 245–49, 255–56, 258–62. Moreover, the CNV regarded the death, in a car crash, of former President Juscelino Kubitschek in 1976 as an 'accident', whereas the State of São Paulo Truth Commission Rubens Paiva (CEV/SP) stated the opposite: Assembleia Legislativa/Comissão da Verdade do Estado de São Paulo 'Rubens Paiva', *Relatório sobre a morte do presidente Juscelino Kubitschek de Oliveira*. São Paulo, tomo IV, 2015, pp. 745–70. Available at < http://comissaodaverdade.al.sp.gov.br/relatorio/tomo-iv/> [accessed 15 November 2020].
[88] CNV, vol. I, pp. 688–89, 863, 892.

Overcoming the Legacy of the Military Dictatorship

the Southern Cone.[89]

Finally, the CNV made good progress in cases of greater repercussion, such as the ones regarding federal representative Rubens Paiva, who had his mandate revoked, and the guerrilla Stuart Angel Jones. Both were victims of enforced disappearance in 1971. The commission, however, did not have enough time to search for the remains of these and other militants.[90] In this regard, Lieutenant Colonel Malhães's testimony had an impact when he revealed the barbaric methods used to hide the bodies of murdered militants.[91]

This critical perspective contrasts with the complimentary assessment of the CNV report given by most of the congresspeople in December 2014, who stressed the relevance of the historical panorama traced, as well as the pedagogical role the text would play in 'national reconciliation'. Very few representatives criticized the lack of justice for the crimes compiled by the commission. On the other hand, Representative Jair Bolsonaro took the floor to reiterate his criticism of the CNV, characterized by him as a 'vengeful' instrument that aimed to damage the image of the Armed Forces.[92]

In effect, the limits and obstacles faced by the CNV can be seen both in the report text and in the final ceremony when it was handed over, which was not as prestigious as the event for the inauguration of the commission, which had been graced by the presence of the five former presidents elected after 1985. It also lacked the optimistic environment of the opening meeting.[93]

Final Remarks

From this critical panorama regarding the establishment of the CNV in Brazil, we can state that enormous difficulties remain in building a public sphere

---

[89] Colonel Sebastião Curió states that he and the soldiers sent at this stage of the attack on the guerrilla movement were trained in Manaus (Nossa, *Mata!*, pp. 161, 382). According to General Manuel Contreras, Head of the National Intelligence Directorate (DINA), Chilean soldiers were sent to Brazil every two months (Marie-Monique Robin, *Escuadrones de la muerte: la escuela francesa*, trans. by Sergio di Nucci and Pablo Rodríguez (Buenos Aires: Editorial Sudamericana, 2004), pp. 364–66, 384). Major Thaumaturgo S. Vaz undertook jungle warfare training at the Escola das Américas between 1962 and 1964, was an instructor at the Jungle Warfare Training Centre between 1968 and 1970, and was a representative from Brazil in the founding meeting of Operation Condor, in 1975, with Lieutenant Colonel Flavio de Marco (CNV, vol. I, pp. 223, 333).
[90] CNV, vol. III, pp. 598–607.
[91] Ibid., pp. 519–28.
[92] Barros, 'O debate parlamentar', pp. 15–18.
[93] It is relevant to mention that Vera Paiva, the daughter of the aforementioned Federal Deputy Rubens Paiva, was invited to make a speech at the commission's inauguration ceremony as a representative of the family members of the dead and disappeared. However, in the event she was not allowed to speak. Vera Paiva, 'Discurso de Vera Paiva na cerimônia de criação da Comissão da Verdade' (2012); available online at: <https://www.sul21.com.br/opiniaopublica/2011/11/discurso-de-vera-paiva-na-cerimonia-de-criacao-da-comissao-da-verdade/> [accessed 5 Oct. 2020]). Also see Bruno Ferraz, 'Ex-integrante diz que comissão teve fim "decepcionante"', *Folha de S. Paulo*, Painel, 21 December 2014; available online at <https://www1.folha.uol.com.br/poder/2014/12/1565515-ex-integrante-diz-que-comissao-teve-fim-decepcionante.shtml> [accessed 14 July 2020].

where the traumatic experiences of the recent past can be shared and debated. And the rights denied to victims of state terrorism committed in the dictatorial period and their relatives are still not as widely debated as they should be. This context has favoured the dissemination of historical 'negationism' and the militarization of politics in Brazil. There were limits to the democratic transition, heavily controlled by the military 'tutelage', that still prevented Brazilian society from accessing memories and experiences that could have shaped a new collective conscience about the dictatorial repression and the status of its victims and survivors, thus rendering the coming to terms with this authoritarian legacy and overcoming it nearly impossible.

Little more than five years after the conclusion of the work of the CNV, Brazil remains a role model of impunity and unapologetic violations of human rights and justice. The agenda of the promotion of human rights is far behind what we expected, and the factual reconstruction of the crimes committed by State actors during the dictatorship are left unresolved. Despite some advances made through the work of the CNV, social and political mechanisms still in place are blocking the dissemination of testimonies about the dictatorship. The prosecutions that might have been expected and the accountability of agents for the crimes committed by the State in this period are not widespread, according to a recent report by the Public Prosecutor's Office.[94] We are still not able to have all the evidence we need to fully debate the legacy of the dictatorship because of those setbacks.

Brazil has moved forward in many respects, but failed to seize the opportunity to give real visibility in the public sphere to the testimonies and facts regarding the violation of human rights as the *modus operandi* of the dictatorial regime that existed between 1964 and 1988. Had the CNV in Brazil fulfilled its duties and followed the path of other commissions, our collective memory could have been reshaped through the acknowledgement of the value of personal testimonies. It could have also been shaped through the collection of pieces of evidence to tell the untold stories and thorough factual investigation to bring forward to our society a new vision based on principles of human rights. Those were the steps needed to set new milestones in the establishment of a new democratic social order. Nevertheless, the legacy of the past remains.

Once again, Brazil missed an opportunity to enforce the rule of law and the value of accountability by denying the violations and the role of State in perpetrating them during the authoritarian regime. The country has also lost the opportunity to give unprecedented visibility to the traumas resulting from slavery and the genocide of the indigenous peoples, which could have helped these populations to gain access to the basic human rights which have been denied throughout their history. There is a continuum between the dictatorship period and the democratic period in Brazil which is mediated by the military

---

[94] Ministério Público Federal, 'Da busca por restos mortais à responsabilização: o longo caminho das ações penais do MPF no campo da Justiça de Transição' (2019) online at <http://www.justicadetransicao.mpf.mp.br/justica-criminal> [accessed 20 February 2020].

tutelage and by the violent practices still put in place by Brazilian democratic institutions, such as our police forces.

In effect, Brazil's experience of (re)democratization contrasts with that of several other Latin American countries, which turned their eyes to their history and came to terms with their dictatorial past, both in juridical and symbolic terms. The return of the military to the centre of the public scene and the evident recent political and social setbacks indicate that the strategy of not prioritizing the promotion of human rights values, principles, policies and legislation, because of our unresolved past — or because of our past 'agreements' — has failed. The social contract sustained by the Amnesty Law might not yet be broken, but it will only change dramatically and for good if we face, once and for all, the legacy of the military dictatorship by dismantling the military tutelage of our democracy.

Challenges to Democracy in the Twenty-first Century: The Current Situation of Brazil — New Variations of the Same Dilemmas[1]

EDUARDO C. B. BITTAR

Universidade de São Paulo

Introduction

Democracy is on the brink. In a time of agony and crisis, contemporary populism throws democracy and its values into a dangerous chasm. The risk of the chasm is contained in the warning by Adorno about the possibility of a relapse into barbarism.[2] The history of the twentieth century has much to say in this regard, in that it serves as a warning, taking into account that historical memory has an important role to play,[3] when it comes to thinking about the destinies of democracy in the twenty-first century.

It is a well-known fact that the twentieth century plunged the world into the spectrum of Nazi-fascism, the Second World War and the concentration camps, from the outbreak of the economic crisis in the 1920s, the economic consequences for Germany of the defeat in the First World War, triggered by the rise of extreme right leaders and authoritarian political schemes. Similarly, the second half of the twentieth century is marked by the Cold War between the USA and the USSR, with disastrous consequences in the nuclear arms race, the political bipolarization between capitalism and communism, with direct consequences in the area of public debate and the political culture of the period. In Latin America, this resulted in dictatorships and authoritarian regimes, not forgetting the serious violations of human rights throughout the region.[4] All this came to an end in May 1968, a political, cultural and social demonstration, in the clash with authoritarianism, the Vietnam War, the suffocating situation of freedom and the emergence of pluralist and pro-minority discourses. The

---

[1] Text translated from Portuguese by Kavita Lamba.
[2] Theodor W. Adorno, *Educação e emancipação*, trans. by Wolfgang Leo Maar, 3rd edn (São Paulo: Paz e Terra, 2003), p. 119.
[3] Márcio Seligmann-Silva, 'Imagens do trauma e sobrevivência das imagens', in *Imagem e memória*, ed. by Elcio Loureiro Cornelsen, Elisa Amorim Vieira and Márcio Seligmann-Silva (Belo Horizonte: UFMG, 2012), pp. 63–80.
[4] Pablo Galain Palermo, 'Desaparición forzada de personas en América Latina', in *Filosofia do Direito*, ed. by Eduardo C. B. Bittar (São Paulo: Quartier Latin, 2019), pp. 169–86.

closing years of the twentieth century would come to represent, in the readings of Eric Hobsbawm,[5] Agnes Heller,[6] and Jürgen Habermas,[7] the depreciation of the very project of modernity and its emancipatory potential. By the end of the twentieth century, the very idea of liberal democracy would also find itself weakened and worn out.

This brief survey of the twentieth century is sufficient to present the existing connection between prosperous economic cycles and unfavourable economic cycles in capitalist societies, for which the rule of a deep connection between economics and democracy is valid. This implies a connection between economic consciousness and democratic consciousness, given that the latter is conditioned by the former. In other words, in times of crisis, when economic consciousness demands economic recovery, authoritarian projects emerge, winning over public opinion and conquering the political scene. Thus, the historical balance sheet drawn from the twentieth century shows that democratic consciousness is fragile, and, therefore easily abandoned, in times of crisis.

Times of crisis are characterized by political division, economic crisis and political discord.[8] The adherence of economic power to narrower political views means that the economic agenda supersedes the democratic agenda. Moreover, it can be stated clearly enough, from these episodes — and indeed, studies of democracy in Latin America tend to point in this direction[9] — that economic elites have a strong attachment to maintaining their economic interests and a weak attachment to republican and democratic principles, adhering to them in an instrumental and opportunistic way, so that democracy is somewhat displaced from the demands and economic interests of the majority.[10]

Hence it is a matter of record that the democracies of the twentieth century are exposed to this type of phenomenon, whether in Europe, the United States or Latin America. But, when it comes to assessing how this happens locally, the weaknesses of the institutions and the existing democratic deficits appear. Therefore, the permanent risk is that of economic consciousness asking democratic consciousness to minimize itself to such an extent that the citizens

---

[5] Eric Hobsbawm, *Era dos extremos: o breve século XX*, trans. by Marcos Santarrita (São Paulo: Companhia das Letras, 2002), p. 562.
[6] Agnes Heller and Ferenc Féher, *A condição política pós-moderna*, trans. by Marcos Santarrita (Rio de Janeiro: Civilização Brasileira, 1998), p. 11.
[7] Jürgen Habermas, 'La modernidad, un proyecto incompleto', in *La postmodernidad*, ed. by Hal Foster, 6th edn (Barcelona: Kairós, 2006), pp. 19–36.
[8] Leonardo Avritzer, 'O pêndulo da democracia no Brasil: uma análise da crise 2013–2018', *Novos Estudos*, 37 (2018), 273–89 (p. 276).
[9] 'The political history of twentieth century Latin America is characterized by numerous breakthroughs to restricted or full democracies, then followed by breakdowns of democracy. Essentially, the economically dominant classes tolerated democracy only as long as what they perceived to be their vital interests were protected' (Evelyne Huber, Dietrich Rueschemeyer and John D. Stephens, 'The Impact of Economic Development on Democracy', *Journal of Economic Perspectives*, 7.3 (1993), 71–86 (p. 78).
[10] Boaventura de Souza Santos, 'E agora, Brasil?' <https://outraspalavras.net/> [accessed 2 August 2019].

relinquish their own rights and freedom, in favour of economic recovery, so that instrumental reason — and, here, it is important to recover this concept (*Instrumentellen Vernunft*) from the Frankfurt philosophical tradition[11] — is placed above everything, to the point of materializing the instrumentalization of the human beings, their dignity, rights and freedoms.

Thus, the destinies of democracy are written according to the logic of cycles and crises. If this is an important conclusion in respect of historical instabilities of democracy, it should also be emphasized that this is how the economic-financial crisis started the weakening of democracy and the Republican crisis in contemporary Brazil.[12] And, in fact, Brazil experienced, since the period of the Direct (Elections) Now (*Diretas Já!*, 1985–88) and the publishing of a new democratic Constitution (1988), a period of restoration of democracy, which was followed by a period of maturing and strengthening of democracy and democratic institutions, which was to last from 1988 until 2013. But, after the 2008 economic-financial crisis, and respective instabilities of the world market and the tendency towards de-globalization, the period 2008–13 was one of growing dissatisfaction, an accumulation of obscurantist tendencies, and the beginning of the collapse of the virtuous cycle that Brazilian democracy had known until then.[13]

The Brazilian democratic crisis in the period 2013–18 — which resulted in public protests (2013), impeachment of the president (2016), a transitional government (2017–18), intense political polarization in the election year (2018), and the election of the new right-wing populist government (2019–22) — is not just a local crisis nor is it something new. What is happening in Brazil is a clear reflection of what is also happening in the United States and throughout Europe, within a global trend of political regimes leaning towards right-wing populism.

This shows that one of the most problematic aporias of democracy is the possibility of being captured by populism. This warning is inscribed in the tradition of the Frankfurt School, from Theodor Adorno[14] and Max Horkheimer, to the more contemporary traditions of Jürgen Habermas,[15] Axel Honneth[16] and Rainer Forst.[17] In this regard, the reconstruction of the meaning of democratic experience is a clear challenge for democracy in the twenty-first century. This points to the need to strengthen the role of democracy and of

---

[11] Max Horkheimer, *Théorie traditionnelle et théorie critique*, trans. by Claude Maillard and Sibylle Muller (Paris: Gallimard, 1974), pp. 20–35.
[12] Lilia Moritz Schwarcz, *Sobre o autoritarismo brasileiro* (São Paulo: Companhia das Letras, 2019), p. 236.
[13] Eduardo C. B. Bittar, 'Crise econômica e crise do direito: a ineficácia dos direitos humanos e o modelo de desenvolvimento', *Revista da Faculdade de Direito*, USP, 105 (2012), 496–508.
[14] Theodor Adorno, *Le Nouvel Extrémisme de droite*, trans. by Olivier Mannoni (Paris: Climats, Flammarion, 2019), p. 53.
[15] Jürgen Habermas, *Direito e democracia*, trans. by Flávio Beno Siebneichler (Rio de Janeiro: Tempo Brasileiro, 2003).
[16] Axel Honneth, *Das Recht der Freiheit* (Berlin: Suhrkamp, 2011).
[17] Rainer Forst, *Normativität und Macht* (Berlin: Suhrkamp, 2015).

its instruments in the light of contemporary debates on the subject. That is why this signalling is decisive, when it comes to discussing the vitality and the quality of democracy in the twenty-first century.

Democracy, Globalization, Crisis and Insecurity

The atmosphere of contemporary societies is characterized by intense relativism, insecurity and instability. In recent years, globalization, cultural fragmentation and a loss of economic growth have generated the most diverse reactions, among them, the revolt of the middle classes, a resumption of nationalism and the reinvention of the social enemy.[18] Fear, despair and economic loss generate mass anti-democratic feeling. For no other reason, the political exploitation of the fascination for authoritarianism is something that brings out the drive for aggression towards and disconnection from the other, leading to violence, anti-democraticism and destructiveness.[19]

At this point, the election of Donald Trump, in the United States, triggered a new process, with three dimensions: i) the use of new technology in the elections; ii) the re-emergence of nationalism; iii) the dissemination of Fake News and the disconnection of political discourse from truth.[20] These facts tie in with the effects of Brexit, with the 2016 referendum in the United Kingdom, and its projections on the political and economic scene of the European Union. From these sparks, authoritarian leaders, extreme right-wing governments and hate speech begin to emerge, rekindling conceptions of the world that were thought to operate only in the century gone by, in a real wave of neo-conservatism which reaches countries such as Hungary, Poland, the United States, Russia, Italy, and Israel, as the Brazilian historian Lilia Schwarcz points out.[21]

In this scenario, the rise of neo-conservative discourses is based on populist propaganda,[22] which has the same compromising effect (inverted) of progressive discourses, generally based on Utopias aimed at the indetermination of the future. However, the rise of authoritarian leaderships throughout the world explores images of an idealized past, shifting the eyes from the universe of the present (inconstant, insecure and uncertain, full of relativism and pluralism) to the idyllic universe of the past-imagined (safe, stable, orderly, straightforward, right), in a reactionary tendency.[23]

---

[18] Fernando Henrique Cardoso, *Crise e reinvenção da política no Brasil* (São Paulo: Companhia das Letras, 2018), p. 158.
[19] Theodor W. Adorno, *Studien zum autoritären Charakter* (Frankfurt: Suhrkamp, 1995), p. 58.
[20] Eugenio Bucci, 'Pós-política e corrosão da verdade', *Revista USP* (2018), 19–30 (p. 22), <http://www.revista.usp.br/> [accessed 2 August 2019].
[21] Schwarcz, p. 25.
[22] Eric Landowski, 'Populisme et esthésie', in *Actes Sémiotiques*, 121 (Limoges: Université de Limoges, 2018), available online at <https://www.unilim.fr/actes-semiotiques/6021>. In this respect, see also Ahmed Kharbouch, 'Manipulation et contagion: le discours ambivalent du populisme politique', in *Actes Sémiotiques*, 121 (Limoges: Université de Limoges, 2018), available online at <https://www.unilim.fr/actes-semiotiques/5982>.
[23] Cardoso, p. 173.

In contemporary Brazil, particularly, this strategy worked, and what was considered a marginal and minor political discourse took its place in present-day politics. Thus, the extreme right parties have based themselves on the ideas of family preservation, religious values, order and progress. Hence, the political discourses could capture the indetermination of the moment, having been able to combine proposals for neoliberal policies, privatization, moralization of politics, controlling criminality and violence, promises of stability and public authority, and public security policies. Here all the characteristics of the discourse of tradition are present, and not of *modernity*, in the history of Brazil.[24]

Add to this the intense media involvement in *Operation Lava-Jato* (run by the Federal Police together with the Public Prosecutor's Office), which led to the imprisonment of politicians and businessmen on charges of embezzlement and corruption — a decisive factor, and one which has been able to generate feelings of frustration, indignation, hatred and revolt among the population, around the facts linked to corruption.

Complete combustion would only be present, when taking in this analytical framework the set of factors which have, gradually, been draining the middle classes, namely, unemployment, the reduction of social rights, the increase in taxes, the loss of consumption capacity, and the blocking of market energies, all direct consequences of the effects of the economic-financial crisis of 2008, which negatively impacted Brazil indirectly throughout the country. If there was no serious crisis in 2008, the period 2008–13 would be one marked by economic loss, tax increases and the decrease in market optimism in the immediately preceding cycle (2003–10).

This is how the 2013 protests erupted in several cities in the country — emerging like a whirlwind[25] — having a huge impact on the legitimacy of governments, mobilized by the emergence of a digital public sphere, within a diffuse set of popular demands, bearing in mind the dissatisfaction with the state of the economic deterioration of the population, among other agendas. This implies that the virtuous period of the Brazilian economy and democracy, which lasted for the period 2000–10, was coming to an end, to be followed by the difficult period of the following decade (2010–20), in which economic losses, high unemployment rates, reforms in the area of social rights (2017), the pandemic (2020), and restrictions on individual rights are evident.

Since then, there has been a strong de-structuring of public debate, which justifies the rise of a political model that values private life, religion and family.[26] Once the political pact is broken, this period will suffer an accumulation of great depreciation, in a succession of protests which will produce an enormous

---

[24] Roberto DaMatta, *O que faz o brasil, Brasil?* (Rio de Janeiro: Rocco, 1986), p. 19.
[25] Eugênio Bucci, *A forma bruta dos protestos* (São Paulo: Companhia das Letras, 2016), p. 16.
[26] Jorge Chaloub, Pedro Lima, Fernando Perlatto, 'Direitas no Brasil contemporâneo', *Teoria e Cultura*, 13 (2018), 9–21 (p. 11).

feeling of political disbelief,[27] in addition to endless criticism of the way in which Brazilian politicians act, the patrimonialism of the Brazilian State,[28] corruption, and the lack of a sustainable economic project for the country, which results in a vacuum that allows the rise of political forces associated with the extreme right.

The Malaise of Brazilian Democracy

For no other reason, the period 2013–18 has been named by Brazilian philosopher Avritzer as being the period of the malaise of democracy in Brazil.[29] Since then, the instabilities have been enormous, which justifies the appearance of a series of theoretical hypotheses, analyses and scientific approaches, based on contributions by political scientists, sociologists, philosophers, economists and jurists, regarding the possible causes of the crisis in Brazilian democracy. It is not possible to list and review all of them here. However, it is relevant to consider some of these approaches, among which are: the hypothesis by Safatle, of the 'exhaustion' of the New Republic;[30] the hypothesis by Avritzer that Brazilian democracy lives in a pendular process, from 1948 until 2018;[31] the hypothesis by Santos, that democracy did not transform the causes that led to civil-military dictatorship (1964–85);[32] the hypothesis by Schwarcz, for whom the uniting of institutions and authoritarian practices forms the current *democra-torship* ('*democra-dura*');[33] and the hypothesis by Cardoso, for whom the current crisis is, partly, a consequence of the economic crisis.[34]

Despite the differences between them, these hypotheses are of decisive importance, in that they point to the deficits of democracy that persist in the configuration of contemporary Brazil. The explanations of these theorists are divergent, but their diagnoses are somewhat convergent as to the country's democratic deficits. And this is because the Brazilian democratic deficits — which stem from the legacy of the country's historical-colonial formation[35] — are responsible for disorganizing the genuine historical attempt to affirm Brazilian democracy, in the context of the last seventy years (1950–2020). One notes, in this period, that only half of the presidents completed their

---

[27] Cardoso, pp. 21–22.
[28] Cardoso, p. 35.
[29] Avritzer, p. 273.
[30] 'Nesse momento da história, é necessário ter claro o fato de que a *Nova República* acabou, morreu' (Vladimir Safatle, 'A Nova República acabou' <http://www.ihu.unisinos.br/> [accessed 27 August 2019]).
[31] Avritzer, p. 288.
[32] Santos, 'E agora, Brasil?'.
[33] Schwarcz, p. 227.
[34] Cardoso, pp. 45–46.
[35] José Murilo de Carvalho, *Cidadania no Brasil: o longo caminho* (Rio de Janeiro: Civilização Brasileira, 2016), p. 88.

mandates, as Brazilian sociologist Fernando Henrique Cardoso points out.[36] Between advances and setbacks, in the cycle of the last thirty years (1988–2018), the lukewarm nature of democracy is due, by all this symptomatic evidence, fundamentally, to a set of historical, economic, political, cultural and social factors,[37] which challenge the advances and achievements that are made on the various internal borders of democracy.

Democratic consciousness is still embryonic in the state of development of contemporary Brazil. Brazilian democracy is, in this respect, prone to a series of local challenges, specific to the history of the country's political and economic development. In this, the Brazilian philosopher Safatle is right to point out the fact that Brazilian democracy is a neo-democracy.[38] The exercise of voting, as a mass phenomenon, is something that dates back only to the 1930s,[39] and, despite the regularity of elections, and the electronic form of current electoral justice, it is important to note that elections and public participation are phenomena that are less than a hundred years old.

Brazilian democracy is recent, but this alone does not explain the turbulence in its consolidation. In Brazil's historical profile, the dichotomous relationship between militarism and social populism shapes the Republican period. Militarism takes up a significant part of the Republican period, and this, as Carvalho points out, has been the case since the beginning of the Republic.[40] In addition, since 1946,[41] with the shift of the axis of power to Brasília, with the demographic explosion and transfer of the population to precarious urban areas, Brazil is divided between two opposing political projects, around two major problems affecting contemporary Brazilian political, economic and social life: (i) reducing poverty; and (ii) combating violence. The left wing, normally, takes on the first proposal; the right wing, normally, takes on the second proposal. Therefore, dialectically, the struggle for power is established in one sense or the other, sometimes based on the discourse of social rights and social inequality (i), sometimes based on the discourse of security and the combat against corruption (ii). For this reason, since 1946, Brazil has experienced democratic moments and anti-democratic moments.[42]

It is clear, therefore, that the country's greatest challenges are the fuel for discord in the exercise of power and the guidance of the electorate. But, regardless of the oscillations in each electoral period, it is clear that Brazil has not yet succeeded in ridding its institutions of the harmful effects of corruption and of patrimonialism, establishing a stable field in the protection

---

[36] Cardoso, p. 89.
[37] Schwarcz, p. 55.
[38] Safatle, 'A Nova República acabou'.
[39] Avritzer, p. 283.
[40] Carvalho, p. 163.
[41] Carvalho, pp. 130–31.
[42] Avritzer, p. 276.

of civil rights,⁴³ which one would assume in a complete liberal democracy, and, yet, it has also failed to establish conditions for the elimination of deep social inequalities,⁴⁴ which one would assume in an agenda of complete social democracy.

Thus, the contradictions manifest themselves very clearly, through anti-democratic symptoms. Some examples are sufficient to clarify this point. Currently, in Brazil, there is a Constitution with a social-democratic profile, but economic policies are neoliberal, which means that they do not provide social rights for the population. In addition, in Brazil, there are numerous democratic institutions in operation, but these are beset by the most diverse crises and threats. To this list, it is still possible to add that Brazil provides for freedom of the press, but journalists continue to suffer attacks and violence in the exercise of their profession. These examples are sufficient to point out that, despite the formal existence of democracy in the country — as its institutions are functioning — a heavy burden of the colonial past⁴⁵ still falls on the conditions of the possibility of the future.⁴⁶

Authoritarian Democracy and the De-institutionalization of Political Participation

Currently, what we have is an authoritarian democracy, in other words, a nominal democracy, a democracy related to the fact that the institutions are functioning and that the election was normal. But, despite the maintenance of the institutions, the practices contrary to democratic life are multiplying, such as: i) the militarization of public office; ii) the closure of all the forums for social participation; iii) the institutionalization of unilateral decision-making by the State; iv) the attempt to free the use of arms by the population; v) the transformation of social problems into policing problems; vi) the re-construction of an imaginary of the 1960s, as a struggle against 'left-wing intellectuals' and 'communists'; vii) the hierarchization of public service; viii) the demand for absolute fidelity to the political leader; ix) the reduction of the role of the State in the economy; x) the disfigurement of social protection bodies; xi) the persecution of political opponents, activists and journalists; xii) the virtual lynching on social networks of opinions critical of the government; xiii) the stigmatization of the stereotypes of 'social enemies'; xiv) the persecution of minorities; xv) the manifestation of hate speech.

---

[43] Avritzer, p. 278.
[44] 'Mão de obra escrava, divisão latifundiária da terra, corrupção e patrimonialismo, em grandes doses, explicam os motivos que fizeram do país uma realidade desigual' (Schwarcz, p. 127).
[45] Eduardo C. B. Bittar, 'Éthos democrático y éthos colonial: la educación en derechos humanos y la democracia como forma de vida', in Derechos y Libertades (Revista de Filosofía del Derecho y Derechos Humanos, Madrid, Instituto Bartolomé de las Casas), 43 (2020), p. 25.
[46] 'A herança colonial pesou mais na área dos direitos civis. O novo país herdou a escravidão, que negava a condição humana do escravo, herdou a grande propriedade rural, fechada à ação da lei, e herdou um Estado comprometido com o poder privado' (Carvalho, pp. 50–51).

In the context of Brazil, these practices only collaborate to transform the Welfare State into a Police State, which intensifies the culture of institutional and social violence that are traditional in the history of the country, hampering the advancement and construction of Republican values, citizenship practices, and the culture of participation and appreciation of social rights. This means the re-emergence in the light of day of the Brazilian anti-democratic past in the guise of the Brazilian democratic present, creating a strong sensation of contradiction between the practices of the State and the desire for democracy, citizenship and justice existing in society.[47]

Thus, currently, the political agenda of the extreme right in Brazil has been dedicated, on the one hand, to economic recovery, and on the other hand, to acting in favour of a world vision that values: i) hate speech towards human rights; ii) the fight against corruption; iii) social punitivism; iv) contempt for the National Congress; v) the scrapping of education, science and universities; vi) the persecution and/or stigmatization of intellectuals, educators and scientists; vii) the attack on human and social sciences; viii) Fake News and the disorientation of public opinion;[48] ix) the spread of threats, violent speeches and forms of expression of political-ideological hatred via social networks; x) the promotion of the self-exile of politicians and intellectuals; xi) the promotion of environmental destruction, particularly in indigenous lands.

With this, in the period 2017–20, Brazil is plunged into the era of the de-institutionalization of social participation, criminalization of politics, hyper-moralization of public debate,[49] discrediting rights and political intolerance. This political scenario has been able to take down the 'mask of Brazilianness' ('máscara da brasilidade') — traditionally associated with 'cordiality', 'tolerance' and 'style' — by moving towards a higher level of social intolerance.[50] As a result, the multiplication of conflict and violence is clearly accelerating in plain view, and, among this whole group of distortions, Law is politicized and torn apart, in a context of high political disagreement, with all the minimal issues exposed to moral, political or social dissent being brought to the field of judicial dispute.

This whole scenario is particularly sensitive for Brazil, in view of the recent past of the last authoritarian government of the twentieth century, the civil-military dictatorship (1964–85) — which came to power with a coup d'état over the elected João Goulart government, during a period of instability and tension, but under the argument of a 'communist threat' — which left a pernicious legacy of human rights violations, authoritarianism, restrictions on freedom of the press and persecution of political opponents. The current Brazilian scenario, from the impeachment-coup of 2016, also during a period

---

[47] Chaloub, Lima, Perlatto, p. 12.
[48] Bucci, p. 27.
[49] Chaloub, Lima, Perlatto, p. 12.
[50] Schwarcz, p. 211.

of instability, initially provoked by the global economic and financial crisis of 2008 — and the scenario of economic decline seen in the period 2008–13 — makes the country not only recall that context of dictatorship, but also revive its imaginary, in the light of the flashes of authoritarian public opinion under the unity of the authoritarian personality,[51] particularly influenced by the occupation of the public sphere by right-wing intellectuals.[52]

Brazilian Democracy: An Incomplete Democracy

According to the Democracy Index 2018 — produced by the Economist Intelligence Unit — it is possible to sense a strong disappointment in the credibility of democracy around the world, given that Brazil is at 50th position, amongst the 167 countries analysed, and has remained among the incomplete or weak democratic regimes.[53] The regimes in the Democracy Index 2018 are classified as an authoritarian regime, a hybrid regime, a flawed democracy or a full democracy, with Brazil classified as a flawed democracy in the years 2015 (with a rating of 6.96), 2016 (6.90), 2017 (6.86) and 2018 (6.97), which places it very far from the last position, occupied by North Korea (1.08), but also very far from the top positions, occupied by Norway (9.87), in first place, or Denmark (9.22), in fifth place. As a country of medium development, it is clear that the huge socio-economic inequalities will create vivid contradictions and endless conflicts and produce a social framework with high homicide rates, as the study of violence in Brazilian life by the Brazilian sociologist Renato Sérgio de Lima shows.[54]

Analyses of Brazilian democracy often differ, but when considering the classification of incomplete democracy given by the Democracy Index 2018, it can be qualified as accurate and adequate. This is because its results coincide perfectly with the set of analyses undertaken by this article, and conclusions drawn from previously published papers, in which I have argued that Brazil is living in an incomplete modernity.[55] Keeping this type of empirical diagnostic in mind is decisively important, as it undoes the mistaken self-image that Brazilian mythology holds, that Brazil would be a full democracy.[56] And, in fact, it is an incomplete democracy, to the extent that it is found:

---

[51] Theodor Adorno, *Le Nouvel Extrémisme de droite*, p. 53.
[52] Chaloub, Lima, Perlatto, p. 9.
[53] Economist Intelligence Unit, *Democracy Index 2018*, <https://www.eiu.com/topic/democracy-index> [accessed 2 August 2019].
[54] Renato Sérgio de Lima, 'Segurança pública como simulacro de democracia no Brasil', *Revista do Instituto de Estudos Avançados da USP*, 96 (2019), 53–68 (p. 59).
[55] Eduardo C. B. Bittar, 'O Decreto no. 8243/2014 e os desafios da consolidação democrática brasileira', *Revista de Informação Legislativa*, Senado Federal, Brasília, 203 (2014), 7–38; Eduardo C. B. Bittar, 'Crise política e Teoria da democracia: contribuições para a consolidação democrática no Brasil contemporâneo', *Revista de Informação Legislativa*, Senado Federal, Brasília, 211 (2016), 11–33. See also Bôas Filho, *Teoria dos sistemas e o Direito brasileiro* (São Paulo: Saraiva, 2009), p. 316.
[56] Schwarcz, p. 22.

I) At a political level:

i) a continuous search for personalism in politics, waiting for a 'saviour of the homeland', instead of relying on institutions;[57] ii) a strong tradition of *mandonismo*,[58] of the association between economics and politics, and of political authoritarianism;[59] iii) the abusive use of the institution of impeachment, which destabilizes democracy;[60] iv) the highest degree of party fragmentation in the last 70 years, compared to all the democracies in the world;[61] v) high levels of corruption, being a historical, endemic and systematic phenomenon throughout the country;[62]

II) At a social level:

i) abyssmal socio-economic inequalities, given that the country ranks ninth in the global income inequality index (2017 data),[63] and is among the five most unequal countries in the world;[64] ii) poverty reaches 40% of the population;[65] iii) unbearable levels of violence, reaching 171 deaths per day, with 553,000 deaths by wrongful murder in the last decade (2016 data);[66]

III) In terms of rights:

i) a framework of 'sub-citizenship' ('sub-cidadania') and social selectivity in the recognition of rights;[67] ii) a fragility of rights and social policies in the face of economic variations; iii) a disconnection between legal provision and the effectiveness of rights; iv) the lack of stability in the implementation of public policies that guarantee rights; v) a strong culture of impunity; vi) a continuous discrediting of human rights discourses;[68] vii) the persecution and extermination of leaders who act in the defence of human rights.

---

[57] 'No entanto, até mesmo no caso desses novos suportes de comunicação, nunca esteve tão firme a imagem de um presidente-pai, um *pater famílias*: autoritário e severo diante daqueles que se rebelam; justo e "próximo" para quem o segue e compartilha das suas ideias' (Schwarcz, p. 63).
[58] Raymundo Faoro, *Os donos do poder: formação do patronato político brasileiro*, 5th edn (São Paulo: Globo, 2012), p. 718.
[59] 'Em um país de resiliente tradição violenta e autoritária' (Lima, p. 65).
[60] 'No caso brasileiro, o impeachment não segue o padrão internacional do presidencialismo, em particular o anglo-saxão, de acordo com o qual impeachments devem ser eventos muito raros' (Avritzer, p. 285).
[61] Cardoso, p. 59.
[62] Schwarcz, p. 90.
[63] Schwarcz, p. 126.
[64] 'nosso país se encontra entre os cinco mais desiguais do planeta, levando-se em conta a concentração e distribuição desigual de renda' (Schwarcz, p. 129).
[65] Schwarcz, p. 232.
[66] Schwarcz, p. 152.
[67] 'Em sociedades periféricas como a brasileira, o *habitus* precário — que implica a existência de redes invisíveis e objetivas que desqualificam os indivíduos e grupos sociais precarizados como subprodutores e subcidadãos, e isso, sob a forma de uma evidência social insofismável, tanto para os privilegiados como para as próprias vítimas da precariedade — é um fenômeno em massa e justifica a minha tese de que o que diferencia, substancialmente, esses dois tipos de sociedade é a produção social de uma ralé estrutural nas sociedades periféricas' (Jessé Souza, *Subcidadania brasileira* (Rio de Janeiro: Leya, 2018), pp. 252–53).
[68] Lima, p. 60.

These are only some indicative elements — considered at the social, political and legal levels — which point to the fragility of Brazilian democracy. A complete and consolidated democracy would not coexist with such levels of distortion and social, economic, political and legal pathologies. The Democratic Rule of Law is, therefore, an inconclusive task in Brazilian reality, and still requires large steps to assert itself in a solid and institutionalized manner.[69]

An Agenda for Brazilian Democracy in the Twenty-first Century

Disbelief, despair and instability have marked democracy in the second decade of the twenty-first century, particularly in regions where it was best established and assimilated, that is, in Europe and the Americas.[70] In this sense, Latin America has been the scene of strong democratic setbacks. Even so, when it was thought that democracy, although weakened, was threatened or condemned in many parts of the world, the results of recent elections confirmed important victories by candidates linked with democratic ideals, in France, Germany, Canada, Holland, and Austria,[71] and, more recently, in the context of the 2020 elections, in the United States. This means that, despite difficult times, democracy is experiencing a temporary crisis, and, probably, will survive the assaults of historical time.

Looking to the future, in Brazil, in order for democracy to be consolidated — as a social and pluralist democracy — there is still a need to secure the central values of modernity, such as, freedom, equality, solidarity, diversity, redistribution, which should be taken as foundations of the Brazilian Republic. Given that life is worth nothing in the country,[72] the inherent dignity in each and every one still needs to be made something unconditional and untouchable by state and institutional violence. In addition, the process of deregulation of public opinion, the overcoming of the culture of individualism and the project of hatred towards social movements are of fundamental importance.

Hence, there is still a long way to go, in that democracy is not only form, but also substance, as Dahl states,[73] so that we can talk about republicanism and democracy in Brazil, as the analysis by Brazilian historian Carvalho points out.[74] Therefore, the challenges for Brazilian democracy are innumerable, if future tasks are considered, which are projected for the twenty-first century:

i) in the field of social justice: the reduction of socio-economic inequalities;[75]
ii) at the level of the protection of minorities: combating all forms of discrimination;

---

[69] Bittar, 'O Decreto no. 8243/2014'.
[70] Cardoso, p. 73.
[71] Cardoso, p. 81.
[72] Lima, p. 64.
[73] Robert A. Dahl, *A democracia e seus críticos*, trans. by Patrícia de Freitas Ribeiro (São Paulo: Martins Fontes, 2012), p. 304.
[74] 'Historicamente, nossa República nunca foi republicana nem democrática' (Carvalho, p. 245).
[75] Cardoso, p. 23; Souza, p. 256.

iii) at the level of public management: the fight against corruption and patrimonialism;[76]
iv) at the level of institutions: the strengthening of democratic institutions;
v) at the level of political parties: democratization, strengthening of political parties and the sense of political representation;[77]
vi) at the economic level: stabilizing the economy, making it sustainable and less vulnerable to instability and cycles of international capital;
vii) on the social level: combating the proliferation of various forms of violence;[78]
viii) on the moral level: combating intolerance and fostering dialogue;[79]
ix) at the level of republican values: the strengthening of democratic values;[80]
x) on the cultural level: the reversal of colonial culture and overcoming the colonial legacy.[81]

This agenda of Brazil's commitments for the twenty-first century would imply social transformation towards democratic consciousness. However, this cannot be achieved with the union of efforts coming from, either the pole of organized civil society, or the pole of democratic institutions of the State. In the dynamics of civil society, it is a question of re-equipping entities and non-governmental organizations for an agenda of transformation. In the dynamics of democratic institutions of the State, it is a question of strengthening democratic institutions, the justice system, social politics and the expansion of the culture in respect of human dignity.[82]

This means a degree of commitment to republican values, liberal premises of citizenship,[83] and awareness of rights that are preventing the appearance of barbarism. Implementation of a participatory democracy, from the perspective of the analysis by Jürgen Habermas (2003), also implies the construction of a source of feed-back of public opinion that makes it sensitive enough for the preservation of minimal human rights values and able to avoid social setbacks.[84]

It is expected that new unfavourable economic cycles will hit the global economy, with repercussions on local economies, throughout the twenty-first century. If the current cycle of crisis and deceleration is generating this group of conflicts and intolerance, institutional and para-institutional democracy must begin to find new mechanisms for creating political and economic stability, in defence of democracy, which will enable it to get through negative cycles.

[76] Schwarcz, p. 65.
[77] Cardoso, p. 223.
[78] 'Vivemos numa guerra muda que parece não mais provocar indignação social desde que circunscrita às periferias e favelas' (Lima, p. 64).
[79] Schwarcz, p. 214.
[80] Cardoso, p. 85.
[81] Carvalho, p. 245.
[82] 'As democracias contemporâneas tendem a ser um espaço coletivo de diálogo e deliberação, e não só um contexto formal de instituições das quais emerge uma "vontade geral"' (Cardoso, p. 102).
[83] Bruce Ackerman, We the People (Cambridge, MA: Harvard University Press, 1991), pp. 298–99.
[84] Maria Pia Lara, La democracia como proyecto de identidad ética (Barcelona: Antropos Editorial, 1992).

Although empirical studies in Political Science and Sociology cannot point to certainties on this path, the association between political democracy and economic inclusion is reinforced here.[85] The mechanisms for this to happen will require new engineering in economic practices, political concepts and legal rules, which are perhaps yet to be found and developed. In any case, their need is already urgent at present, and will be even more so in the future.

It can already be said that the risks to which democracy is exposed should be shielded by the formation of a democratic public opinion, resistant to the appeals of an authoritarian minority. Therefore when one thinks of democracy as a defence of pluralism, dialogue and the centrality of participatory processes,[86] in line with the analysis by Habermas,[87] or even, when discussing the importance of the right to justification as a form of control of one's will and a guarantee of the quality of democracy, in line with the analysis by Rainer Forst,[88] currently, it is clear that contemporary Brazil (2019-22) exemplifies the opposite of this process.

Conclusions

Brazilian democracy is going through an intense period of turbulence, and its challenges for the twenty-first century are not inconsiderable. The turbulence of the period 2013-20 is, clearly, the result of the global economic-financial crisis — as Brazilian sociologist Fernando H. Cardoso states[89] — which has affected the entire economic and political life of the country through economic stagnation. Thus, the crisis of Brazilian democracy is closely related to the global economic crisis. The current economic crisis puts Brazilian democracy in a scenario of high risk, which makes it slip into its opposite, into dictatorship. For no other reason, some analyses — as with the analysis undertaken by Brazilian historian Lilia Schwarcz[90] — have used the term '*demo-cradura*' (democracy + dictatorship) in order to elaborate the caricature of contemporary politics in the country. Authoritarianism can reappear under the guise of democracy, when democracy is taken only as form and not as substance, as a procedure of access to power, and not as practice and consciousness. Hence, one can see that the local effects of the global crisis are always very particular. In Brazil, these effects have allowed the historical democratic deficits of the country to emerge, which are a result of slavery, the latifundium, corruption and patrimonialism, predominant since the colonial period.

---

[85] Kenneth A. Bollen and Robert W. Jackman, 'Democracy, Stability and Dichotomies', *American Sociological Review*, 54 (1989), 612-21 (p. 618).
[86] Cardoso, p. 103.
[87] Habermas, *Direito e democracia*.
[88] 'The basic claim of political and social justice with regard to this process is to establish a "basic structure of justification"' (Rainer Forst, *Justification and Critique: Towards a Critical Theory of Politics*, trans. by Cirian Cronin (Cambridge: Polity Press, 2014), p. 107).
[89] Cardoso, p. 45.
[90] Schwarcz, p. 227.

Thus, modern-Brazil clashes with retrograde-Brazil, once again. The Brazilian historical cycle, structured by a dialectic of modernity and tradition — following Brazilian anthropologist Roberto DaMatta's hypothesis — is restored, now in an environment of new technology and accelerated communication.[91] It is in this sense that Brazil experiences new variations of the same dilemmas. In its present stage of development, Brazilian democracy is not only very recent, it is also affirmed in the present with difficulties, given that its future challenges point to the need for a cure of its more basic ancestral problems. Perhaps, the greatest lesson of the crisis is precisely the persistence with which the deepest social and economic problems — not yet resolved — return to the surface. At the end of the cycle of re-democratization of the last thirty years (1988–2018), this set of issues continues to demand the need to promote changes in the sense of citizenship, democratic culture, social participation and the development of democratic institutions.

This allows for the diagnosis that Brazilian democracy is an 'incomplete democracy' ('democracia incompleta'), a thesis that I have been developing and supporting in several studies in recent years.[92] Consequently, its current configuration has characteristics of the universe of democratic values and characteristics of the universe of authoritarian values. This allows the insight that democratic stability depends on several factors, among them: i) economic stability; ii) political consensus; iii) mediation of the institutions; iv) the degree of development of the public sphere. Maturation will require numerous tasks, before it can be said that Brazilian democracy is consolidated. And, in fact, it has not yet reached this point, and the risk of simply slipping back into dictatorship is already sufficiently high as to confirm that the democracy of the future needs to be stronger than is currently the case. In the future, a stable and complete democracy will call for present efforts towards social justice, sustainable development, social peace, the control of various forms of violence, the expansion of human rights educational policies,[93] the universalization of citizenship, and the expansion of social participation. These are aspects of democratic life that have the character of an agenda that is at once economic, political, cultural and legal, and that requires them to be supplied in order to minimize the pull that economic conscience exercises over democratic conscience in social life.

---

[91] DaMatta, p. 19.
[92] Bittar, 'O Decreto no. 8243/2014'; Bittar, 'Crise política e Teoria da democracia'.
[93] Eduardo C. B. Bittar, 'Art, Human Rights Activism and a Pedagogy of Sensibility: The São Paulo Human Rights Short Films Festival — *Entretodos*', *Human Rights Education Review* (University of South-Eastern Norway), 3.1 (2020), 69–90.

Torture:
Notes and Perspectives in a Context of Governmental Support for Gross Violations of Human Rights in Brazil[1]

Paulo Endo

Universidade de São Paulo

Taking into account the rights set out in the Universal Declaration of Human Rights (UDHR) of 1948, it is quite common, if naive, to believe that human rights violations have already been eradicated. This is a common belief because many of us wish that those moral and civilizing standards that we cherish and consider represented in the UDHR become achievable and, if put into practice, could, by transmission, teaching or persuasion, become a global reality. Unfortunately, no country has fully made this achievement and it is highly improbable that any country will make it. We have not been able to eradicate human rights violations with the same effectiveness that malaria, measles or childhood paralysis were eradicated in some countries.

The comparison is not arbitrary. These are two distinct epistemic fields, two different ways of combating human suffering that presuppose coping strategies that only coincide at one point or another for their realization. Maybe the main way is through the resolute willingness of governments to do it. Mass vaccination is something feasible, but applying human rights for all can only be achieved through profound changes in institutions and in the way of thinking, feeling and living of people, so that these rights become inertial forms of conviviality and justice, which only occasionally resort to justice for their realization. It is therefore possible to find communities, groups and places where human rights predominate without the intervention of any judicial apparatus to achieve them.

But nations must also act in concert, and measures to consolidate a culture for human rights must be more prevalent than actions to destroy them. Unfortunately, this has not happened yet either. At the end of World War I, which devastated entire countries and claimed the lives of millions of European citizens, Freud noted: 'From preceding discussions we find solace that our bitterness and painful disillusionment with the uncivilized conduct of our

---

[1] The research on which this article is based is supported by São Paulo Research Foundation (FAPESP).

fellow-citizens of the world in this war were unjustified. They were based on an illusion to which we had given way. In reality our fellow-citizens have not sunk so low as we feared, because they had never risen so high as we believed.'[2] This ironic sentence, when transposed from the psychoanalytic in which it originated, suggests at least two things:

1) That the fantasies we have about ourselves, about who we are, are elements that condense shared facts and ways of feeling and thinking that, however, are not proved in the face of reality. Thus there is a cloud of obscurity that signals that the desire for the new has not in fact produced the new and it would be necessary to invent ways that still don't exist to reach it. Due to this fact, the possibility of retroceding, retroacting and retrograding to the known is immense and an effect of what Freud calls illusion.

2) Repetitions of social patterns unconsciously determined and reproduced by subjects and institutions mock the most auspicious intentions and turn them into unrealities, masks and skirmishes that permanently postpone achievements which are more or less definitive or stable. As long as people and institutions keep clinging to these unrealities, it is impossible to meet the challenges they conceal.

In a recent article (2018), I further developed a reflection that has often come to my mind since 2006.[3] Particularly in the last article published, I sought to briefly assess the inaction of the Brazilian State and institutions in terms of controlling and combating torture in the country, at least in the past fourteen years. Since 2001, when the report on torture in Brazil by Nigel Rodley, then UN rapporteur on torture, was presented, it is possible to note that virtually none of his thirty recommendations was seriously considered and implemented with all the due urgency and even the ease indicated by the report. On that occasion, I used data on places of detention collected by the National Mechanism for Prevention and Combating of Torture in its latest report in 2016. From this comparison it is clear that the practice of torture is an ongoing crime in places of detention and that the magnitude of the problem is completely overlooked in security policies of governments and parliamentarians in different states of the federation. To make things worse, this issue is not properly focused by the media spotlight.

Juan Méndez, UN rapporteur on torture, visited Brazil again in 2015.

---

[2] Sigmund Freud, 'Considerações atuais sobre a guerra e a morte', in S. Freud, *Introdução ao narcisismo: ensaios de metapsicologia e outros textos (1914-1916)*, trans. and notes by Paulo Cezar de Souza, OC, vol. XII (São Paulo: Companhia das Letras, 2010), p. 214.

[3] Paulo César Endo, 'Tortura: aspectos psicológicos', *Polêm!ca*, 16 (2006), n.pag.; idem, 'Violência, elaboração onírica e o horizonte testemunhal', *Temas em Psicologia*, Ribeirão Preto, 17 (2010), n.pag.; idem, 'Banido, bando, bandido, bandeirante', *Percurso: Revista de Psicanálise*, São Paulo, 3 (2014), 61–70; idem, 'Sonhar o desaparecimento forçado de pessoas: impossibilidade de presença e perenidade de ausência como efeito do legado da ditadura civil-militar no Brasil', *Revista Psicologia USP*, 27 (2016), 8–15; idem, 'Freud, o inconsciente, a des-memória, a in-memória e os paradoxos do esquecimento, do sonho e do real em Auschwitz', *Percurso: Revista de Psicanálise*, São Paulo, 60 (2018), 77–88; idem, 'O arquivo de sonhos de ex-prisioneiros de Auschwitz do Museu-Memorial de Auschwitz-Birkenau', *Percurso: Revista de Psicanálise*, São Paulo, 60 (2018), 89–96.

His report pointed out problems very similar to those observed in 2001: mistreatment and widespread torture, threats to those who denounce or report abuses inflicted on them, abusive use of non-lethal weapons, and unnecessary generation of tension in the prison environment, creating a permanent state of disquiet, discomfort and fear in detainees. During inspection of places of detention, heavily armed state security agents could be seen with rifles, shotguns, pistols and even a grenade launcher. A lawless state of war without limits constitutes the prison environment in Brazil. The Special Rapporteur on torture further added that: 'Torture and this sort of abuses constitute a deep-rooted and pervasive practice which has been so trivialized that prisoners do not mention it, unless they are asked about it'.[4]

Fourteen years earlier, in 2001, Nigel Rodley concluded in his report:

> Torture and similar ill-treatment are meted out on a widespread and systematic basis in most of the parts of the country visited by the Special Rapporteur and, as far as indirect testimonies presented to the Special Rapporteur from reliable sources suggest, in most other parts of the country. It is found at all phases of detention: arrest, preliminary detention, other provisional detention, and in penitentiaries and institutions for juvenile offenders. It does not happen to all or everywhere; mainly it happens to poor, black common criminals involved in petty crimes or small-scale drug distribution. And it happens in the police stations and custodial institutions through which these types of offender pass. The purposes range from obtaining of information and confessions to the lubrication of systems of financial extortion. The consistency of the accounts received, the fact that most detainees still bore visible marks consistent with their testimonies and that the Special Rapporteur was able to discover in almost all police stations instruments of torture as described by alleged victims such as iron and wooden bars make it difficult to refute the numerous torture allegations brought to his attention.[5]

Undoubtedly, torture remains widespread in Brazil as a continuous practice that has not been eliminated since the end of the civil-military regime, particularly in places of detention throughout the country. The lethargy for over a decade indicates the explicit tolerance by governments of such practices maintained by state security agents. As for the findings and the persistence of serious violations of human rights in the country, the reports mentioned are abundant and explicit in confirming a true epidemic of cruel and degrading practices.

The aim of this article is to reflect on how a government composed mainly of military men is behaving from 2019 on, having as its leader a president who

---

[4] 'Report of the Special Rapporteur on torture and other cruel, inhuman or degrading treatment or punishment on his mission to Brazil (January 2016). UN General Assembly. 31st session. Human Rights Council'. Available at: <https://digitallibrary.un.org/record/831519/files/A_HRC_31_57_Add-4-EN.pdf> [accessed 1 March 2019], p. 11.
[5] 'Report on Torture in Brazil produced by Nigel Rodley, Special Rapporteur on Torture for the UN Human Rights Committee, Geneva, April 11, 2001', paragraph 166. Available at: <http://www.dhnet.org.br/dados/relatorios/dh/br/relatores_onu/rodley/index.html> [accessed 1 March 2019].

overtly supports the practice of torture and other discretionary practices from the past, such as those committed by former president Augusto Pinochet of Chile and well-known Brazilian torturer and killer Carlos Brilhante Ustra. However, it is also very important to consider that the current government, which took office in January 2019, is the direct heir to a context of almost total inaction of previous governments in the fight against torture in Brazil since the beginning of the democratic period that started in 1985.

This situation, which today is extremely serious due to the record of impunity and proliferation of such practices by the security forces in the country, naturalizes the practice of torture as part of a system that has maintained, consecrated and deepened it in Brazil for decades, either implicitly or explicitly. This system is not necessarily inherent in military governments, although such practices have been commonly used in these cases as a very violent tool in interrogations to allegedly and paradoxically obtain 'national security' information by threatening, torturing and killing citizens of their own country.

The establishment of this direct and inertial correlation between the practice of torture and military governments is obviously due to the large-scale use of such practices by military governments in Latin America in the recent past and also to their constant use as an illegal practice by the security forces nowadays operating with very high levels of violence in most Latin American countries. It is worth mentioning that such countries are regarded as places where, theoretically at least, democratic regimes prevail.

The persistence of this theme in the Americas, presently including the United States, under the recent administration of Donald Trump and particularly the current presidency of Brazil under the direct influence of the United States of America, is an indirect focus of interest in this article, but we need to consider overseas influences. There are many specific aspects of the persistence of torture practices in the respective Latin American countries. However, there are also aspects that can only be better understood considering the mutual influences between these countries, both those that occurred between them and those coming from outside.

The present study will seek to accentuate the little-mentioned influence of the French army in the torture practices that spread throughout Latin America, especially between the 1960s and the 1980s. Many researches carried out during this period highlighted the well-known American influence in the coups d'état in Latin America,[6] others offered important readings on the 'Latinization' processes of the practice of torture, as part of the strategies of repression and control adopted by military and coup governments during this period.[7] In

---

[6] Luís Fernando Ayerbe, *Estados Unidos e América Latina: a construção da hegemonia* (São Paulo: Editora da UNESP, 2002); Felipe Victoriano Serrano, 'Estados, golpes de Estado y militarización en América Latina: una reflexión histórico política', *Nueva Época*, 23.64 (2010), 176–93; Marcos Roitman Rosenmann, *Tiempos de oscuridad: historia de los golpes en la América Latina* (Buenos Aires: Ediciones AKAL, 2013).

[7] F. Bendfeldt-Zachrisson, 'Torture as Intensive Repression in Latin America: The Psychology of its

addition to these studies, we will try to highlight a social concept and practice that continues to influence the Latin American and Brazilian security forces and whose main spokesperson is today the current president of the republic: the 'enemy within'.

Let's start by highlighting a well-known excerpt from the testimony of Argentine General Martín Antonio Balza, who commanded the Argentine Army from 1991 to 1999, during the two terms of President Carlos Menem. In 1995 he was the first senior member of the Argentine military to break the silence, after years of military muteness about crimes committed during the Argentine dictatorship. I quote below that excerpt from his long testimony:

> Without looking for innovative words, but by appealing to the old military regulations, I take this opportunity to once again order the army, before the whole society: no one is obliged to comply with an immoral order or one that departs from the laws and military regulations. Whoever does it engages in vicious conduct, worthy of the punishment its gravity requires. Without euphemisms I say clearly: 'Whoever violates the national Constitution commits an offense. Whoever gives immoral orders commits an offense. Whoever obeys immoral orders commits an offense. Whoever uses unjust and immoral means to achieve an end he believes just, commits an offense. An understanding of these essential aspects makes the republican life of a state. Understanding this, abandoning once and for all the apocalyptic vision, pride, accepting dissent and respecting the sovereign will... This is the first step we are taking in many years to leave the past behind, to help build the Argentina of the future, an Argentina matured in pain that can come someday to a fraternal embrace. If we cannot elaborate the pain and heal the wounds, we will have no future. We must no longer deny the horror we experienced, so that we can think of our lives as a society that advances, overcoming pain and suffering.[8]

It is important to highlight in this testimony an attempt to retake the principles that rule the 'old military regulations' in Argentina, which would be contaminated by the French influence. The French advisers would successfully teach the Argentine military strategies for subverting the very institutional function of the military in the name of a greater danger, above any regulations. The prompt adherence to these teachings would permanently tarnish the reputation of the Latin American military in the future. For Balza, the most

---

Methods and Practice', *International Journal of Health*, 18.21 (1988), 301–10; Samantha Viz Quadrat, 'Operação Condor: o "Mercosul do Terror"', *Estudos Ibero-Americanos*, PUCRS, 28.1 (2002), 167–82; John Dinges, *Os anos do Condor: uma década de terrorismo internacional no Cone Sul*, trans. by Rosaura Eichenberg (São Paulo: Companhia das Letras, 2005); M. M. L. Rocha, '"El río nos quedó adentro": direitos humanos e os debates sobre desaparecimento forçado e genocídio na justiça de transição do terrorismo rio-platense' (unpublished doctoral thesis, Universidade de São Paulo, 2018); Andra Nicolescu et al., *Respondiendo a la tortura: perspectivas Latinoamericanas sobre un desafío global* (Bogotá: International Bar Association's Human Rights Institute and Universidad Externado de Colombia, 2020).

[8] Available at: <es.wikisource.org/wiki/Declaración_del_General_Martín_Balza_del_25_de_abril_de_1995_(Autocrítica)> [accessed 1 March 2019].

fundamental point in this strategy was the French invention of the existence of the 'enemy within'.

In an interview with Marie-Monique Robin in 2003, Balza points out the French influence on Argentina:

> The horror that unfolded in Argentina from 1976 to 1982 is so extraordinary, so enormous, that unthinkable is the first term that comes up because we cannot even think of it. [...] I would say it was a political, ideological, military and religious cocktail that engendered the most criminal regime in our history. And the teachings by the French military advisers from the 1950s onwards played a key role in the preparation of this cocktail. The influence of the Americans would follow shortly after — but the greatest evil had already been done.[9]

Marie-Monique Robin then asks: 'Why do you speak about evil?' And Balza says:

> Because the French brought to Argentina an evil and perverse conception that literally poisoned the spirit of the officers of my generation: that of the 'enemy within'. Before their arrival, men in our army, as in any army in the world, were trained to defend our country from any aggression from a foreign enemy; that could be a neighbouring country like Chile or Paraguay. From the moment the concept of 'enemy within' was introduced, we all internalized the fact that the enemy we had to confront was our own fellow-citizen: he could be anyone who was with us on the train in the morning, the teacher of our children, or our neighbour; in short, all those with whom we do not share the same ideas and who could have close or vague affinities with communism presented as the absolute evil, or with the Peronist movement presented as a by-product of the former. In other words, in their conferences, articles in military magazines and engagement drills, the French advisors, and then their Argentine students, who would eventually surpass their 'masters', kept telling us that the battlefield was the Argentine territory itself and that, in order to destroy the subversive ideas that endangered the Christian values of our Western civilization, it was necessary to destroy man himself. In fact, from the late 1950s until the coup in March 1976, the army was preparing to unleash a fratricidal war and to behave like a real occupying army in its own territory.[10]

This well-known and peculiar testimony addresses relevant points, of which three aspects that should be highlighted:

1) The long technical, theoretical and psychological preparation for the practice of torture, deaths and disappearances was started in the 1950s by the French school and it would be triggered, more than 20 years later, in 1976 in Argentine territory, as well as in Brazil, Venezuela and Chile;

2) The perversion and weakening of the role of the military based on the definition and internalization of the 'enemy within' concept;

---

[9] Marie-Monique Robin, *Escadrons de la mort, l'école française* (Paris: La Découverte, 2008), pp. 200–01.
[10] Ibid, p. 201.

3) The conviction manifested in serious violations that continued to occur, even after the UN had adopted the UDHR in 1948, demonstrates the use of the UDHR as a veil to conceal practices incompatible with the nascent culture of human rights — completely despised by the French government, but fully compatible with the domination strategies learned and developed by the victorious countries in World War II and, in the case of France, in the colonial wars. What had been learned and transmitted by the war allies then mocked what was announced in the newly declared UDHR.

* * * * *

Military governments in South America knew that they committed illegalities by systematically using torture and that is why they did not publicly admit it as a government practice. The French government also knew that it violated the 1948 UDHR, one of the effects of the victory of the Allied countries which promptly condemned the atrocities found in German concentration and extermination camps.

In addition to having turned their back on the UDHR, to which France adhered to as a member state of the UN, French governments have practised, replicated and transmitted such practices to other continents, producing incurable wounds in the countries under their influence. Among those several practices, one stands out: the possibility of continually committing serious human rights violations in colonized countries and on other continents, thus disrespecting the Universal Declaration, while defending those same rights on the public scene and in international politics. The pedagogy of cynicism was added to the teaching of techniques and instruments of torture and repression.

Although systematically using torture practices in the late 1940s in Indochina and recurrently in Algeria from 1957, the French army boasted that they had been one of the co-founders of the UDHR a few years earlier and were proud of the so-called 'French Resistance', as well as of being one of the protagonists among the Allied countries that had defeated Nazi barbarism in 1945. The concepts that create conditions favourable to torture in South American countries in terms of its authorization, logistics, equipping and common practice are those of 'national security' and the 'enemy within'. However, the French doctrine of the 'enemy within' precedes that of American national sovereignty.

These concepts gained strength and notoriety in practices learned, transmitted and developed in the tensions between colonized and colonizing countries in the twentieth century. France was an exporter of such concepts and practices to Argentina and Brazil. The same concepts and practices would later spread to other South American countries and are still present in torture practices and techniques such as drowning, electric shocks and the macaw's perch (*pau de arara*), as well as in the way victorious nations in World War II presented and still present themselves as democracies respectful of human rights before international courts and international human rights bodies. The French government, for example, did that in the late 1940s and the 1950s in colonial conflicts. The French heritage in South American countries includes not only concepts, techniques and insurmountable traumas that became national features, but also hypocrisy concerning false commitments and false protagonism in the preservation and consolidation of practices compatible with democracy and the human rights. The so-called dirty war waged in Indochina since the 1940s, at the same time that the Universal Declaration of Human Rights was formulated, corroborates this point. I quote Marie-Monique Robin:

> On July 29, 1949, journalist Jacques Chegaray would denounce the French army's use of torture during the Indochina War in an article published in *Témoignage chrétien*, a French Christian newspaper, reporting his visit to a non-commissioned officer's office in Phul Cong, Tonkin:
> 'This is my office', said the French officer to the journalist. 'The desk, the typewriter and the toilet, and in the corner the machine to make people talk. [...] Yes, the dynamo [an electrical generator]. It is very convenient for interrogating prisoners. These are the contact, the positive pole and the negative pole; we turn them on and the prisoner spits!'
> Henry Ainley, former legionnaire of the French Foreign Legion, testified in 1955: 'We didn't talk about kidnappings, appropriations, torture, but about punitive expedition, material recovery, and interrogations.'[11]

A few years later, the French army would widely use torture and create clandestine detention centres in Algeria where there was the usual practice of interrogation during the conflicts of the colonial war between the nationalist groups (mainly the National Liberation Front) and the French government and army.[12] Therefore, after the end of World War II, France was an obstinate transnational human rights violator, committed for decades to the development, application and transmission of the practice of torture in colonized countries, as well as in the United States and South America.

The French school of death and torture squads gathered followers in Latin America, and the practice of torture was underpinned by the 'good results' achieved in the conflicts between the French army, led by Colonel Philippe Mathieu, and the groups that rose up in 1957 for the independence of Algeria. Mathieu was a war veteran, having served in the French resistance force against the German occupation, the Indochina War and the Battle of Algiers. He mastered the methods that made the military proud and the motivation that the 'humanitarian' function of torture can prevent the deaths of women and children, commented Paul Aussaresses, a former French Secret Service agent and veteran of the Indochina and Algerian wars who directly contributed to the civil-military regime in Brazil during the years 1964–85, in an interview in 2008.[13]

---

[11] Robin, pp. 54–55.
[12] Robin, pp. 92–104.
[13] Available at <https://www1.folha.uol.com.br/fsp/brasil/fc0405200809.htm> [accessed 1 March 2019].

Of course, for Aussaresses, communism was an imminent risk to women and children, so communism and communists, including women and children, had to be wiped out, as had happened in Algeria. The production of falsifications of judgment has as its main shield the horror and constant practice of threats posed by the higher authority of the state against those who have been definitively characterized as communists (the internal enemies). That is the way to articulate the fracture between categories of citizens proved a posteriori by the violence that will be inflicted on them. 'He was tortured, murdered and disappeared because he was a communist or he was not a communist so he was tortured [...]'. Such characterizations would not resist the demonstration, even because this demonstration was often conceptually condemned by the grotesque caricature that post-WWII national sovereignty policies made of the so-called communists. Violence then comes to form this definition and carries with it, as a strategy, the demonstration of the consequences and risks of deciding to be an 'enemy within'.

The fratricidal wars in Latin America during the civil-military dictatorships reveal that the same strategies used by the current president of Brazil to build the 'enemy within' are unclear and unconvincing, depending to a large extent on a significant part of disorganized civil society. Nowadays torture as an enduring practice does not apply to the communist category, but to the poor, blacks and inhabitants of the peripheries of Brazilian cities. This is the category that has become socially convincing as a prime target for violations, but it has not met the political and social conditions yet to become a relevant topic in the presidential rhetoric and in social policies.

Today the president himself and his family are suspected of being connected to organized crime and they also lack a definite right-wing social agenda to clearly indicate those ('internal enemies') who are hindering or impeding its implementation. The president and his group cannot characterize friends and enemies only on the basis of the performance and attacks conducted by individuals and groups on social media sites. Gradually, everything becomes a fight between the president and those who are not his friends or do not agree with his ideas.

Today, the use of torture against the 'enemy within' paradoxically is not yet viable as a public government practice although the current president has frequently defended it. Yet the same practice of torture is still mainly directed against the vulnerable people inside the prisons and places of detention. The presidential discourse to support the transposition from the torture committed secretly by the security forces inside the walls, still has not managed to convince the population to the point of becoming an open authorization for the practice of torture. But he will probably keep trying until the end of his term.

More than two years after the beginning of the new administration, the current president and his family also do not represent the identity ideals desired by most Brazilians. An effective use of the same post-Second World War concepts and modus operandi, including the notion of 'enemy within' and national sovereignty, cannot be implemented on a significant scale due to a formidable obstacle: the abandonment of these concepts by the very countries that generated them and put them into practice, such as the US government to which the Brazilian president conforms as a vassal.

Among the three vertices that hold the current president in power are the support from the US government and a still significant support from the right-wing and/or conservative Brazilian electorate and the armed forces, but none of them has ever supported torture in a systematic and overt way as part of government security policies, and all of these would be important to turn it into a reality in Brazil, as the government would not only have to amend the 1988 Constitution, but also would have to break all international and regional human rights agreements, declarations and treaties entered into to date.[14] Nowadays, the elected president still seems to be the only one who would publicly support the use of torture as a government practice. But the responsibility of their predecessors for letting torture be used against the poor and vulnerable for decades, since the end of dictatorship, may open up an opportunity for the current administration to legally pursue many activists who are at risk of being persecuted and tortured when conducted to the prisons — places operating outside the law where arbitrariness is rife.

Even worse, we are now facing the imminent risk of deepening the disastrous and discriminatory prison policy by replacing it with the total absence of consistent social projects and policies. Arrest and kill are still the main proposals of the federal government to fight crime and violence. This programme can be read between the lines of the presidential campaign of the current president in the recent past and it will certainly be used in the future during the presidential campaign in 2022, when the president-elect will openly attempt his re-election. The discourse of war on drugs and bandits is already a cherished belief of the government and many Brazilians. As a matter of fact, similar promises were made by past right-wing candidates. From now on, however, as a strategy it could become a belief based on mass incarceration

---

[14] At an international level, Brazil is a member state or supporter of the core UN human rights treaties that prohibit torture and abuse. They include the International Covenant on Civil and Political Rights and its two optional protocols; the Convention against Torture and Other Cruel, Inhuman or Degrading Treatment and its optional protocol; the International Convention for the Protection of All Persons from Enforced Disappearance; the Convention on the Rights of the Child; the International Convention on the Elimination of All Forms of Racial Discrimination; the Convention on the Elimination of All Forms of Discrimination against Women; the International Convention on the Rights of Persons with Disabilities; the International Convention on the Protection of the Rights of All Migrant Workers and Members of Their Families; the Convention on the Status of Refugees; and the Convention on the Status of Stateless Persons. Brazil is also a signatory party to the Rome Statute of the International Criminal Court. At a regional level, Brazil is part of the major human rights treaties of the Organization of American States, including the American Convention on Human Rights; the Inter-American Convention to Prevent and Punish Torture; the Inter-American Convention on Forced Disappearance of Persons; the Inter-American Convention on the Prevention, Punishment, and Eradication of Violence against Women; and the Inter-American Convention against Racism, Racial Discrimination, and Related Forms of Intolerance. The State also recognizes the jurisdiction of the Inter-American Court of Human Rights.

programmes, police violence and mitigations offered to ordinary armed citizens mobilized on social networks on the internet. Thus, inside prisons, torture will still occur in a socially invisible and consistent manner and prisons may be among the government's strategies to pursue and eliminate opponents.

Millennium Starts: Morphological and Seminal Embryos of Contemporary Brazilian Literature[1]

Roberto Vecchi

Università di Bologna

If space is undoubtedly the 'deuteragonist' of Brazilian contemporary narrative, another relevant role is played by the means — not only aesthetical, but also in a broader sense of the word — that configure this space and allow us to trace some of the urban space's incisive topographies which can be transposed to contemporary Brazilian literature. The notion of 'contemporary' thus delineated, not through a comprehensive and impossible list of works, but from a strict selection of only a few novels, presents — and this is the hypothesis this article aims at building — a potential exemplarity, its implied darknesses included,[2] in a much broader literary, geographic, cultural, historical landscape: the representative part of a whole.

Not only that, but literature also becomes, in this way, a powerful tool to bestow and articulate the shape of a space that is quite — contradictorily — composite with the city's space: Luiz Ruffato's novel, *Eles eram muitos cavalos*, 2001 (translated and published in English as *There Were Many Horses* in 2014), that represents São Paulo, and the narrative *Passageiro do fim do dia* by Rubens Figueiredo (about Rio de Janeiro) read in an equally *paulistano* counterpoint by Sérgio Capparelli in *O rapaz do metrô*, combine, in their respective motions, the fragments and the multiplicity, the parts and the whole, and they present themselves as a representative sample of literature's potent ability to capture something that occurs in the deepest ganglions of Brazilian society. They are outside of any easy illusion of 'realism'.

More than just a collection of fragments, *Eles eram muitos cavalos* is a project that actually puts to good use the immanent power of the fragment. This — the use of fragments — is a trace that, in the first two decades of the current century, constitutes a sharply dominating tendency in contemporary Brazilian literature. In this sense, the fragment does not see itself restricted to a simple building element, but rather is a strategic aspect of the project that

---

[1] The English version of the present article was prepared thanks to the support of the Cátedra Eduardo Lourenço (Università di Bologna/Camões). The text was translated from Portuguese by Rodrigo Seabra Neves da Rocha.

[2] See Giorgio Agamben, *Che cos'è il contemporaneo?* (Rome: Nottetempo, 2008), p. 13.

stems from its use. There is a kind of antithetical movement in this element's building, as if its smallest possible quantity could amplify its potential to gather an enormous amount of 'realness' which would be impossible otherwise. To sum up, it is not just about a fragment, or the remains of some destruction, but about a part that accentuates its expressive potency in relation to an absent totality, but one that has left considerable, if partial, traces behind.[3] And this highlights, against the 'real', that 'São Paulo', the very image of the ruin, as an indication of a temporality that has largely lost itself and that left a significant residue that allows for contemplation. In Ruffato's novel, the broken vestiges of a specific day, precisely defined at the 'header',[4] give substance to the novel's first fragment, in the chaotic uncertainty of the unavoidable city.

From an etymological point of view, and with ample resonance in the conceptual sphere, 'fragment' is a deverbal from the Latin *frangere* that points to the chaotic result of a rupture, a liberation from pre-existing forms, whereas 'aphorism', also a deverbal, but from the Greek *aphorizein*, to divide or separate, points in the opposite direction towards a strict limitation, from which one can extract the meaning of 'definition' (from *aphorismos*).[5] This combination of oppositional forces seems to explain the use of the fragment as an aphorism,[6] which substantially resignifies and adapts the fragment, exploiting this material in multiple unforeseeable potentialities. Therefore, its *dynamis* stems from the double movement of maximum expressive concentration, on one side, and, at the same time, the widest possible opening to the universal, on the other. It is as if there were, in the aphorism-fragment, a centripetal force concerning the form and a centrifugal force when it comes to the meaning, and they both come into action linguistically.

Actually, using the fragment as an aphorism implies not only a rupture with the 'real', but also, and above all, operating a selection, an adaptation, an adjustment that turns into a monad something that, in itself, would be nothing more than a shard, a shrapnel, a residue destitute of any meaning except for the metonymical and immediate one of being the result of a rupture. The conciliation of a dialectics of the limited and the unlimited — the limitation of

---

[3] It is possible to note, from this reconstruction, the presence of Schlegel's romantic reflection, who, in a famous fragment of the *Athenäum* (n. 22), points out that 'the project is the subjective embryo of a developing object', which makes it then 'a fragment from the future', the final shape being constituted by the fragmentary whole, a space filled with gaps and presences, silences and words, a place of 'shadows and mixtures'. See Franco Rella, *Limina: il pensiero e le cose*, 2nd edn (Milan: Feltrinelli, 1994), p. 18.
[4] 'São Paulo, May 9 2000. Tuesday', in Luiz Ruffato, *There Were Many Horses*, trans. by Anthony Doyle (Seattle, WA: Amazon Crossing, 2014), p. 11; original edition, *Eles eram muitos cavalos*, 11th revd edn (São Paulo: Companhia das Letras, 2011), p. 13.
[5] Françoise Susini-Anastopoulos, *L'Écriture fragmentaire: définitions et enjeux* (Paris: PUF, 1997), p. 17.
[6] About this use of a fragment in *Elefante*, by Chico Alvim, see Roberto Vecchi, 'O real como projeto poético de *Elefante* de Francisco Alvim', in *Transliterando o real: diálogos sobre as representações culturais entre pesquisadores de Belo Horizonte e Bologna*, ed. by Roberto Vecchi and Sara Rojo (Belo Horizonte: Faculdade de Letras POSLIT, 2004), p. 62.

the aphorism and the boundlessness of the 'real', of the experience of the real, of the space — of the opened and the closed, balances a set of forces in which the maximum concentration of form works hard to grasp the horizon of meaning in its widest amplitude.

In Ruffato's project of fragments, the impression of the cartographic cut of the city that situates the scene can stand out, sometimes: 'Na esquina com a rua Estados Unidos, o tráfego da Avenida Rebouças estancou de vez. Henrique afrouxou a gravata, aumentou o volume do toca-cedê, Betty Carter ocupou todas as frinchas do Honda Civic estalando de novo, janelas cerradas, cidadela irregatável, lá fora o mundo, calor, poluição, tensão, corre-corre' [The traffic flatlined on the corner of Estados Unidos and Rebouças Avenue. Henrique loosened his tie and turned up the volume on the CD player, Betty Carter spilled into every nook and cranny of his brand-new Honda Civic, the windows rolled up around his unassailable citadel, leaving the world outside, with its heat, smog, tension, bustle and hustle].[7] The detail, due to its connotative effect, confirms that the place evoked functions on the basis of its bond with the powers-that-be: in the city, space is divided, fragmented, torn apart by economic and social extremes sometimes invisible, but actively present.

Above all, the stratigraphy underneath the solely explicit dimension of space becomes outlined, thus demarcating the many other spaces that constitute that dimension. Such is the case of a fragment (within a picture where violence and social turmoil are the structural axes of a disjointed sociability that crosses through and fractures the urban space) like 'Diapers', where the conflict that stems from the race–social class prejudice exposes all the sides of a complex polygon: the anaphoric use of the image of the security guard — 'O segurança, negro agigantado, espaduado, impecável dentro do terno preto' [the security guard, a big black guy wide as a door, impeccable in his black suit] — as opposed to the 'negro franzino' [skinny, boney black guy], the 'otário' [punk] who, by the looks of it, was intending to subtract a few essential items from the store (a connection structured by the use of the adverb 'discretamente' [discreetly]), and finds himself blocked right from the start by the suspicion that arises due to his racial and social conditions, is operated in this public-private space of the supermarket along with the head of security (with no racial connotations involved), saying: 'Olha cara, se tem uma coisa que eu conheço é malandro... vagabundo... Conheço pelo cheiro... Se conheço' [man, if there's one thing I can recognize a mile away it's a newjack... a punk... I can smell 'em...].[8] The comment the black security guard makes, marked by at least one background ambiguity covered by obscenity ('man, that Souza is one bitchin cold-ass motherfucker!'),[9] values and confirms an aspect defined by Beatriz

---

[7] Ruffato, *Cavalos*, p. 71; *Horses*, p. 72.
[8] Ruffato, *Cavalos*, p. 51; *Horses*, p. 50.
[9] Ibid.

Resende as the 'retorno do trágico' [return of the tragic],[10] seconded exactly by the use of the fragment: beyond the immediate meaning of the modern tragic, the amphibology of meanings in one same sentence must be reconducted to the tragic, or, in other words, whoever belongs in the *polis* or out of it will interpret the rule in a different way, just as pointed out by Jean-Pierre Vernant in the case of classical Greek tragedy.[11] The urban space arises away from an exhaustive mapping process, in absolute infeasibility, stemming from a partiality, a duality that, besides posing a dilemma, legitimates again the social opacity of a country's formation that is complex and unfinished: 'são paulo é o lá fora? É o aqui dentro?' [is são paulo the out-there? is it the in-here?].[12]

In *Eles eram muitos cavalos*, in which hundreds of voices, stories, obsessions, phobias, wishes, fragments get mixed together in a visual tableau governed by forces and conflicts, there is the refounding of an alternative urban poetic that, at the same time, re-reads the catalogue of representations that lies on top of the urban space. The inextricable combination that forms the territory, between urban space and social entanglement, reinstates the old theme of the city as being grey — a chromatic trace consecrated by literature, from Ribeiro Couto to Mário de Andrade, amongst others[13] — offering an alternative perspective for re-reading. The opacity gets somewhat disassembled from its composite stratigraphy already present in traditional images, a characteristic the fragment isolates, emphasizes and suspends:

> terça feira
> fim de semana longe
> as luzes dos postes dos carros dos painéis eletrônicos dos ônibus
> e tudo tem a cor cansada
> e os corpos mais cansados
> mais cansados
> a batata das minhas pernas dói minha cabeça dói e
>
> [tuesday
> weekend far away
> the streetlights headlights lights on the electronic panels of the buses
> and everything is the color of tiredness
> and the bodies are even more tired
> more tired
> my calves are killing me my head is killing me my][14]

The consistency of the colour grey confers a thicker materiality, constituted

---

[10] Beatriz Resende, *Contemporâneos: expressões da literatura brasileira no século XXI* (Rio de Janeiro: Casa da Palavra–Biblioteca Nacional, 2008), p. 29.
[11] Jean-Pierre Vernant, 'Tensioni e ambiguità nella tragedia greca', in *Saggi su mito e tragedia*, ed. by Jean-Pierre Vernant and Pierre Vidal-Naquet (Turin: Einaudi, 1994), pp. 35–36.
[12] Ruffato, *Cavalos*, p. 82; *Horses*, p. 83.
[13] Nicolau Sevcenko, *Orfeu estático na metrópole: São Paulo sociedade e cultura nos frementes anos 20* (São Paulo: Companhia das Letras, 1992), p. 15.
[14] Ruffato, *Cavalos*, p. 83; *Horses*, p. 85 (the interruption after the possessive pronoun — a conjunction, in the original — figures in the original work).

by a space that is non-symbolic or poetic (and present, at the same time), but, above all, by the anthropic layer interposed, thus incorporating, side by side with the overcast skies established from the very beginning, the social opacity of a complex and unfinished building of the country.

In its abuses and innocences, its prejudices and ideologies, where language recomposes itself, sometimes stridently, poetics gives concreteness to that grey colour. This happens, for example, in the case of the old employee ('The continuous old-fella') who is invited by his employer not to go to work, because, when dressed in a suit and tie as she demands of him, he could be taken for a policeman and become a target for the shootings the city has been experiencing. And then he 'saiu do banheiro, olhos chãos, o rio morto, os carros indiferentes, os prédios futuristas, a cortina escura do horizonte: *a velha coitada*' [leaves the restroom, eyes down, the dead river, the indifferent cars, the futuristic buildings, the dark curtain on the horizon, *the old dear, bless her*].[15] This is another shade of grey that liquefies, but does not eliminate, the class discrimination diluted in the attentive cordiality between servant and boss, which only in appearance is seen as 'modern' and 'innocent', but in actuality is the fruit of the persistence of a domesticated barbarity.

Therefore, it is in this unresolved tension between fragments and project that the 'São Paulo' of *Eles eram muitos cavalos* situates itself, attributing measure and a paradoxical (although possible) shape to the metropolitan boundlessness. This is a book that through literature — and through the intersection of forces, dislocations and relations — brings everyone close to the impossible, phantasmagorical simultaneity of a day with the name of the rewritten city. And, effectively, 'they were many horses', *quod erat demonstrandum*, as says the line of verse by Cecília Meireles that gives this book its title, as shown in the epigraph.

Ruffato's project, even if inscribed into a clear line of modern tradition, takes on a singular and self-owned challenge, as if the insufficiencies that always arise from designing the text of a city — and this text never exhausts its idealistic propensity, falling always short of a verisimilar coincidence — would serve as a platform for a radically new project. From this stems that duplicitous and contradictory trace the novel has, as if it were something familiar and, at the same time, drastically divergent and otherly, in its disturbing strength. In fact, the city is an accumulation of multiple spaces, times, experiences, which problematically let themselves become isolated also because its strength is particularly founded in relationships that narrow down one to the other in sometimes unexpected ways, but that, when combined, can provide for a relevant meaning. In the city, centre and periphery converge, which is another recursive element in the typical Brazilian narrative dating from the turn of the millennium, where public realm and private sphere, *polis* and *oikos*, converge and crisscross, reflecting themselves even in the very means that combine the relationship between the parts and the whole — the whole that is the city. It is

---

[15] Ruffato, *Cavalos*, p. 57; *Horses*, p. 57.

also where the means represent a fundamentally relational thread, in a certain way, foundational of its constitutive network.

In fact, the bus, the subway, or the train are not a tribute to a conventional narrative isotopy of urban modernity. There is a quotational residue of this past in the present, always modern (but of a modernity that can only be acknowledged in contradictory and drastically plural ways), that becomes evident in the restructuration of perceptions that movement, through technique, makes possible and finds itself the founder of a modernization of the very idea of representation (the fragmentary, the swift, the ephemeral, the rest) torrentially explored by the historic vanguards and by modern literature. However, it is a residue that, in itself, does not justify the macroscopic emergence of a theme — the passage through the public means — but its evidence seems to have a whole other density.

The presence of the theme, and its possible function within contemporary Brazilian literature, has already been made evident by many critical gazes. From this point of view, a quite lucid contribution by Regina Delcastagnè in her article 'Deslocamentos urbanos na literatura brasileira contemporânea' maps the different means — public or private — by which displacements happen in novels by Marcus Vinícius Faustini, Rubens Figueiredo, Sacolinha and Vário do Andaraí.[16]

Space emerges as a social dimension, a contemporary coexistence of different temporalities, one that allows us to think like the subjects that practise it — from this stems the aesthetical, but also political, importance of being in transit, because 'apesar de toda hierarquia estabelecida nas grandes cidades, apesar de todo esforço de exclusão empreendido pelas elites dominantes — seja no mundo concreto, seja no âmbito das representações — essa passagem, e sua narrativa, transformam o espaço que tocam, promovendo uma espécie de alargamento do universo dos possíveis' [despite all the hierarchy established in the big cities, despite all the effort towards exclusion employed by the dominant classes — be it in the concrete world or in the realm of representations — this passage, and its narrative, transform the space they touch, promoting a kind of enlargement in the universe of possibilities].[17]

Actually, this reflection inscribes itself aside from an analysis of the displacements, because it elects a particular form in which they occur, the one concerning the public means. This is not about an option for a theme or the attempt to second a simple narrative isotopy. More than that, it is an attempt to analyse the thick conceptual layer that the notion of 'public means' brings to the critical theory — and that a few novels, in elucidating manner, problematize, by means of dissolving many founding dichotomies such as the one between public and private realms and that between means and ends.

From this point of view, the connection one refers to when mentioning

---

[16] Regina Delcastagnè, 'Deslocamentos urbanos na literatura brasileira contemporânea', *Brasiliana: Journal for Brazilian Studies*, 3.1 (2014), 31–47.
[17] Delcastagnè, p. 46.

'means' as shown in Giorgio Agamben's book *Mezzi senza fine: note sulla politica*[18] (published in English as *Means without End: Notes on Politics*) is not a voluntary one. It actually aims at discussing, in theoretical terms, what politics becomes when the indistinction of conventional categories is introduced and another *nomos* establishes itself from a critical reconfiguration of space. *Mezzi senza fine* follows the publication of *Homo sacer: il potere sovrano e la nuda vita*[19] (published in English as *Homo Sacer: Sovereign Power and Bare Life*) by the same author (as part of a cycle that was closed in 2014 with *L'uso dei corpi*,[20] published in English as *The Use of Bodies*), which rethinks the theme of power from an extreme gesture, even if one that has already been founded on ample elaboration: the inscription of politics in life, something that leads towards a redefinition of the very idea of sovereignty. In building this new quadrant of how contemporary power works, the old categories of classical sovereignty are disassembled and recoded, thus showing how the new paradigms of modernity — identified not in the classic and lustral example of the city, but in the 'camp' (as in extermination camp) — make the differentiation between politics and its outside impossible. This lack of distinction affects, for example, and directly, the classic separation (present even in Aristotle's *Politics*) between *oikos* and *polis*, between household and city, between private and public.

There is also the link between means and ends, with which the phenomenon of violence, for example, is often reconsidered — an appropriate moment to bring up a key text in order to rethink modern violence, that by Hannah Arendt, *On Violence*,[21] which, in this relationship between means and ends, calls attention to the predominance of the means. This leads us to think of a progressive distancing of the ends by the means, so much so that Walter Benjamin, in a hermetic essay such as *Zur Kritik der Gewalt* (published in English as *Critique of Violence*), points out the very evident weight of 'means themselves'.[22] Agamben accentuates even further Benjamin's line of thought, showing the irreversible fracture of the means that are no longer alternative to the objectives. And the conceptual topic is interesting if referred to the 'public means'. In current thinking, to sum it up, the term 'means', from a theoretical point of view, figures as an extremely slippery object at a moment when both the means and the public realm seem only problematically apprehensible.

The crisis that the notion of public means goes through does not translate only as a temporary turbulence. It owes a lot more to the erosion that the concept of public realm, ever since its first Kantian configuration, has come to suffer in the empirical plane as well, where it means social practices. Besides possible normative definitions, the public sphere, which goes from an abstract form to

---

[18] Giorgio Agamben, *Mezzi senza fine: note sulla politica* (Turin: Bollati Boringhieri, 1996).
[19] Giorgio Agamben, *Homo sacer: il potere sovrano e la nuda vita* (Turin: Einaudi, 1995).
[20] Giorgio Agamben. *L'uso dei corpi. Homo sacer IV, 2* (Vicenza: Neri Pozza, 2014).
[21] Hannah Arendt, *Sulla violenza* (Parma: Guanda, 1996).
[22] Walter Benjamin, 'Per una critica alla violenza', in *Angelus novus: saggi e frammenti* (Turin: Einaudi, 1962), p. 6.

the contact with real substance, in modern times faces the degradation of the idealistic view that one could identify with the Greek *agorá*. The philosopher who most updated the concept of the public sphere, Jürgen Habermas, in his classic book *Strukturwandel der Öffentlichkeit* (published in English as *The Structural Transformation of the Public Sphere*),[23] redefines it as a discursive dissolution of power in which the selective element of argumentation, in modernity, ends up subrogating power itself — which, however, finds its basis of legitimacy in it, and not in customs or tradition.

In the society of the spectacle, where the social bonds of an identitarian notion of community can be found weakened to the point of exhaustion, this substitution becomes even more flagrant, since politics, which, as often noted by Agamben, only coincides imperfectly with the idea of being public, would characterize itself by being an 'extreme expropriation of language',[24] something that leads us to rethink, through another conceptual apparatus, the figures of historical conscience (a proposed example is that of the refugee as compared to national identities).[25] This way, politics becomes, in its mediatization, pure mediality, a sphere of absolute means — means that have exactly no ends.

What are the consequences, however, of a precarious determination of the concept of public means if we try to situate it in the Brazilian context? The theme becomes more complex because, from classic interpretations (and we can think, in particular, of Sérgio Buarque de Holanda and his book *Raízes do Brasil*, published in English as *Roots of Brazil*), it is problematic to define a public sphere if, from the conditioning elements of its formation, it is problematic to assume this sphere as being constituted when personalism or the ideology of cordiality rule, and this includes the processes of modernization in the twentieth century.[26] In a way, one could say that the focus on the Brazilian side of this matter leads to a reflection with ample theoretical consequences. The incompleteness of the public sphere, for reasons that remit to a tortuous historical process — the effect of something we usually call 'coloniality' — transforms the Brazilian experience into a significant laboratory that helps understanding the contemporary world.

If politics, these days, has reached a point where it is thought in terms of the emptying of its constituent functions as the opposite of the public, in a moment when biological life is presumed as the political task *par excellence*, the prevailing paradigm is that of the household, the private dimension, the unpoliticizing *oikonomia*.[27] The household here can be seen as the national, the private, the closed, the class, anything that impedes the broadening of 'I' into 'we', with a surge for a new possibility of a 'common' thought. At this point, it

---

[23] Jürgen Habermas, *Storia e critica dell'opinione pubblica* (Bari: Laterza, 1984).
[24] Agamben, *Mezzi senza fine* p. 91.
[25] Agamben, *Mezzi senza fine*, p. 21.
[26] About this, see Lilia Moritz Schwarcz, *Sobre o autoritarismo brasileiro* (São Paulo: Companhia das Letras, 2019), p. 63.
[27] Agamben, *Mezzi senza fine*, p. 109.

only makes sense to remember the example proposed by Agamben, by using Kafka's short story *Der Bau* [*The Burrow*], which talks about an animal (a rat or a fox or something like that — it is not identified) that digs obsessively in order to build itself a safe burrow, a burrow which ends up turning into a lethal trap.[28] By means of this figure that so belongs to the contemporary, with the substitution for the private whenever and wherever something should be public, we see ourselves facing the spread of a condition that goes in the opposite direction, and that, in Brazil and in other 'souths' around the world, historically, has been affirming itself: the privatization of community spaces where the political subject should be a collective subject, and not just a simple expression of an oligarchy or the elite.

We learn from the studies on the dynamics of violence that the privatization of the public realm is the precondition that allows for violence in its pure state as used in a massacre or a genocide, but also for the paradoxical and, at the same time, rational 'construction' of that public realm, according to Wolfgang Sofsky.[29] The anteriority of a hypotrophy of the public sphere within an extremely complex network of power relations led the public means to become not services *for* citizenship, but urged them to make evident a class mark, in a way. These means detach themselves from their completely public goal, becoming autonomous and bringing into discussion both a politics of the means and public politics.

What is left of the community when the biological and the political bodies grow more and more coincidental, at each moment less distinguishable? In Brazil and in Latin America, in general terms, this is a wildly vibrant and present theme. It can be said that Brazil anticipated the social claims movements — which now, in 2019, occupy Latin America's contemporary scene — with the 2013 Mass Protests: at that moment, the *Movimento Passe Livre* [Free Fare Movement], concerning the public means, in a way invoked an alternative standing of the masses in order to shift the power relations when it comes to space, in the name of a possible dissolution of the discourse of power. Is this instance still possible, or should it be rethought in more complex terms, within a global quadrant that seems to limit the rescue of something — i.e., the shared, inclusive dimension of an indistinctive public policy — that is currently going through a crisis or even a dissolution process?

Spanish philosopher Daniel Innerarity, in his key book about this subject, *El nuovo espacio publico* (2006; loosely translated as 'The New Public Realm'), analyses this limit, suggesting an extreme rethinking of the very concept of public realm, which also deeply modifies the notion of 'common' — leading to the redefinition of a 'public sphere' that is no longer the one produced by the Enlightenment, but one that poses the need to rethink the rules of participation according to another context of references when other classes and forces have

---

[28] Agamben, *Mezzi senza fine*, p. 108.
[29] Wolfgang Sofsky, *Saggio sulla violenza* (Turin: Einaudi, 1998), p. 81.

occupied the 'public' scenario.[30] What is at stake here is the need to rethink the concept of community not from an identitarian body of work, as could happen in the foundational times of the national narratives, but from within its own plural and unfinished view, marked by differences and internal ruptures inside a logic of more social complexity.

Two books can help us understand, considering their somewhat extreme character, how to think the limits of the public means and the demand for new topographies, especially when it comes to the urban space within a political idea that matches a conceptual reading of literary texts. Those two books are quite different from each other: one, the novel *Passageiro do fim do dia*, by Rubens Figueiredo (2010; loosely translated as 'The Passenger at the End of the Day'), has been acclaimed and is already a subject of discussion; and the other, *O rapaz do metrô*, by Sérgio Capparelli (2014; loosely translated as 'The Boy from the Subway'), is a hybrid work based mainly on poetry and potentially aimed at a young-adult audience. In both, and in the critical combination of both, one can see that a kind of hypertrophy emerges, a kind of narrative or poetic maximum exposure of the means of public transportation, which brings to the forefront the characteristics of the public means in Brazil (with a social class connotation) and the limits of the public realm and means that are made evident by the crumbling of the notion of 'common'.

The narrative in *Passageiro do fim do dia* as a whole fits in one bus trip, from downtown to the suburb of Tyrol, the protagonist Pedro's neighbourhood. That happens in spite of the many ruptures that criss-cross the narrative — the traumatic scene of a past incident, the reading that takes him into the anachronism of Darwin's passage through Brazil which allows for a recovery of the times of slavery[31] — and the path through that public means of transportation that threads the continuity of the narrative, thus marking its sequentialization.

In the case of Capparelli's work, the poetry that sometimes, exceptionally as it may be (even though a progressive dilution of the poetic can be perceived), turns into prose (but this prose is always present as a palimpsest in the poetic montage of the book) is always protagonized by a sixteen-year-old lad who is the recurring poetic persona in the poems. He works as a train maintenance apprentice in São Paulo's subway service and, as he tells us in Chapter 3, he casually films a 'chacina' [slaughter] conducted by some boys involving the protagonist's own friends in the neighbourhood where they all live, Campo Limpo. The work is structured in eight chapters that are also called 'slaughters' (one for each chapter, as in 'first slaughter', 'second slaughter' and so on), thus confirming that the theme of representation of violence — and of the possible writing of this violence — is dominant in the economy of this work, which

---

[30] Daniel Innerarity, *Il nuovo spazio pubblico* (Rome: Meltemi, 2008), pp. 42–43.
[31] See Paulo Roberto Tonani do Patrocínio, *Cidade de lobos: a representação de territórios marginais na obra de Rubens Figueiredo* (Belo Horizonte: Editora da UFMG, 2016), pp. 161–62.

aims to encompass, from the victim's point of view, the 'war of São Paulo'.[32] The element that horizontally and integrally structures the printing area of the book is the *paulistano* subway line, meaning that the continuing and circular trip around town — stations, neighbourhoods, places, streets, maps and public signs — also crosses the whole of the work, despite the hiatuses that the poetic form itself somehow constantly produces. São Paulo's subway works, then, as a scaffolding that supports the book and through which the book builds itself, as if the outside has stayed, this time, within the work.

The emphasis on the means in both case studies here, and the conversion of transit into permanence — a little bit like Guimarães Rosa's *travessia* [crossing], as one might observe — accentuate even further the detachment between means and ends, as could be expected in a context where both cases are dominated by the progressive and unstoppable emptying of the notion of public space and, therefore, of the public realm. As is often the case, especially in contemporary literature, literary writing is able to provide proper shapes to conceptual aggregates that would be difficult to represent plastically in any other way, thus subtracting from them the theory of an abstract dimension and giving them effective concreteness.

Something occurring in both works is that violence seems to take over the narration, spreading a sense of dread and the uncomfortable impression of a fear that penetrates deeply, defiling that narration with the daily banality in which the subway or a bus line should represent the usual means that allow for the citizens' dislocation. Both texts attest that it is not quite like that, and that the anomaly — the distortion in the means' workings — happened because some citizenship pact has been broken or because the context of urban violence, which has as main victims the peripheral populace, has grown to become dominant. However, there are those who seek some kind of rescue of the public dimension.

In *Passageiro do fim do dia*, the poor people look up to the State and seek inclusion within the perimeter of citizenship: the public college represents a trace of qualification,[33] as well as treating each other 'as equals'. This is seen as such by Rosane, Pedro's girlfriend, who lives in Tyrol and represents a border between inclusion and exclusion, citizenship and 'just another face in the crowd' — someone who risks, and turns precarious, the viability of a notion of 'the people' — with a favourable connotation, since, in such a diversified society, it is not 'common' to see how 'pessoas que à primeira vista traziam marcas tão diferentes e mesmo opostas' [people who, at a first glance, carried marks so different and even opposite] would face off on the same level.[34] However, in the reproduction of the classic dichotomy that constitutes the social character, between the *polis* and the *oikos*, the precariousness of the borders becomes evident, as well as, deep down, the impossibility of assuming,

---

[32] Rubens Figueiredo, *Passageiro do fim do dia* (São Paulo: Companhia das Letras, 2010), p. 138.
[33] Figueiredo, p. 48.
[34] Figueiredo, p. 46.

unless in idealized fashion, the conventional binomial: 'para Rosane, *direito* significava que tinha de tomar alguma coisa de alguém — alguém que tinha tomado uma coisa dela' [to Rosane, *having a right* meant that she'd have to take something from someone — someone who had taken something from her].[35]

But it is the public means itself, when related to the passengers, that makes evident another mediality, which does not conciliate with a means–end relation, brought forth, as it is, by the context of urban violence and inscribing the means as an instrument in the state of exception that empties it of any destination of public use. The 'travel contract' cannot be fulfilled anymore; the problem now is to reach a destination, any destination. It does not matter where, because the original route has become impossible due to threats. This is how the means itself, the bus, gets somewhat subtracted from the public dimension and goes forward from the informality of the drivers' conversations and the tricks for route changes.

This (induced, of course) privatization of the public sphere is so strong that it even produces a kind of metamorphosis in the means: 'o ônibus agora seguia bem devagar, sempre em segunda ou terceira marcha, um longo trecho sem parar. Avançava com velocidade baixa e constante por um corredor lateral que se formara na pista da direita, onde os ônibus seguiam de perto uns dos outros — a dianteira de um bem perto da traseira do outro, numa espécie de comboio' [the bus now moved on quite slowly, always in second or third gear, for long stretches with no stops. It went on in a low, constant speed through a side corridor that just formed by the right lane, where buses followed one another closely — one's front close to the other's rear, forming a kind of convoy].[36]

At the same time, there are traces of a public dimension that have been lost, if not on the outside then at least on the inside, in the inner part of the bus. Here, the conversations — better still, Pedro's indictment-driven intuition, when it comes to the other passengers, but also to the two communities in which they are all inserted, Rio's and Tyrol's — operate a critical disassembling of power, of the very use of the public space to other intentions. Examples are myriad, but the most impressive of all is perhaps the episode of the social programme's magnetic card that fails to work in a supermarket and exposes to shame Rosane's father and aunt when they have to return everything they bought, especially considering they are on a rival group's turf.

Capparelli's hybrid work, one that takes on the challenge of verse without abandoning a very clear narrative line, articulated from an ample literary and cultural quotational play, also has a public means of transportation, the São Paulo subway, as its core. The public means, the metropolitan network, cuts out fragments of the uncontourable city that can be assembled on a personal board that says a lot about the main voice of the text, that of the sixteen-year-old train maintenance apprentice who faces unwritten rules that are reserved in

[35] Figueiredo, p. 159.
[36] Figueiredo, p. 179.

the public realm, rules apparent only to people of colour (and that also allows for the surfacing of a relation between race and class that reveals the limits and prejudices that turn precarious that same political notion).

It could be stated that the protagonist and owner of the predominant poetic voice, when he traverses the subway stations — an artificial map, since fabricated by the subway line, but still realistic — avoids, through the imagination of that cut in reality, opening a breach — an imaginary one — into nature, as if the disconnect in the relation between the realm of technique and nature, a mother notion when it comes to the idea of 'modern', were always marked by turbulence and limits: 'Edifício Copan': Um edifício | que ondula | saudades | do mar' [Copan Building: A building | that undulates | a longing | for the sea]; or 'Composiçao a céu aberto: O metrô | Como quem não quer nada | Compõe toda | uma paisagem' [Composition under an open sky: The subway | nonchalantly | builds the whole | of a landscape].[37]

The book, in reality, travels in a way that can be seen as inverse as that of Rubens Figueiredo's novel, grafting the visions and violences of the suburbs onto images of downtown, articulated by the subway circuit: periphery can actually disseminate itself anywhere, which is reminiscent of a famous verse by Racionais MC's (in their album *Sobrevivendo no inferno* [Surviving in Hell]).

However, the erosion of the idea of 'public' emerges, above all other instances, in the theme of justice, which consolidates itself as the dominant theme, especially in the end part of the book, when, in the supplement that can be deemed essay-like — the topic in question being 'Human rights and the application of the law' — the public power tries to react to the threats that the apprentice from Campo Limpo received after witnessing a slaughter. Fiction and reality mix once more when, in the epigraph to the final text of 'slaughter 7' (in typical newspaper language, which seems to appear here in order to evoke modernist poetry), a piece of factual data is provided: 'Das 24 chacinas do ano passado, só uma foi esclarecida' [Of the 24 slaughters committed last year, only one has been solved].[38]

The meeting between the boy from the subway and the public prosecutor (in the poem titled as such) makes clear not only his complete distrust when it comes to the security institutions, but also the near certainty of the violent death that awaits him. The collusion between the military police officers and the criminals with the intent of executing the 'private' massacres, and the macabre slush fund of some police battalions functions in the same vein. The (poetic) denouncement, however, is unequivocal (even if, in the end, the murdering police officers are arrested), and it shows the definitive rupture of any possible integration in a space that is private — that private space of violence abuse, and not that of citizenship:

---

[37] Sérgio Capparelli, *O rapaz do metrô: poemas para jovens em oito chacinas ou capítulos* (Rio de Janeiro: Galera, 2014), p. 24 and p. 85 (unpublished in English as of 2020; loosely translated here).
[38] Capparelli, p. 137.

> No espaço de um mês
> Assassinaram trezentos
> Na cidade de São Paulo
>
> Sem falar nos sumiços:
> Na periferia somem
> Negros e mestiços.
>
> A polícia militar:
> 'Tudo o que é sólido
> Desmancha no ar!'
>
> Boatos desencontrados
> Do estouro da guerra civil,
> Nas favelas e becos.
>
> Dois poderes conflituantes:
> De um lado o poder armado
> E do outro o armado poder
>
> [In the space of a month
> They murdered three hundred
> In the city of São Paulo
>
> Not to mention the disappearances:
> In the peripheries, they vanish
> The blacks and the mixed-bloods.
>
> The military police:
> 'All that is solid
> Melts into air!'
>
> Mismatched rumours
> Of the breakout of a civil war,
> In the slums and alleys.
>
> Two conflicting powers:
> On one side, armed power
> On the other, power that is armed.]
>
> ('Culpa dos Maias' [Blame it on the Mayans])[39]

In the quite ruined landscape of the public means and spaces, so macroscopically connected to the civic degradation that makes precarious the very notion of citizenship, what is left, then, of the (re)integrationist illusion that is structured as more of a rhetorical component than as an effective possibility for consolidation of a space that is unequivocally public?

The texts themselves give us a possible vanishing point in order to answer that crucial question. The crisis in, and the collapse of, the distinction between public and private permeate the narratives of *Passageiro do fim do dia* and *O rapaz do metrô*. In the former, Pedro sets up, in the mini-community of suffering (or of victims) that is formed, from the mistakes and the threats that

---

[39] Capparelli, p. 124.

mark this group, a different attitude, a complex one, but one that inaugurates another notion of 'common' that puts into play a banalized sense of belonging in order to remit to another potential dimension of community:

> Pedro quase lia os pensamentos daquela gente. Já eram familiares. Mas, como na fila, no início da viagem, Pedro sentiu também que não era um deles. Sentiu aquilo com perfeita certeza e junto veio uma sensação de alívio, mas também de remorso: a sensação de uma ponta de maldade — maldade velha, repetida, que nem era dele, pessoal
>
> [Pedro could almost read the minds of those people. They were already familiar. But also, as had happened in that queue at the beginning of the trip, Pedro felt he wasn't one of them. He felt that with perfect clarity, and that came to him together with a sense of relief and also one of remorse: the feeling of a hint of evil — and old, repeated evil that wasn't even his, not personal][40]

Analogously, the subway apprentice, now free from danger, finds himself establishing another relationship (of a 'community of lovers', as Blanchot would put it)[41] that also shows how the emptiness that now lodges the disarrangement between public and private can be rethought from an alternative notion of 'common':

> Ela me disse, vamos!
> E a segui sem saber aonde
> E então pensei, estranho,
> Me paga um dia essa mulher,
> Sigo-a que nem boi na canga,
> Com ela, aonde ela quer.
>
> Eu disse a ela, vamos!
> Ela veio, sem saber aonde.
> Sem nada achar de estranho.
> Confiei de cara nessa mulher,
> Comigo, que nem boi na canga,
> Para o que der e vier.
>
> [She told me, let's go!
> And I followed her without knowing where to
> And then I thought, that's weird
> She'll pay me back someday, this woman
> As I follow her like a yoked ox
> With her, wherever she pleases.
>
> I told her, let's go
> She came, without knowing where to
> Without ever finding it weird
> I trusted this woman right away

---

[40] Figueiredo, pp. 195-96.
[41] Maurice Blanchot, *La comunità inconfessabile* (Milan: Feltrinelli, 1984), p. 84.

> With me, like a yoked ox
> Come hell or high water.]
>
> ('Canga' [Yoke])[42]

The restructuring of the relationship between the 'I' and the 'we' thus becomes the way to rethink the atrophy of the political horizon, in the irruption of the private as public, when the political body and the biological body become indistinct, in the impossibility of thinking politics from the viewpoint of another mediality that does not allow for us to see an ending it would determine. The possibility of a 'new common', where the community essentialisms do not work even in discourse (nation, language, religion and so on), or they work as radical irrationalities, which is yet another form of malfunction, founds itself on top of another — extreme — speech possibility, after the disappropriation of the language of the spectacle-state. It goes through, as Agamben always says, a 'being-in-means',[43] which is a being-in-language as a condition to rethink politics as a place that effectively turns a means visible as it should be: a pure and endless mediality.[44]

The 'common' as such, in an undetermined ground between the proper and the improper, inaugurates another grammar in which the experience in a public means, as shown by the works in question, makes it possible to find a condition beyond mediality and public space: a rescue-as-potency that inscribes itself in the border threshold between two undifferentiated conditions — but they also, in the tension of touching one another, cause an event of language, and, as nature and technique, reality and artifice, touch one another and do not mix in the event-language of the poetry of a trip in the public means:

> Das fachadas da Faria Lima
> Às seis da tarde
> Até Guarulhos, já noite,
> São vinte e cinco quilômetros.
> Nas duas margens,
> *Shoppings, fast-foods* e financeiras
> Vão ficando para trás.
> Refletem-se no para-brisa
> As primeiras estrelas
>
> [From the façades of Faria Lima
> at six o'clock in the afternoon
> until Guarulhos, evening already,
> it's twenty-five kilometres.
> On both margins,
> malls, fast-food joints and financial companies
> are left behind.

---

[42] Capparelli, p. 142.
[43] Agamben, *Mezzi senza fine*, p. 92.
[44] Agamben, *Mezzi senza fine*, p. 93.

Reflecting on the windshield
are the first stars].

('Deixando a Faria Lima' [Leaving Faria Lima])[45]

It is from this undetermined, yet necessary, point that the politics of another 'common' can begin to be rethought, and then create ways to imagine — something that literature allows — other community relations, away from the usual standoffs and, in particular, the ones of today.

The Brazilian novel, to which we add the adjective 'contemporary' — as seen in the select constellation of works by Ruffato, Figueiredo and Capparelli, which are parts of a much wider whole, between fragments and means, private dimension and public space, peripheries and centre — becomes the preferential place for an aesthetically constituted elaboration of a new notion of 'common' and of 'public'. It is a Brazil made out of paper that could, nevertheless, foreshadow a future completely other and, desirably, real.

---

[45] Capparelli, p. 110.

The Predicament of Contemporary Brazilian Fiction and its Spatiotemporal Modalities

KARL ERIK SCHØLLHAMMER

Pontifícia Universidade Católica do Rio de Janeiro

How to write about Brazil today? In what times do we live? After the hope that came with the new century, the present restages the atrocious return of an authoritarian period before that of the recent and fragile democracy. According to Karl Marx,[1] history happens first as tragedy and repeats itself as farce, but in Brazil, Veríssimo counters, 'history does not repeat itself as farce, farces repeat themselves as history'.[2] In Joca Reiners Terron's most recent novel, *A Morte e o Meteoro* [Death and the Meteor] (2019), the author performs a fictional archaeology of the future of whoever already experiences the beginning of the end. The retrofuturistic narrative takes readers to the verge of the apocalypse that they will already recognize as if it were old news. Eternally lying in the so-called 'splendid cradle', to which the Brazilian national anthem refers, the country is lagging behind and the catastrophic future of daily life in the present is narrated. The protagonists, the Kaajapukugi indigenous tribe, face unavoidable extermination in what remains of the Amazon forest, under the threat of mining, land grabbing, drug trafficking, and the ruthless exploitation of their habitat. Only fifty Indians are left, all men, who are barely surviving, and the moment is one of an international rescue operation. On the plateaus of the state of Oaxaca in Mexico, a local indigenist anthropologist tries to help Boaventura, a lonely Brazilian Northeasterner whose destiny is fatally intertwined with the Kaajapukugi and who sees himself called to the mission to protect the Indians. When Boaventura dies on arrival in Oaxaca in obscure circumstances, the tale gains the air of a detective story set in the refuge of the Brazilian Indians, now led by enigmatic metropolitan Indians, a militant action group inspired by the student revolt movement in Rome, during the 1970s.

The story of *A Morte e o Meteoro* explores the design of a fragile geography between threatened peoples and between regions exposed to disaster in the larger Latin American continent. The extermination of the forests is confused with the disappearance of hallucinogenic beetles, native languages, and a whole cosmology and worldview. Terron inscribes himself in the contemporary

---

[1] *The Eighteenth Brumaire of Louis Napoleon*, trans. by Ben Fowkes, in *Surveys from Exile*, ed. by David Fernbach (Harmondsworth: Penguin, 1973), p. 146.
[2] <https://www.diariodocentrodomundo.com.br/essencial/verissimo-aqui-a-historia-nao-se-repete-como-farsa-as-farsas-se-repetem-como-historia/>, 21 May 2018 [accessed 16 April 2021].

narrative, abandoning the big cities, which in their time were the heir to the national scene, and exposing the margin of an apocalypse that in certain parts of the country and the continent has become an everyday condition. He offers a narrative of resistance in a tragic account of loyalty and commitment, vocation and destiny, and love and betrayal. At the same time, he creates a view of a dystopian future that readers paradoxically recognize in a frightful déjà vu of contemporary reality. Such contemporary fiction therefore expresses the environmental, economic, sociopolitical, and cultural crisis through a disjunction, a temporal mismatch that shuffles historical times which coexist in the complex social reality, and that is dramatically expressed in this tension between pasts which are experienced in the present and futures which are uncertain and threatening.

The English philosopher Peter Osborne is probably one of the thinkers who has most profoundly examined the understanding of the term 'contemporary' within the history of present art and also within the historiographic discussions on the topic.[3] One of the main points of his argument begins with the differentiation between the idea of the 'present' in modern thought, for example in Baudelaire, in which the present is described as the passage from the past to the future, and the concept of the present in the contemporary, which appears as the negotiation in the present of the relation between the different layers of time in the past. Osborne mentions three moments of different meanings of the contemporary: one that coincides with the post-war and that, for example, is expressed in the foundation of the Institute of Contemporary Arts (ICA) in London, in 1946; another that coincides with the post-conceptual art of the 1960s; and finally, the worldview that accompanies the fall of the Berlin Wall in 1989. With the fall of the wall, world communism starts to collapse and, in a way, the period of modern revolutionary hope that began in 1917 comes to a close. At this moment, China enters the global market with a new model of capitalism, and a victorious neoliberal globalization begins at the cost of the cultural policies of an independent Left. Within the world of art, Osborne adds, this moment provokes 'the apparent closure of the historical horizon of the avant-garde; a qualitative deepening of the integration of autonomous art into the culture industry; and a globalization and transnationalization of the biennale as an exhibition form.'[4]

Thus, the contemporary for Osborne is, on the one hand, different from a simple synchronicity or simultaneity of events that occur at the same time. On the other, it is different from what he calls *coevalness*, which refers to a phenomenological and intersubjective sharing of 'the same time'. Examples of these distinctions will be explored later, but what is important is Osborne's approach to understanding the contemporary as a 'typological' time that in itself builds a horizon of co-occurrence. This *constructive* aspect is

---

[3] Peter Osborne, *Anywhere or Not at All: Philosophy of Contemporary Art* (London: Verso, 2013).
[4] Osborne, *Anywhere or Not at All*, p. 53.

fundamental to Osborne's key argument, which defines the contemporary as a heuristic fiction, a construct through the concept of historical temporalization. It concerns a problematic, albeit real and necessary, fiction. He projects the historical present as a 'living disjunctive unity of multiple times',[5] that is, 'there is no socially actual shared subject position of, or within, our present from the standpoint of which its relational totality could be lived as a whole, in however epistemologically problematic or temporal existentially fragmented form.'[6] Nonetheless, the contemporary is approached 'as if' this subjective position really existed, thereby updating the Kantian argument on forms of contemplation. Only, in Osborne's approach, the contemporary dialectically projects a disjunctive spatial unity of various times in contrast to a present temporal unity of various spaces.

Leaving aside the complexity of Osborne's theoretical argument, an understanding of this conflictual relation makes it possible to think of the contemporary as connected to the transnational reality of the postcolonial world after the Cold War. As Osborne asserts:

> With the historical expansion, geopolitical differentiation and temporal intensification of contemporaneity, it has become critically incumbent upon any art with a claim on the present to situate itself, reflexively, within this expanded field. The coming together of different times that constitutes the contemporary, and the relations between the social spaces in which these times are embedded and articulated, are thus the two main axes along which the historical meaning of art is to be plotted.[7]

From this double perspective, cultural spaces are related within a geopolitical complexity that transcends the hierarchical design of colonial imperialism, and historical times coexist as superimposed layers within what Ernst Bloch called a 'simultaneity of the non-simultaneous' (*Gleichzeitigkeit des Ungleichzeitigen*),[8] that gains reality in the contemporary present. This argument fits the recent Brazilian experience well.

During the 1990s and 2000s, Brazil began to experience a certain prosperity accompanied by social achievements and slight democratic progress on human rights and by a public effort to seek justice. The fall of the Berlin Wall in 1989 sparked a global hope for an overcoming of the Cold War, and in Latin American countries, a path was cleared for another, different approximation to the developed world through a more equal dialogue that challenged traditional ideas of economic and cultural dependency. Theories of 'unequal exchange' were challenged along with the Eurocentric view that delegated to Latin

---

[5] Peter Osborne, 'Global Modernity and the Contemporary: Two Categories of the Philosophy of Historical Time', in *Breaking up Time: Negotiating the Borders between Present, Past and Future*, ed. by Chris Lorenz and Berber Bevernage (Göttingen: Vandenhoeck & Ruprecht, 2013), pp. 69–86 (p. 79).
[6] Osborne, *Anywhere or Not at All*, p. 59.
[7] Osborne, *Anywhere or Not at All*, p. 69.
[8] Ernst Bloch, *Heritage of our Times*, trans. by Neville Plaice and Stephen Plaice (Cambridge: Polity Press, 1991) [first pub. as *Erbschaft dieser Zeit*, 1935].

America a position on the global periphery destined to be always oriented toward the centre of the Western world. In this manner, globalization and digital technology not only introduced the notion of contemporaneity for a more egalitarian debate with the art and literature of the 'First World', but also established, from the perspective of Brazil, a way to be included in the global financial market as a supplier of commodities and also of art and literature, which had never before enjoyed a similar attention and global interest.

With the new democratic constitution of 1988, followed by the achievement of economic stability during the 1990s, Brazil not only gained global political recognition, but also emerged as an innovative contributor to the debates on the inconclusive legacy of modernity. Thus, the end of the twentieth century closed in light of the question of postmodernity based on a decolonial geography that was beginning to design its independence in a challenge to Western thinking. The celebration of the five-hundredth anniversary of the so-called 'discovery' of the Americas in 1992, and its coincidence with the seventieth anniversary of the Brazilian Modern Art Week, instigated the reformulation of the legacy of Brazilian and Latin American modernism for a more inclusive modernity with a positive and plural recovery of its periphery. Brazil was beginning to find its unique role in the postcolonial scenario, in which it simultaneously represented the legacy of economic underdevelopment, marked socially by its history of slavery, and a certain vanguard of sensible experiments in popular culture. Its corporal and musical expression seemed, in the light of re-readings, to propose examples for the inclusive, multi-ethnic, and cultural policies of the twenty-first century. Facilitated by new global circuits of digital communication and by media ubiquity, local encounters arose in new interactive spaces, thus introducing the emergence of an anachronistic agency that allowed the updating of the past to serve as a guide for the future.

The new regional topologies were what destabilized the customary hierarchical relation between the developed 'First World' and the 'Third World' under development. Historical time became so complex that it challenged the very concept of nation and especially the perspective of nation building.[9] In the 1970s, the economist Edmar Lisboa Bacha referred to Brazil as 'BelIndia', a monster whose small head represented a 'Belgian' upper class and whose fat body represented a level of poverty and deprivation comparable to that of India.[10] At the beginning of the twenty-first century, the minister Delfim Neto opted for the image of 'Enghana' to characterize the high level of public taxation, comparable to that of England, and the low level of public services, comparable to those of Ghana. Afterwards,[11] under pressure due to the crisis in public

[9] Silviano Santiago contrasted the idea of nation-building (*formação*) with what he called the episteme of inclusion (*inserção*) ('Formação e Inserção', *Estadão*, 26 May 2012).
[10] Edmar Lisboa Bacha, 'O Rei da Belíndia', 1974. PDF file available on the website of the Instituto de Estudos de Política Econômica/Casa das Garças [accessed 2010].
[11] Michael Lind, *The Next American Nation: The New Nationalism and the Fourth American Revolution* (n.p.: Free Press, 1995).

security, the metaphor of 'Brazilianization' foresaw Brazil as the vanguard of 'favelization' in the world, which was causing a situation of violence and crime that was driving the middle and upper classes to imprison themselves in gated communities heavily protected by private security services. In other words, the nation is not a single and defined territory any more, as regions and locations disconnect and reconnect with other territories and locations that are often distant, depending on social and cultural conditions which are superimposed on geopolitical borders in a sort of 'local' internationalization or 'globalization of the poor', in the words of Silviano Santiago.

Instead of a national space, from the topological point of view Brazil thus offers plural demographic spaces that reveal an absurd inequality and also an internationalization of social, economic, and cultural characteristics in certain spaces that are no longer configured in traditional regional descriptions such as states and cities. Such dystopian affinities of a certain urban wretchedness place Brazil at the vanguard of the apocalypse of the developmentalist ideology that predominated in the postcolonial scene. From this perspective, the 'First' and 'Third' worlds are synthesized and wealth is confined to the new transnational territories that are exclusive to authoritarian neoliberalism, while wretchedness encloses the great majority of the population in peripheries with more and more inhumane environmental and demographic conditions.

In the Lula administrations from 2002 to 2010, the country defied this fate and began to dream of a place among the big shots, by achieving recognition as the fifth largest economy in the world and a surprising jump in social mobility as a result of its income redistribution policy, its continental leadership in Latin America, and its global ambition to become a member of the UN Security Council. There seemed to be no limit to the country's good fortune, as Brazil naturally earned the right to host the 2014 World Cup and the 2016 Olympic Games, much earlier than the onset of the 2013 economic crisis, which, along with the corruption scandals, made evident the critical situation of the Workers' Party governmental policies that led the country to its worst moment of depression and unemployment since the return of democracy in 1985. With the 2018 elections and the victory of Jair Bolsonaro, an improbable representative of a 'new old Brazil' committed to a great dismantling of everything considered to be the fruit of the young democracy, and even of 'democracy' itself, an unpleasant state of revenge and hatred, if not direct violence, took over the public sphere, thereby creating a never-before-seen challenge for literature. Today it is not enough to act in defence of freedom of expression against the attempts at ideological control and direct censorship, nor to defend the abstract right for art and literature to exist in the face of the ignorance of a government that only sees in them an ideological threat. There must be a concern with showing the real relevance of literature in its capacity to respond to life as experienced, before being questioned, and to intervene in all possible ways, from critical revelation to affective realization.

Understanding this situation is related to the perception of our time, and to how writing literature today can intervene in the way that present time becomes history. An initial example of this, and perhaps representing the most insistent answer to this question, is the author Ricardo Lísias, who straight after the 2018 presidential election began a diary project written online as a daily commentary on the new president and his unstable government and released as pamphlets covering three months and later in books with a yearly frequency. The first volume is called *Diário da Catástrofe Brasileira Ano I — O inimaginável foi eleito* [Diary of the Brazilian Disaster: Year 1 — The unthinkable was elected] and covers from October 2018 up to the end of 2019, and its continuation in Year 2 — *O presidente tem ciúmes do vírus* [The President is jealous of the virus], which has so far been launched in a version to the end of March 2020. As a novelist, Lísias is known for his autofiction in novels like *O Divórcio* [The Divorce] (2013) and his experimental challenges of the boundaries of fiction as in *A vista particular* [The special view] (2016). In the diary, the driving impulse is the 'necessary', not to say 'compulsory' comment, which gives the project the character of a kind of 'writing in the present' with the aim of intervening in the immediate situation, in the *status quo*, with a critical comment, with irony or distance, or simply with the impossible insistence on having the last word.

Another way of dealing with a similar political perplexity in the realm of fiction is the most recent novel by Chico Buarque de Holanda, *Essa Gente* [These People] (2019). The book was released on 14 November 2019 and is composed of a series of diary entries by a writer named Duarte, a resident in Leblon, Rio de Janeiro, who relates how difficult it is for him to overcome writer's block and manage his personal relationships with his ex-wife, his son, his editor, his neighbours, and a wide range of other typical characters from this upper-class *carioca* neighbourhood. The brutalization of social relations, intolerance, violence, and constant stupidity provide the general tone of the dialogues. Recent occurrences in the real life of the city are mixed with fiction, and the result is a portrait of the current state of affairs that is close to a chronicle. The chronology of the chapters, always marked by very recent dates, offers the reader the sensation of a daily blog that reconciles everyday incidents and sociopolitical events from a very recent past. Beginning on 30 November 2018 and ending on 29 September 2019, the narrative covers the fateful year of 2019 and is only interrupted by some flashbacks and letters from the past, the oldest of which dates from 12 February 1999. The back cover of the novel informs the reader that the first edition was published on 14 November 2019. Thus, the supposed distance between what is described and the act of writing is radically diminished, and an effect of *simultaneity* is produced that is normally not achieved in literary fiction. It is a story about the present written 'in medias res', as it occurs, and the time is neither that of the epic of grand narratives nor that of the revelatory account focused on the privileged instant of a sudden transformation. The text thus gains a hallucinatory resonance by including itself at the moment of the events in question, which is in line with the author's explicit intention to comment upon and intervene in current affairs.

To the extent that it characterizes contemporary fiction, Chico Buarque's writing tends to erase the difference between fiction and reality, the temporal distance between writing and its scene, and excels through its desire to intervene by fictionally interacting with real events. Everything is fiction and everything is real, not only because the context appears in some achingly real events, such as the execution of an innocent musician with eighty gunshots by the public security forces, as actually happened in April 2019 in Guadalupe, on the outskirts of Rio de Janeiro, but also because the novel is an *act* of listening to a certain tone and to certain voices of Brazil today. Some fragments are messages, letters and notes that circulate among the characters. Others are brief accounts, as if they were personal records of the protagonist. The novel's ironic narrative does not try to interpret the historical logic behind the actions reported and it is converted into an activity which in itself is an act of storytelling as the action takes place. It thus explores the 'presence of the present', the here and now, and seeks its authenticity in this blatant 'ontology of the present' that is contemporary to the extent that it does not try to explain the ballast of history and rejects promising any relief in the future.

Without a doubt, the contemporary in art and literature has been perceived since the turn of the century as a temporal complexity that has challenged the modern historiographic certainties of a sequential continuity in historical time that supported a whole hermeneutic universe of causes and effects. In the heated discussion of 'the postmodern versus the modern', critics of modernity such as François Lyotard recognized that the 'post' argument in itself arose from the modern view and therefore represented, strictly speaking, its genealogical defence. As a result of this type of sophism, the quarrel between the modern and postmodern camps has lost its explanatory power and a discursive space has been opened up for the question of the contemporary.

In its colloquial sense, the contemporary only registers the temporal coincidence between two phenomena, but the discussion has gained importance to the extent that the contemporary has begun to mean something beyond this strictly chronological argument (X happened at the same time as Y), by evoking the perception of a multiplicity of coexisting times and therefore an exacerbated permeability among the conceptual boundaries of past, present and future. Nonetheless, the contemporary does not only concern an epistemological relation between a chronological time and a duration that makes it possible to pass through different levels of chronology; it also concerns, from the geopolitical perspective of globalization, local spaces (cities, neighbourhoods, everyday events, private experiences, etc.) that, within global spaces (the media, technology, the economy, and the public sphere), establish material perspectives of temporal experiences and their simultaneous coexistence. This is how the space of the nation loses relevance and retreats in the face of the global mobility acquired as a result of circuits of approximation and interaction in restricted spaces of commerce, migration, art and culture, as well as of political resistance and utopian or alternative thinking that disregard national borders and often traverse the hierarchical relations of centre and periphery.

Just as Appadurai, in the 1990s, identified the five '-scapes' in postmodern society — mediascapes, technoscapes, ethnoscapes, financescapes and ideoscapes[12] — we are witnessing today a plural density of globalized spaces that create the material conditions for the complex temporalities of the contemporary. In the 1980s, the anthropologist Johannes Fabian criticized the Western view of the 'other' as backward in its development and not fully contemporary with the First World as a result of a spatiotemporal distance that he called 'allochronism'.[13] For Fabian, the requirement for a critical anthropology was to demand full contemporaneity for all cultures against the 'chronopolitical' tendency that perpetuated colonial inferiority. From this perspective, the contemporary as a politics of the present established a real platform of dialogue without imperial hierarchies, and, in Brazil, it was translated into the experience of being recognized at the same table, as a global partner. Nonetheless, even though the historian Dipesh Chakrabarty (2008) agrees with Fabian's critique of the 'backwardness' of non-Western cultures, he insists on the potential for recognition of moments of an authentic 'heterotemporality' in relation to the global 'present' and therefore of a certain coexistence of different temporal layers.[14]

From the point of view of the experience of time as lived, this heterogeneity of time in certain local and autonomous cultures in relation to the globalization of measured temporality opens the field to what Foucault called 'heterochrony', a time that interrupts or is removed from the globalizing historical time of the contemporary. Jacques Rancière has recently said that this 'heterochrony is a redistribution of times that invents new capacities for framing a present'.[15] In the history of modern literature, the simultaneity among disassociated narrative actions pointed towards a transhistorical and qualitative duration of time that merged the past and the future into a profound possibility of a present and a presence, as Auerbach argued with the examples of Proust, Joyce, and Woolf. Contemporary narrative, however, exercises its anachronistic freedom in a way that accentuates the interruptions between phenomenological temporalities, the radical disassociation of living conditions in a homogenizing historical globality.

---

[12] Arjun Appadurai, 'Disjuncture and Difference in the Global Cultural Economy', *Public Culture*, 2.2 (1990), 1–24.
[13] Johannes Fabian, *Time and the Other: How Anthropology Makes its Object*, 2nd edn (New York: Columbia University Press, 2002) [first pub. 1983].
[14] Dipesh Chakrabarty, *Provincializing Europe: Postcolonial Thought and Historical Difference* (Princeton, NJ: Princeton University Press, 2008).
[15] Jacques Rancière, 'In What Time Do We Live?', in *The State of Things*, ed. by Marta Kuzma, Pablo Lafuente and Peter Osborne (Oslo: Office for Contemporary Art; London: Koenig Books, 2008), p. 34.

That is how recent fiction manages to give a testimony of local spheres within the national sphere itself, in which the temporalities of the past and even of the future coexist in their historical presence. Two examples are worth mentioning: the novel *Torto Arado* [Crooked Plough] (2018), by Itamar Vieira Junior, and *Verão Tardio* [Late Summer] (2019), by Luiz Ruffato.

In his striking debut novel from 2018, the young Bahian author Itamar Vieira Junior manages to create an environment with a paradoxical universality in his description of a small community in the state of Bahia. Set at Água Negra, a farm in the region of Chapada Diamantina, the story accompanies the sisters Bibiana and Belonísia, daughters of Zeca Chapéu Grande, a leader of the Afro-Brazilian Jaré religion practised by the mostly black rural workers in the region. Based on ethnographic work in the region, the author recreates in narrative language the social fabric of a *quilombola* or maroon community in which slavery penetrates and is made present in all of the relationships revealed. With the magic touch of a Juan Rulfo, the 'time of violence' gains a transhistorical and 'heterotemporal' dimension. Just as in the narratives of *Pedro Páramo* and *El Llano en Llamas*, the representational markers are erased and what emerges as ontological ground is the violence detained in the social and economic relation to the landowners and their authorities but also in the family ties and in the community. All of a sudden, one perceives the past of slave society recover its contemporary reality in the farm's hierarchical structural relationship between the owners and the peasants who live there for free in exchange for working the land without pay, and only caring for their own survival in their spare time. The land ownership in itself maintains the exploitation of entire families for generations. The novel's strength, however, is not only to document this regional condition but to give concreteness to the resilience of the inhabitants, in the rhythm of the narratives, in the enchanted environment, in the pacing of the story, and in a material way in certain places and in certain simple objects, such as a sharp knife that the grandmother kept from the past of violence and which will mark the sisters' lives as destiny.

At the centre of the story there appears the *quilombo*, which is simultaneously both a place in the past, of refuge for runaway and freed slaves without rights or property, and in the present, as the communitarian and the spiritual cement that holds the family of Zeca Chapéu Grande together. In the third part of the novel, a spirit tells the story in the name of this condition, and the historical account of modernity is then no longer the backdrop of the action but that which forces its way into the community from the outside by introducing present economic and political interests cloaked in a foreign judicial legality against the permanency and rights of the *quilombolas*. However, it is also from the abyss between this political contemporaneity and the survival of the community of Água Negra under the yoke of coloniality that the reactive violence emerges, along with the resistance immanent in the very memory of the place and its long history. In the first two parts of Itamar Vieira's novel, the narrative develops in a heterochronic layer that becomes the very means of the independent action of historical time. The context is not identified with precision due to the persistence of the strong relation among generations and the weight of an archaic inheritance on the actions of the characters, which seems to determine their destiny. In the third part, the historical present appears in a way that threatens the community and its integrity. The insightful reader would recognize the implicit attempts to question the constitutional rights that guarantee land possession to the *quilombola* communities. However, this present, that could be converted into a documentary reference to the difficulties of *quilombola* communities under the current government, does not ultimately override what is preserved in the narrative journeys of the sisters and their family. The strict regional focus on this small community projects through its narrative an analogous human condition in other countries and on other continents and allows us to perceive a transnational reality at the margin of global modernity.

In 2019, the Minas Gerais author Luiz Ruffato released the novel *Verão Tardio*, which reflects the failure of hopes for a fulfilling life in an exploration of the dissolution of family and community ties in Brazilian society. All of Ruffato's work somehow explores the theme of the impossible recovery of the past based on the story of the Zona da Mata in Minas Gerais where the author was born and grew up. His recent novel expresses like never before the melancholy of a historical present that is trapped by the past and that becomes an allegory for the country. For six days, Oseias returns to Cataguazes, his hometown, and looks for his friends and family in search of some understanding of a life that now seems to be coming to a pathetic close because of the presence of disease and his finding no comfort in the little that is left of affective and social ties. Oseias looks for answers without recognizing the questions. He abandoned the town forty years ago in favour of a life in São Paulo and had visited it for the last time in 1995, before his mother's death. Thus, he himself is part of the dissolution, and what seems to remain is disaffection, separation, and guilt. Why did his sister Lígia kill herself? Oseias' melancholy and the presence of the past are superimposed on the chronological present that organizes the novel into six straight days, and the encounters or 'disencounters' on the character's path do not lead to anything but the tangled threads of what has passed. Thus, the historical present only reflects a certain past that does not pass, or else it would foreclose any possibility of mourning and overcoming and convert the present into a macabre and sick repetition of past traumas.

The odyssey of Oseias (a partial anagram of 'odisseia' [odyssey]?) offers a sinister image of a past that not only 'does not pass' but also hinders and obstructs the present as a path and a possibility. Thus, the ballast of the past is not unburdened, and unlike Ulysses, Oseias is not truly 'recognized' upon his return to Ithaca nor is his past epically redeemed. Instead of an understanding of his own story, melancholy for Oseias is converted into a deep sadness for the missed opportunities of a life that was not lived. Thus, Ruffato's novel becomes a politically allegorical mirror of a present that is negatively bound by the mistakes committed, in contrast to *Torto Arado*, by Itamar Vieira Junior, in which the presence of the past is a device of resistance and survival, a historical and cultural diversity that has been reencountered.

In the novel *Enterre seus Mortos* [Bury Your Dead] (2018), by Ana Paula Maia, the focus is on a future that appears as the menace of ecological entropy at the margin of global modernism and this retrofuturism opens a dialogue with Joca Terron's apocalyptic phantasy *A Morte e o Meteoro* [Death and the Meteor]. The heterochrony survives in the impossible and tragic activity of the main character, Edgar Wilson, who makes a living by collecting the carcasses of dead animals on the highways of a grotesque and dystopian future Brazil that is strangely recognizable. It is a fatally Anthropocene world that is collapsing and heading towards environmental disaster, and in which the exploitation of natural resources is translated into the uncontrollable proliferation of carcasses. Against this machinery of death, Edgar Wilson is a strange hero who makes a living by collecting, grinding and processing the carrion that he encounters on the highways. When human corpses begin to appear on his path, he assumes responsibility, along with his friend Tomás, an excommunicated priest, in order to defend the dignity and history of these bodily remains and thereby avoid the erasure of what seems to be the last boundary of humanity.

It is no coincidence that the narratives commented upon are organized according to a spatial logic, a constrained topology that binds the flow of time and frames the historical present, revealing the superimposition of disjunctive temporal layers. I will conclude this brief problematization of the understanding of the contemporary in Brazilian literature with a final striking example. It concerns Milton Hatoum's trilogy, *A noite da espera* [The Longest Night], whose first two volumes — *O lugar mais sombrio* [The Darkest of Places] (2018) and *Pontos de fuga* [Points of Escape] (2019) — have already been published. In an experimental approach to memorialism, Hatoum manages to offer a literary image of the open yet also vulnerable space of Brasília — the new capital of the country — during the so-called 'years of lead' of the 1960s. This image takes shape in the story of the student Martim, who has recently entered the University of Brasília (UnB), and his friends and acquaintances. Among students and artists, professors and diplomats, bourgeois and employees, many of whom have recently arrived from various regions of the country, Martim goes around in search of his mother, who ran away with a painter. Seduced by his newly conquered adult freedom, Martim ends up involved in a fragile attempt at opposition against the military dictatorship that forces him to escape to São Paulo, where in the second volume he will be accepted at the University of São Paulo. In a parallel narrative, Martim appears in exile in Paris, in a closed and claustrophobic environment, between 1978 and 1979, writing letters and telling stories of encounters with friends and companions from the time of resistance to authoritarianism. Without scrutinizing the complexity of the narrative, or entering the autobiographical dimension of the account, it is important to emphasize the spatial perspectivism of Hatoum's style and the playing with the labyrinthine blindness in which one did not realize what was in fact happening in the dark times. Hatoum abandons the descriptive virtuosity that characterizes his previous work and employs a narrative economy that is organized according to the prevalence of recognizable spaces of the dreaming architecture of a new Brazil, which in the novel is challenged by authoritarianism and menaced with no longer existing. Instead of the 'point of escape' that opens and organizes the optical representation of space, the title of the second volume thematizes a line of flight bound to cross uncertain territory under the control of repression. In this way Hatoum plays on the contrast between the open architecture of modernist optimism in the vast empty landscape of the *cerrado* [savannah] and the mental closure of repression in which the narrative opens a space of freedom, resistance and revolt, but also of exile and survival.

Without a doubt, there are many other examples worthy of commentary in the recent literary production in Brazil. I have attempted here to offer a reading and understanding based on the possibility of establishing a dialogue among current writers who through their narrative interpretation of national space and historical time have managed to express their general discomfort with the historical moment of the country and, in some cases, their explicit critical position in the face of a new governmental regime and its rhetoric of violence and intolerance, but also of a deeper-lying historical inequality that is now returning with a neoliberal, moral and even religious Pentecostal legitimation. The latest literature addresses a contemporary authoritarianism that seeks to rewrite history and negates the destruction of the future. To write in the Brazilian present is to write against this ideological dictatorship of negationism and ignorance where freedom of speech has become a disguise for fake news and where the walls of censorship are raised daily in the name of hostility against diversity and freedom of thought.

Recently, the author Julián Fuks characterized the Brazilian dystopia with the following precise words:

> When behaviour is not dictated by necessity, it seems to respond to an intricate system of ideological positions and personal tendencies, a tangle of ideas, impulses, moods and fears. The abysses already known between right and left, between defenders of individual freedom and those who prefer to embrace a social vision, are then overlapped by an endless series of other disputes fought with the same antipathy. The cautious against the ruthless, the obedient against the subversive, the healthy against the timid, the optimistic against the pessimistic who, with their contradictory reading of graphs and curves, all face each other with virulence, as if they did not know that others are responsible for the tragedy. The most complex protagonists, and there are not a few of them, are tragically confronted with themselves.
>
> Perhaps that was the intention — here lies a possible interpretation of this eccentric dystopia — as an alternative goal for its terrible leaders:

namely, the destruction of all social ties, of any intention directed towards the common good, of any possibility of an enlightened and peaceful dialogue. In the triumph of individualism, any debate will be fought with complete distrust: any proposal in a collective name will be understood as a defence of a unique, personal, narcissistic interest, any public stance will be considered inconvenient from the outset.[16]

---

[16] Julián Fuks, 'Distopia à brasileira: a não-ficção do desgoverno e do individualismo...' — see <https://www.uol.com.br/ecoa/colunas/julian-fuks/2020/09/05/distopia-a-brasileira-a-nao-ficcao-do-desgoverno-e-do-individualismo.htm?cmpid=copiaecola>.

The Arts as a Space of Memory and Resistance to Denialist Policies in Brazil Today

MÁRCIO SELIGMANN-SILVA

Universidade Estadual de Campinas

Brazilian history in the twenty-first century has been marked by the thirteen-year-long government of the Workers' Party (PT), followed by a struggle on the part of the conservative parties, associated with the Federal Prosecution Service and the judicial system, to put an end to PT's 'reign'. President Lula governed from 2003 to 2011, while President Dilma was in power from 2011 to 31 August 2016, when, early in her second term, she was impeached and replaced by Vice-President Michel Temer. In January 2019, the far right came to power, through elections, for the first time since the dictatorship period of 1964–85. The process to overthrow PT had started in the judicial system which, on 17 March 2014, launched a supposedly anti-corruption investigation (named *Operação Lava Jato*) which gradually undermined PT's political base. The culmination of this process was the imprisonment on 7 April 2018, with no documentary evidence, of former President Lula, who was presidential candidate and ahead in all polls. The judge who presided over *Operação Lava Jato* and who ordered Lula's arrest was to be appointed Minister of Justice in the Bolsonaro government. Another eighteen members of *Operação Lava Jato* (Federal Police chief officers, Federal Revenue auditors and Federal Justice civil servants from the state of Paraná) were awarded government positions. Michel Temer, who was Dilma's vice-president, later acknowledged in 2019 that she had committed no criminal misconduct and that the impeachment was a coup. Temer himself was prosecuted for corruption and arrested (and later released) in 2019.[1]

The Advance of the Right and the Return of Censorship in Brazilian Culture

This reaction of right-wing and conservative forces of Brazilian politics also had deep consequences in the field of culture. Since June 2013, a year before *Operação Lava Jato* was launched, street protests triggered by the economic crisis and with specific targets, such as rising public transport fares, had been infiltrated by new far-right groups that appropriated those demands. A series

---

[1] Cf. 'Jamais apoiei o golpe, diz Temer sobre impeachment de Dilma', in <https://exame.abril.com.br/brasil/jamais-apoiei-o-golpe-diz-temer-sobre-impeachment-de-dilma/> [accessed 10 Jan. 2020].

of demonstrations in 2014 and 2015 broadened the targets of the protests and boosted these new groups, strengthening the wave that culminated in Bolsonaro's election in 2018. One of the main banners of these movements such as *Endireita Brasil* (created in 2012), *Movimento Brasil Livre* (MBL) and *Vem pra Rua* (both created in 2014) is a moralizing defence of a self-proclaimed Christian model, critical of a supposed 'moral decay' vaguely identified with the left. In the words of Messenberg:

> The demonstrations that took hundreds of thousands of people to the streets in the main Brazilian cities in the months of March, April and August 2015 brought to light the activism of certain social actors who had not participated so intensely in public affairs for decades. Such demonstrations revealed the privileged presence of groups of a conservative profile that — despite their differences in ideological shades — publicly exposed segregating and authoritarian beliefs.[2]

Evidently, as shown by Wendy Brown among others,[3] this conservative movement defends a markedly neoliberal agenda which reverberates through practically the whole world today. In the specific case of Brazil, it involves an alliance between segments of big business, conservative politicians and religious sectors, especially neo-Pentecostal. One must bear in mind that the organization of this highly conservative front should be viewed as a reaction to a series of achievements in the field of human and minority rights, enhanced by the 1988 Constitution (the so-called 'citizenship constitution', promulgated three years after the end of the dictatorship) and reinforced by PT's thirteen-year administration. In an issue of *Cadernos Pagu*, an important publication from the University of Campinas (UNICAMP) focused on feminist studies, the editors of the dossier on 'Conservatism, Rights, Moralities and Violence' wrote:

> The current conservative struggle against the achievements and visibility of minority movements seems currently to be one of the main obstacles to ensuring the fundamental rights of a number of people. The focus on sexual morality in the conservative agenda has especially targeted rights related to gender equity and sexual and gender diversity. On the one hand, due to growing religious pluralism in Brazil and a diversity of views and interpretations of state secularism, Christian actors have achieved significant public representation. Markedly diverging from the classic forms of influence of the Catholic Church, Pentecostal evangelical leaders have been massively entering political life and running for elected positions, mainly as legislators and for centre-right parties. Organized as a caucus in the National Congress, a large part of these parliamentarians evokes an idealized view of a united 'people of God' as a supposed national majority in order to stir moral anxieties through an apocalyptic narrative in

---

[2] Débora Messenberg, 'A direita que saiu do armário: a cosmovisão dos formadores de opinião dos manifestantes de direita brasileiros', *Revista Sociedade e Estado*, 32.3 (December 2017), 621–47 (p. 621).
[3] Wendy Brown, *Undoing the Demos: Neoliberalism's Stealth Revolution* (New York: Zone Books, 2015); ead., *In the Ruins of Neoliberalism: The Rise of Antidemocratic Politics in the West* (New York: Columbia University Press, 2019).

which women's and LGBT rights and policies, besides restricting religious freedom, threaten the moral integrity of children and the Brazilian family.[4]

Since September 2017, therefore since the government of President Michel Temer, we have witnessed increasing censorship of art exhibitions, plays, musical performances and books deemed 'immoral'. In 2019 alone, more than three hundred complaints against censorship were filed.[5] If during the Temer administration such censorship was the result of intimidation campaigns orchestrated by the aforementioned right-wing movements and politicians most often associated with the neo-Pentecostal sector, since 2019 members of the actual government have taken the initiative. It should be noted that these campaigns are part of the government's strategy to ensure support and have been used increasingly, as its total inability to improve the economy becomes clear. For example, on 10 September 2017, the exhibition *Queermuseu — Cartografias da Diferença na Arte Brasileira* [Queermuseum — Cartographies of Difference in Brazilian Art], which had opened on 15 August of the same year at Santander Cultural, in Porto Alegre, was cancelled following protests. The exhibition, curated by Gaudêncio Fidelis and displaying works that addressed gender and differences, was scheduled to run for another three weeks. A vigorous online campaign accused the exhibition of promoting 'paedophilia, zoophilia, pornography and desecration'. The exhibition featured works by eighty-five artists, including some of the leading figures of contemporary Brazilian art such as Lygia Clark, Adriana Varejão, Leonilson and Yuri Firmeza, besides Cândido Portinari, an exponent of Modernism and one of the most influential Brazilian artists internationally in the twentieth century. The Santander Cultural venue is linked to an important financial institution that decided to close the exhibition. In the public statement issued to justify the closure, it agreed with the allegations raised by MBL and other right-wing factions: 'We have heard the protests and we understand that some of the works in the "Queermuseu" exhibition disrespected symbols, beliefs and people, which is not in line with our view of the world'.[6]

Shortly before this event, which caused a strong repercussion in the press, works displayed in two exhibitions, one in Campo Grande, Mato Grosso do Sul, and another in Guarulhos, São Paulo, were criticized by authorities and censored for addressing paedophilia in the Catholic Church.[7] A theatrical performance based on a play by the English playwright Jo Clifford, *The Gospel*

---

[4] Regina Facchini and Horacio Sívori, 'Conservadorismo, direitos, moralidades e violência: situando um conjunto de reflexões a partir da Antropologia', *Cadernos Pagu*, 50 (2017). Epub e175000, 26 June 2017, <https://doi.org/10.1590/18094449201700500000>.

[5] The journalist and president of the São Paulo Art Critics Association (APCA), Celso Cunha, speaking at the opening of the International Theatre Festival, São Paulo, 5 March 2020.

[6] *Folha de S. Paulo*, 10 September 2017, <https://www1.folha.uol.com.br/ilustrada/2017/09/1917269-apos-protesto-mostra-com-tematica-lgbt-em-porto-alegre-e-cancelada.shtml?origin=folha> [accessed 10 Jan. 2020].

[7] <http://censuranaarte.nonada.com.br> [accessed 10 Jan. 2020].

According to Jesus, Queen of Heaven, was censored both in Jundiaí, São Paulo (on 15 September 2017), and later in Garanhuns, Pernambuco (on 30 June 2018). In both cases the play was challenged by authorities (judicially in the Southeast and by the executive in the Northeast) but performed thanks to a successful legal battle. For its advocates, censorship was justified because, in the words of judge in Jundiaí, the play 'injures the feelings of ordinary people'. At the core of the aversion of judges and politicians to the work was the main actress, Renata Carvalho, a transsexual. Underlying the censorship was pure homophobia and transphobia.[8]

In the same month, on 26 September 2017, the performer Wagner Schwartz, who was staging a performance at the São Paulo Museum of Modern Art (MAM) called *La Bête*, inspired by the work of one of the most important contemporary artists in Brazil, Lygia Clark, was the target of a series of attacks on social media and in the press for having performed naked, and for having a child approach him during the show. Evangelical leaders compared the artist to Satan, criminalizing his work. Schwartz's performance actually drew on one of the guiding principles of Lygia Clark's work, that of public intervention in the creation of her works. Her 'Bichos' [Animals] series, of neo-concrete inspiration, comprises foldable pieces intended to be handled by the audience. For the artist, her animals should be seen as 'a living organism, an essentially active work. Between you and them, total, existential integration is established. In the relationship established between you and the Bichos there is no passivity, neither yours nor theirs'.[9] The child who approached the artist was accompanied by his mother, and both were participating in the performance's proposal. But for members of the new conservative wave, it represented an opportunity to attack an artist and one of the most important art venues in Brazil. Wagner Schwartz was interviewed for more than four hours by police officers of the paedophile unit. It is important to stress the focus of these acts of censorship as an attack on culture, trying to associate cultural production with immorality, paedophilia, pornography, etc. It was clearly orchestrated by right-wing movements in Brazil at that crucial time of self-affirmation of right-wing politics in the Brazilian political scene, following thirteen years of PT governments, seeking to mobilize society as a whole against cultural producers and supporters. As would happen again when Bolsonaro came to power, in 2017, during the Temer administration still, this mobilization to attack culture and demonize cultural actors and their defenders was also intended to distract

---

[8] 'Justiça derruba liminar que proibia peça em Jundiaí' <https://www1.folha.uol.com.br/ilustrada/2018/02/justica-derruba-liminar-que-proibia-peca-em-jundiai.shtml> [accessed 20 Feb. 2020]. As a reaction to these and other attacks suffered by the actress Renata Carvalho and other transgender actresses, she was invited to direct the opening session of the 2020 São Paulo International Theater Festival.

[9] Larissa Chagas Daniel, 'Obra estática: um bicho de Lygia Clark na Pinacoteca do Estado de São Paulo', in III Encontro Nacional de Estudos da Imagem, 2011 — Londrina — PR III Encontro Nacional de Estudos da Imagem 03 a 06 de maio de 2011 — Londrina — PR, p. 1759.

the population from the government's failure to boost the economy. In the first fifteen years or so of this century, culture became more and more a bastion of democracy, freedom and the construction of other subjectivities, transgressive and non-binary. If right-wing movements are turning brutally against culture, thus building the false idea that a 'Messiah' is needed to save the country from the sins of the 'left', the world of cultural agents and producers of cultural policies has increasingly responded by leading the coordination of other political conceptions, critical of the neoliberal and neoconservative wave.[10]

In August 2019, Roberto Alvim, the then head of FUNARTE (National Arts Foundation), prohibited the performance of the play *Res Publica 2023*, by Companhia Motosserra Perfumada, which proposed a reflection on the political split that has marked Brazil since 2013. The head of FUNARTE claimed he would not support a work with an 'ideological bent'. It is important to remember that this same official of the current government was later appointed as Secretary of Culture (equivalent to Minister of Culture in the current federal administration) and in that capacity presented his new national cultural project aimed at producing great national art in the following terms, which clearly echoed a speech by Joseph Goebbels: 'The Brazilian art of the next decade will be heroic and it will be national. It will be endowed with great capacity for emotional involvement and it will be equally imperative, given that it is profoundly linked to the urgent aspirations of our people, or else it will be nothing'.[11] Following the release of this video by the Secretary, President Bolsonaro announced that he approved his proposal. However, Alvim was dismissed after national and international protests, including from the Israeli authorities.

In August 2019, the Ministry of Citizenship cancelled the public call for the selection of works to be aired on public TV stations, for which LGBT-themed works such as *Afronte* (a feature film by Bruno Victor Santos and Marcus Azevedo on the lives of young black homosexuals in the Federal District) and the five-episode documentary series *Transversal* (by Émerson Maranhão and Allan Deberton, about transsexuals in Ceará), which had been shortlisted. The cancellation came after criticism of the films by the actual president, made live on Facebook, in which he condemned the producers of those works for seeking funding from Ancine (Brazilian Film Agency), as well as the Regional Far South Development Bank (BRDE) and the Brazilian Communications Company (EBC).[12]

[10] Márcio Seligmann-Silva, 'Decolonial, des-outrização: imaginando uma política pós-nacional e instituidora de novas subjetividades', in 21ª Bienal de Arte Contemporânea Sesc_Videobrasil: Comunidades Imaginadas: Leituras / Serviço Social do Comércio; Associação Cultural Videobrasil; organização: Luisa Duarte; coordenação editorial: Teté Martinho (São Paulo: Sesc: Associação Cultural Videobrasil, 2019), pp. 20–44.
[11] 'Em vídeo, Alvim copia Goebbels e provoca onda de repúdio nas redes sociais', <https://www1.folha.uol.com.br/ilustrada/2020/01/em-video-alvim-cita-goebbels-e-provoca-onda-de-repudio-nas-redes-sociais.shtml> [accessed 10 Jan. 2020].
[12] 'Estas são as séries com temática LGBT que Bolsonaro "garimpou" de edital da Ancine' <https://

In the first week of September 2019, the exhibition *O Riso é Risco: Independência em Risco — Desenhos de Humor* [Laughter is Risk: Independence at Risk — Humorous Drawings], which opened at the Porto Alegre City Council, was forced to close less than 24 hours after its inauguration, on the orders of the president of the City Council, a member of PP, a right-wing party. As would be expected in any democratic country, the thirty-six drawings by nineteen artists, dedicated to humour and caricature, naturally included cartoons involving the Brazilian president, who had the support of the president of the City Council. Some works critically addressed the current government's project of genocide of indigenous populations, others execrated the current criminalization of human rights, and some opposed the policy of devastating the Amazon rainforest and the entire environment. The cartoonist and university professor Celso Schröder stated that the argument of the council's president for closing the exhibition, namely, that 'the cartoons are offensive to President Bolsonaro', evoked that of the perpetrators of the *Charlie Hebdo* shooting in 2015, who accused its cartoonists of disrespecting Mohammad. In his words: 'It is the same argument used for the attack in Paris, it is an unsustainable argument. It is state censorship. It is the state preventing people from expressing themselves. This is censorship'.[13]

That same week, the Mayor of Rio de Janeiro, Marcelo Crivella, a Protestant pastor, ordered books with 'LGBT themes' to be seized at the Rio de Janeiro Book Biennial (the most important book fair in the country). When visiting the fair, he apparently felt uncomfortable seeing a scene of two men kissing in a comic book. The law-enforcement agents he sent to the fair did not find any 'LGBT-themed' books, which had promptly sold out following the censorship announcement. After successive court decisions first forbidding and then authorizing Crivella's attitude, the Supreme Federal Court (STF) finally ruled that the seizure of books was illegal. The work that triggered the moralistic crusade is a simple Marvel album, *Avengers: The Children's Crusade*.[14]

Lastly — it is impossible to summarize here the more than 300 cases of censorship — I report the case of an attack on a work that addresses the continuity of racist colonial violence against blacks in Brazil. This is essential because, as we will see, the arts have restructured themselves from a decolonial viewpoint also in response to these attacks stemming from a vigorous return of neocolonial thought. On 19 November 2019, almost at the end of the first year of the far-right president's term, the *Trajetórias Negras* [Black Trajectories] exhibition, held in the Chamber of Deputies in Brasília to celebrate Black

---

www.huffpostbrasil.com/entry/filmes-lgbt-bolsonaro_br_5d5b3a68e4b05f62fbd414d7> [accessed 10 Jan. 2020].
[13] 'Câmara dos Vereadores censura exposição de charges críticas a Bolsonaro em Porto Alegre', <https://www1.folha.uol.com.br/cotidiano/2019/09/camara-censura-exposicao-de-charges-criticas-a-bolsonaro-em-porto-alegre.shtml> [accessed 10 Jan. 2020].
[14] 'Justiça veta censura homofóbica de Crivella na Bienal do Livro do Rio', <https://brasil.elpais.com/brasil/2019/09/06/politica/1567794692_253126.html> [accessed 10 Jan. 2020].

Awareness Day (20 November), was attacked by a federal deputy, who tore one of the works off the wall and smashed it up. The work was by the cartoonist Latuff, depicting police violence against the black population. It is important to note that during the PT governments there was an enormous expansion of higher education in Brazil, and the introduction of social and racial quotas produced an upheaval in the public university system, which was previously reserved for the white middle class, but today has more blacks than whites.[15] This inclusion process caused unease on the right, a bastion of racist thought of colonial origin. Federal Deputy Colonel Tadeu, a member of the same party as the current president, the PSL, had smashed a drawing portraying a police officer right after shooting a handcuffed black boy wearing a T-shirt printed with the Brazilian flag. In Brazil the police often kill residents in peripheral areas, mostly blacks, later attributing the fact to *'autos de resistência'* [acts of resistance], i.e., the police were supposedly only defending themselves. Thus, police officers who kill, on- or off-duty, are rarely convicted in Brazil. In 2017 the homicide rate among young blacks and browns reached 185 per 100 thousand inhabitants, almost three times the homicide rate among whites.[16] The number of peripheral residents killed by the Rio de Janeiro police reached a record high in 2019. Of the total deaths computed up to April of that year, 434 were considered 'records of resistance'. 'Acts of resistance' is the expression used by the Rio police bureaucracy; in São Paulo the term used is *'resistência seguida de morte'* [resistance leading to death], but both terms of the police lexicon imply *a defence of lawfulness (exclusão de ilicitude)*. Evidently, there is legal support for these excuses used by the police, such as Article 292 of the Penal Code, but what happens is an abuse of the prerogative of self-defence, since the police themselves are in charge of investigating these crimes.[17] The current president has always been an enthusiast for police violence and is a known supporter of militias, praising them when a parliamentary deputy and now again as president. Moreover, during the campaign the current president associated blacks with cattle, explicitly revealing his prejudice against the black population. Such an attitude coming from the highest authority in the country clearly encourages genocidal practices among the police.

---

[15] IBGE, 'Desigualdades Sociais por Cor ou Raça na Brasil', <https://biblioteca.ibge.gov.br/visualizacao/livros/liv101681_informativo.pdf > [accessed 10 Jan. 2020].
[16] 'Homicídios entre jovens negros são quase três vezes maiores do que brancos e chegam a 185 por 100 mil', <https://www1.folha.uol.com.br/cotidiano/2019/11/homicidios-entre-jovens-negros-e-quase-tres-vezes-maior-do-que-brancos-e-chegam-a-185-por-100-mil.shtml> [accessed 10 Jan. 2020].
[17] 'Mais de 400 em 2019', <https://www.justificando.com.br/2019/05/25/mais-de-quatrocentos-em-2019-sete-por-dia-no-rio-precisamos-por-fim-aos-autos-de-resistencia/> [accessed 10 Jan. 2020].

Art as Resistance

As is evident from the above, the cultural field has been transformed into a battlefield with the gradual rise to power of the right. If up to the mid-2010s one saw a process of change, moderate but nonetheless important, in the extreme inequality of income distribution in Brazil, accompanied by a series of artistic manifestations of voices previously deprived of opportunities of expression, since then there has been a counter-process of censorship and a curbing of these new subjectivities and group identities manifested in the cultural field.

The arts, according to Walter Benjamin, are a means of expanding our scope of action, which he also thought of as literally a play space (*Spielraum*).[18] They expand our field of playful action through the construction of a new image-space (*Bildraum*) that is also an extension of our bodies (*Leibraum*).[19] They make it possible to formulate dreams, utopias, political agendas, they help draw identity boundaries for individuals and groups, they expand our bodies and senses. If in the nineteenth century and the early twentieth century the arts and literature were transformed into strongholds of nationalism, since World War II, and especially with the advent of genocide and violence on an unheard-of scale, the arts have gradually shed this nationalist rancidity to increasingly become a means of self-writing and resistance. The artistic field steadily frees itself from the shackles of the museum (introduced in the nineteenth century) and the white cube (created by Modernism in the twentieth century), just as the theatre pulls down the barrier of the 'black box' to which it was limited in bourgeois theatre. Literature and all the arts start to play a key role as an inscription of violent processes and histories, which were previously repressed.[20]

This helps us understand the stance that artists and curators in Brazil have taken in the face of this recent history marked by persecutions against certain groups of the population, especially blacks, women, LGBTQI+ individuals, and peripheral and poor populations. The twenty-first century has witnessed a boom in curatorial initiatives related to both Afro-Brazilian art (that is, by artists who address Afro themes) and art produced by Afro-descendants. At MASP and Instituto Tomie Ohtake in São Paulo in 2018, the *Histórias Afro-Atlânticas* [Afro-Atlantic Stories] exhibition, curated by Adriano Pedrosa, Ayrson Heráclito, Hélio Menezes, Lilia Schwarcz and Tomás Toledo, was undoubtedly one of the high points of these initiatives, exhibiting Brazilian artists in the Atlantic context of the African diaspora. Inspired by the survey made by Hélio Menezes for his text in the catalogue of *Histórias Afro-*

---

[18] Walter Benjamin, *Das Kunstwerk im Zeitalter seiner technischen Reproduzierbarkeit. Werke und Nachlass. Kritische Gesamtausgabe*, ed. by Burkhardt Lindner (Frankfurt a. M.: Suhrkamp, 2012), p. 109.
[19] Walter Benjamin, 'Der Surrealismus: Die letzte Momentaufnahme der europäischen Intelligenz', in *Gesammelte Schriften*, Band. II: *Aufsätze, Essays, Vorträge*, ed. by Rolf Tiedemann and Hermann Schweppenhäuser (Frankfurt a. M.: Suhrkamp, 1977), p. 309.
[20] Márcio Seligmann-Silva (ed.), *História, Memória, Literatura: o testemunho na era das catástrofes* (Campinas: Editora da UNICAMP, 2003).

Atlânticas, I highlight the following exhibitions in Brazil and in other countries addressing this Afro-Brazilian theme: *Incorporações — Arte afro-brasileira contemporânea* [Incorporations — Contemporary Afro-Brazilian Art] (Oct. 2011–Jan. 2012), at the International Arts Festival Europalia, Brussels, curated by Roberto Conduru; *Afro como ascendência, arte como procedência* [Afro as Ancestry, Art as Origin] (Dec. 2013–Mar. 2014), at SESC Pinheiros, São Paulo, curated by Alexandre Araújo Bispo; *Histórias Mestiças* [Mixed-Race Stories] (Aug.–Oct. 2014), at Instituto Tomie Ohtake, curated by Adriano Pedrosa and Lilia Schwarcz; *Territórios: artistas afrodescendentes no acervo da Pinacoteca* [Territories: Afro-Descendant Artists in the Pinacoteca Collection] (Dec. 2015–Jun. 2016), at the São Paulo Pinacoteca, curated by Tadeu Chiarelli; *A cor do Brasil* [Brazil's Colour] (Aug. 2016–Jan. 2017), at the Rio de Janeiro Art Museum, curated by Paulo Herkenhoff and Marcelo Campos; *Diálogos ausentes* [Absent Dialogues] (Dec. 2016–Feb. 2017), at Instituto Itaú Cultural, São Paulo, curated by Rosana Paulino and Diane Lima; *Agora somos todxs Negrxs?* [Are We All Black Now?] (2017), at Galpão VideoBrasil, curated by Daniel Lima; *PretAtitude* [BlackAttitude] (2018), at SESC Ribeirão Preto, curated by Claudinei Roberto;[21] and I add the more recent exhibition *Rosana Paulino: A costura da memória* [Rosana Paulino: The Sewing of Memory] (Dec. 2018–Mar. 2019), displayed at the São Paulo Pinacoteca and curated by Valéria Piccoli and Pedro Nery.[22] I would also include in this list of exhibitions dedicated to Afro themes and approaches the Videobrasil Biennials, curated by Solange Farkas, and the exhibition *A empresa colonial* [The Colonial Company] (Dec. 2015–Feb. 2016). Farkas is head curator of the Contemporary Art Festival Videobrasil, first held in 1983. Her focus on the Global South has played an important role in the affirmation of art committed to decoloniality themes. In 2000 she curated *Mostra Africana de arte Contemporânea* [African Contemporary Art Exhibition], together with the South African critic Clive Kellner, held at SESC Pompéia, in São Paulo. Despite not being an exhibition with an ethnic curatorial approach, *A empresa colonial*, held at Caixa Cultural São Paulo in 2015/16 and curated by Tomás Toledo, fittingly addressed the continuity of colonial power in contemporary Brazil.[23] Its openly decolonial approach is still rare in Brazil, a country marked by an impressive continuity of colonial thought and practices.

---

[21] *Histórias afro-atlânticas: [vol. 2] antologia*, ed. by Adriano Pedrosa, Amanda Carneiro and André Mesquita (São Paulo: MASP, 2018).
[22] *Rosana Paulino: a costura da memória*, curated by Valéria Piccoli and Pedro Neri, texts by Juliana Ribeiro da Silva Bevilaqua, Fabiana Lopes and Adriano Dolci Palma (São Paulo: Pinacoteca de São Paulo, 2018).
[23] Tomás Toledo, *Empresa Colonial* (São Paulo: T. Toledo, 2016).

The New Afro-Descendant Decolonial Art: The Example of Jaime Lauriano

Among the most outstanding artists who self-identify as Afro-descendants and produce decolonial art, Jaime Lauriano has produced a series of works that aim to offer a revision of Brazilian history from the viewpoint of the continuity of racial violence against blacks, but which simultaneously locate this violence within a system of capitalist and neocolonial power. On entering the aforementioned exhibition at Caixa Cultural São Paulo, *A empresa colonial*, visitors would soon come across Jaime Lauriano's work *Quem não reagiu está vivo* [Those Who Didn't React Are Alive] (2015). It consists of a series of ten boards (each 48 × 35 cm) with pages framed in transparent material, each with an image at the top, a title in the middle and a text in Portuguese and English in the lower part. It is not by chance that this format resembles the Baroque *emblem*, which consisted of interplay between a title, a text in verse or prose, and an image. The title would announce the 'moral' of the emblem. In this work by Lauriano, the title of each board is a message that aims to re-interpret Brazilian history from the point of view of the losers and the downtrodden. It realizes the need to 'brush history against the grain',[24] in Walter Benjamin's expression. As Benjamin notes in the same thesis *On the Concept of History*, the critical historian, the historical materialist must withdraw (distance himself) critically from the notion of traditional history (or monumental history, to borrow from Nietzsche),[25] which sees in history a procession of winners and identifies with it. In Benjamin's words:

> [...] Whoever until this day emerges victorious, marches in the triumphal procession in which today's rulers tread over those who are sprawled underfoot. The spoils are, as was ever the case, carried along in the triumphal procession. They are known as the cultural heritage. In the historical materialist they have to reckon with a distanced observer. For what he surveys as the cultural heritage is part and parcel of a lineage which he cannot contemplate without horror. It owes its existence not only to the toil of the great geniuses, who created it, but also to the nameless drudgery of its contemporaries. There has never been a document of culture, which is not simultaneously one of barbarism.[26]

Thus, we follow in Lauriano's boards a rewriting of a history that seemed familiar and known, but which is transformed and revealed in its background of repressed violence. The first board recalls the resistance of the enslaved African population in Brazil who founded the *Quilombo dos Palmares* community of fugitive slaves. The image, a reproduction of Manuel Vítor's familiar 1955 painting, *Guerra dos Palmares* [The Palmares War], portrays

---

[24] Walter Benjamin, 'On the Concept of History', trans. by Dennis Redmond <https://folk.uib.no/hlils/TBLR-B/Benjamin-History.pdf > [accessed 20 Jan. 2020].
[25] Friedrich Nietzsche, 'On the Uses and Disadvantages of History for Life' [1874], trans. by Ian Johnstone <https://www.leudar.com/library/On the Use and Abuse of History.pdf> [accessed 20 Jan. 2020].
[26] Benjamin, ibid.

the repression against the *quilombo*, and the text stresses that this massacre meant the perpetuation of 'the right of man over man'. The second board reproduces the well-known 'Terra Brasilis' map (1519), whose images celebrate the Portuguese conquest, in the style of empathy with the winners that we read critically with Benjamin. In this case, the motto/title ('forced labour of native peoples') and the text deconstruct the map's image (and a certain triumphalist image of history). If the first board stirs empathy with the enslaved and massacred African populations, the second directs the gaze to the suffering of indigenous populations:

The famous Terra Brasilis map — commissioned by Manuel I of Portugal, produced by the cartographers Lopo Homem, Pedro Reinel and Jorge Reinel and illustrated by António de Holanda — glorifies the Portuguese invasion of the 'new world'. In this copy we can see how the authors describe and illustrate the new continent, extolling the exploitation of the 'Brazilian' land from the colonization and enslavement of the bodies of dozens of indigenous peoples.

The third board focuses on the 'extermination and dissolution of self-organized communities'. In this case, the image reproduces an archive photograph of the followers of the messianic political-religious leader Antônio Conselheiro in Belo Monte (Canudos). The text emphasizes that this population that resisted the 'landowning logic that structured Brazilian land and society' was massacred, with over 25,000 dead, in 1897. The fourth board also looks at the conflict over land, but stresses the 'concession of land exploitation to foreign companies'. It is as if the kind of exploitation presented in the Terra Brasilis map was continued in the twentieth century. The fifth board shows a sign put up on 9 October 1970 in the city of Altamira, in the heart of the Amazon region, during the civil-military dictatorship, which served as a landmark for the beginning of the construction of the Trans-Amazonian highway (BR 230, which cuts across the entire Amazon rainforest from east to west). The motto emphasizes the 'devastation of forests and extermination of indigenous peoples' and the explanation links the 'pharaonic works' of the dictatorship period with the desire of military presidents for everlasting fame, which resulted in the death of 'thousands of indigenous peoples'. The sixth board addresses the current theme of 'police repression as a genocidal tactic', exemplified by the 1993 Candelária massacre in Rio de Janeiro, stating that 'the episode revealed the genocidal policy of social cleansing'.[27] The seventh board, which also unfolds ideas from boards three and six, focuses on 'massacre as a tactic for dispersing social protests'. The text recalls another massacre of resisters, in this case the peasants of Eldorado dos Carajás, savagely killed by the military police of the state of Pará in 1996. The eighth board is dedicated to the motto

---

[27] On 23 July 2003, there was a massacre close to the Candelária church in the city of Rio de Janeiro, in which six teenagers and two adults sleeping on the street were killed. The eight were poor and black. The perpetrators were identified as being 'militiamen' and military police. None of the killers was arrested.

'devastation of communities to ensure the nation's progress'. It focuses on the construction of one of the huge hydropower dams in the Northern region of Brazil, which causes socio-environmental destruction and destroys local communities, a project headed by a violent conglomerate comprising the Brazilian state and its national and international business associates. The ninth board highlights once again the resistance to the alliance between big business and state. The motto quotes the words of the São Paulo state governor on the occasion of the massacre of the community of Pinheirinho in the state of São Paulo, in yet another barbaric act of repossession: 'Those who did not react are alive', the cynical motto of a government that openly acknowledges its policy of exterminating those who resist the impositions of the capitalist state. The housing policy is also revealed here as social cleansing. The last board announces: 'institutional segregation and racism transfigured as social security measures', exposing the hypocritical racist policy of the police forces, in this case of Rio de Janeiro. The photos of the emblems used by Lauriano highlight the images of the resisters: the resistance of those enslaved in the colonial period, the population of Canudos, the burial of the Candelária massacre victims, the members of the Landless Workers Movement of Eldorado dos Carajás, the indigenous community, victim of the hydropower dams, the armed population of Pinheirinho ready to face the military police of São Paulo. With this focus on resistance struggles and repressive violence, he works to build a new image of the history of a country that still tends to worship its 'heroes' from the elites. The resistance to the genocide of the black population is associated with a widespread struggle to reconstruct and take ownership of a past hitherto erased and repressed.

Memory of the 1964–85 Dictatorship

In Brazil, the final report of the National Truth Commission (2011–14) officially established that 434 people were killed or had disappeared due to action by the Brazilian state between 1946 and 1988 (but in fact emphasizing the period 1964–85). In that same report, 377 public officials were identified as being involved in these crimes. Those officials were not or cannot be tried, because in Brazil there is an amnesty law in force protecting these perpetrators of state terrorism. Although the official number of victims is 434, the chapter of the report on crimes against indigenous peoples stated that at least 8,350 indigenous individuals were killed by state action during the 1964–85 dictatorship. This figure was not added to the 434 on the official list for 'lack of more accurate data'. In other words, the necropolitics of the dictatorship period continues in Brazil through the impediment of justice and the erasure of history and of access to the truth of that period. The disappearance of the bodies of political victims, a perverse practice that prolongs suffering and halts the entire process of mourning and working through, is duplicated by this 'disappearance' of justice that closes the courts' doors to the executioners and prevents access to the truth.

If during the dictatorship some Brazilian artists resisted with many important works (Claudio Tozzi, Cildo Meireles, Antonio Manuel, Artur Barrio, Evandro Teixeira, Nelson Leirner, Claudia Andujar, Gontan Guanaes Netto, among others), in the post-dictatorship period, with rare exceptions, artists engaged in more formalist poetics or other thematic agendas. However, since 2013–14 there has been a change of scene. A new line of production (after the June 2013 protests and the National Truth Commission, whose final report was released on 10 December 2014) has embraced the challenge of inscribing the dictatorship's past in the present. The need and urgency of this inscription became evident throughout the 2018 presidential campaign and the first year of the Bolsonaro government, marked by a succession of denials (ranging from global warming to the violence of the dictatorship period, via the 'forgiveness' of the Jewish Holocaust in World War II, which also erases and denies it).

Among these new artists of memory who recognize the importance of building from the narratives of dictatorship violence an active depository of images capable of driving the struggles for human rights and justice today, I recall the following names: Rosângela Rennó, Clara Ianni, Fernando Piola, Laís Myrrha, Jaime Lauriano, Fúlvia Molina, Leila Danziger, Paulo Nazareth, Xadalu and Rafael Pagatini. For lack of space I mention here only an impressive work by Leila Danziger which she displayed at the *Hiatus* exhibition (held at the São Paulo Resistance Memorial in Oct. 2017–Mar. 2018), which I curated. Leila Danziger's installation, *Perigosos, subversivos, sediciosos* (*Cadernos do povo brasileiro*) [Dangerous, Subversive, Seditious (Notebooks of the Brazilian People)], links the violence and censorship of the dictatorship period with present times. The work consists of two panels, placed next to each other in the corner of the room: on one wall there are three columns of books that were censored or placed under suspicion during the dictatorship ('left-wing' or 'pornographic' works). On the other wall there are three columns of shelves with photos of people who disappeared during the dictatorship and of victims of violence in the post-dictatorship period, such as the bricklayer Amarildo (1965–2013), a victim of military police violence, who 'disappeared' in Rio de Janeiro, in 2013. Over these images the artist reproduced a few pages of the censored books. She thus created an artistic device to trigger reflection on censorship and disappearance in which images and books disappear and appear. A key detail is that the books are nailed to the wall with huge copper nails; they are 'crucified', sacrificed, like the missing flesh and blood victims. For centuries, books have accompanied humanity as a powerful archive. In them we inscribe ourselves and, as in photography, try to challenge death. In a way books are people, and Heine knew this when he wrote: 'Where they burn books, they will in the end also burn people'.[28] By creating this powerful device

---

[28] The phrase comes from Heine's play *Almansor: Eine Tragödie*, when, on hearing that the Crusaders

about disappearance and censorship, Danziger also makes it possible to bridge the gap between the dictatorship past and the present time, marked once again by security policies that repeat the practices of torture and disappearance.

Final Words

In the twenty-first century, two clear moments can be identified in the field of cultural activities in Brazil: if until the end of the left-wing PT governments there was an evident and effective boom in the arts that supported the self-affirmation of new gender, ethnic, individual and collective identities, as of the 2016 coup we have gradually witnessed an escalation of censorship and restriction in the freedom of the arts and artists. The response has been a reaffirmation of art engaging in retrieving the memory of the dictatorship period (1964–85) as a basis of comparison to understand our time. We also have artists who reaffirm the struggle for the rights of black bodies and culture, such as Sidney Amaral, Charlene Bicalho, Dalton Paula, Janaína Barros, Antônio Obá, Juliana Santos, Priscila Rezende, Lídia Lisboa, Renata Felinto, the curator and artist Daniel Lima, Tiago Gualberto, Moisés Patrício, Marcio Marianno, Peter de Brito, Ana Lira, Ayrson Heráclito, Jota Mombaça, the dancer and performer Luiz de Abreu, the comic book author Marcelo D'Salete, and Frente 3 de Fevereiro (one among several art collectives that have emerged in recent years). There is also a powerful new art focused on the affirmation of indigenous culture, once again threatened with extinction, such as the photographer and artist Claudia Andujar, whose works (from the late twentieth century) are increasingly appreciated and exhibited.[29] In the field of ecological art there is also the rediscovery and revaluation of the works by Frans Krajcberg (1921–2017), who collected the debris of burnt forests in the Amazon region and other areas of Brazil to build devices for inscribing the natural history of violence.[30] Artists, curators and art critics and historians have taken an increasingly determined stance in the face of the insistent attacks on culture and the arts. As a place of resistance, they also configure, beyond survival in dark times, new and challenging spaces of dream and struggle.

---

have burnt the Quran during the sack of Granada, the character Hassan says: 'Das war ein Vorspiel nur, dort wo man Bücher verbrennt, verbrennt man auch am Ende Menschen' [That was but a prelude; where they burn books, they will ultimately burn people as well].

[29] Claudia Andujar, *A luta Yanomami* (São Paulo: IMS, 2018).

[30] Gustavo da Silva Ribeiro, 'Fragmentos de Luz, memórias da destruição', in *Literatura e Autoritarismo*, June 2012, Santa Maria.

From 'Flocking for Rights' to the Politics of Death: Indigenous Struggle and Indigenous Policy in Brazil (1980–2020)[1]

OIARA BONILLA and ARTIONKA CAPIBERIBE

Universidade Federal Fluminense, Niterói, and
Universidade Estadual de Campinas

> [...] we must put an end to all that causes suffering, that kills, that destroys life.
> [...] we don't even have to build anything new, the indigenous people already have a project, the riverside communities already have a project, we just have to stop, look, reflect and act.
>
> ANTONIA MELO[2]

On 9 April 2020, Alvanei Xirixana, a fifteen-year-old Yanomami, died of Covid-19 at the General Hospital of Roraima. He was the first indigenous victim of the pandemic to be officially recorded. The Yanomami people, who live on the border between Brazil and Venezuela, have survived major epidemics, the most recent of which only fell short of wiping out the entire population because their land was demarcated in 1992, momentarily stemming invasions by gold miners, the main cause of contagion.[3] The youth's death comprises elements that will provide the starting points for our reflection here.

The Yanomami land is inhabited by 27,000 indigenous people,[4] and is

---

[1] We thank Tânia Stolze Lima for her valuable suggestions, Diogo Campos dos Santos for designing the maps and Ronaldo de Almeida for the careful copyediting. We emphasize that any mistakes or estimations are our sole responsibility. The authors thank Espaço da Escrita — Pró-Reitoria de Pesquisa — UNICAMP – for their support in translating this article into English.

[2] Available at <http://revistadr.com.br/posts/antonia-melo-lideranca-do-movimento-xingu-vivo-para-sempre/> [accessed 8 May 2020].

[3] The demarcation of indigenous lands is a long administrative process that involves several technical and bureaucratic steps, under the responsibility of the indigenous agency (FUNAI): 1) identification of the land through a detailed study carried out by technical staff; 2) approval of the detailed report by FUNAI; 3) time-limit for challenges; 4) declaration of the area's limits; 5) physical demarcation; 6) ratification by the President of the Republic; 7) registration with the relevant notary and the Office of Federal Property (SPU). Available at <https://pib.socioambiental.org/pt/Demarcações> [accessed 23 April 2020].

[4] Available at <https://pib.socioambiental.org/pt/Povo:Yanomami> [accessed 8 May 2020].

currently invaded by about 25,000 gold miners.[5] Illegal small-scale mining in indigenous lands is an unhealthy activity with intensive use of techniques and substances that are harmful to the environment, causing silting up of rivers and polluting them with mercury and other chemicals.[6] In addition, the incessant movement of labour introduces diseases and alcoholism, while favouring activities such as prostitution and drug trafficking.

Alvanei took more than twenty days to be diagnosed, dying a few days after being tested.[7] Similar situations of neglect have been common for decades. The ethnocide recipe is complete: epidemics, land-grabbing, exploitation and degradation of natural resources, undermining of rights, faulty or non-existent public policies, religious conversion.[8] Our purpose here is to retrace a recent historical and political process in which elements of this recipe are renewed while highlighting the existence of a confrontation in which the indigenous struggle emerges as a significant political force.

* * * * *

Analysing this process in the twenty-first century requires looking back to include the transition period between the civil-military dictatorship and the restoration of democracy in Brazil (1980–90). In the last three decades three periods, in turn, stand out in relation to indigenous rights and indigenous policy. The first occurred in the wake of the enactment of the 1988 Constitution (CF-88), when the current indigenous legislation was designed and started bearing fruit (1990–2006). In the second, the government's economic and political choices opened up the field of indigenous rights to negotiation, exposing them to multiple attacks and attempts at undermining (2006–18). And the third is marked by the dismantling of democratic advances, with the election of Jair Bolsonaro installing a process of radicalization and an openly genocidal policy.

---

[5] Bruce Albert, *Agora somos todos índios*, Coleção Pandemia (São Paulo: N-1, 2020).
[6] Luiz César Marques Filho, *Capitalismo e colapso ambiental* (Campinas, SP: Editora da Unicamp, 2018), p. 230.
[7] Albert, *Agora somos todos índios*.
[8] Ethnocide is used here in a sense widely employed in anthropology, meaning the extermination of difference (or sociocultural distinctiveness) for the purposes of its assimilation into a dominant sociocultural context. In the case of Brazilian indigenous peoples, it occurs through these multiple actions. For a broader discussion of this notion of ethnocide, associated with the concept of genocide and applied to indigenous peoples in Brazil, see Orlando Calheiros, '"No Tempo da Guerra": algumas notas sobre as violações dos direitos dos povos indígenas e os limites da justiça de transição no Brasil', *Re-vista Verdade, Memória e Justiça*, 9 (2015), and Eduardo Viveiros de Castro, 'Sobre a noção de etnocídio com especial atenção ao caso brasileiro' (mimeograph, undated).

The Virtuous Cycle

The flocking of indigenous people for rights

In 1978, the civil-military dictatorship tried to issue a decree for the emancipation of indigenous peoples, seeking to end the tutelage regime introduced in the early twentieth century. This regime was based on the Indian Statute (Law 6001/1973), guided by the Civil Code of 1916, whereby indigenous people, married women and children over 16 but under 21 were considered to be 'relatively capable' of managing their own lives.[9] That meant that indigenous people were deemed either 'primitive', living according to their own customs and traditions, or 'acculturated', and therefore destined for emancipation, with the consequent dissolution of their differences.[10]

The attempt at emancipation led to the uniting of militant forces and culminated in the founding of the Union of Indigenous Nations (UNI), the first Brazilian national indigenous movement.[11] UNI was born from the recommendations of the 1st Indigenous Studies Seminar of Mato Grosso do Sul, held in Campo Grande in 1980. This gathering brought together representatives of fifteen indigenous peoples, including Mário Juruna, who would become the first indigenous federal deputy,[12] and was attended by anthropologists such as Darcy Ribeiro and Carmen Junqueira.[13]

The momentous occasion was marked by strong regional and national mobilization, with alliances driven by the conjuncture, as described by Ailton Krenak:

> The coordination of this thing they call indigenous movement was like a flock of birds [...] that come together in flight and then break up. [...] People ask what so many different people who met on that occasion, different indigenous ethnicities, riverside dwellers, rubber tappers, might have in common. What they had in common was fear of progress![14]

---

[9] Manuela Carneiro da Cunha, 'Índios na Constituição', *Novos Estudos Cebrap*, São Paulo, 3.3 (2018), 429–43 (pp. 430–31).

[10] Manuela Carneiro da Cunha 'Compartilhar a memória', in *Os Índios na Constituição*, ed. by Camila L. Dias and Artionka Capiberibe (São Paulo: Ateliê Editorial, 2019); Ailton Krenak, *Ailton Krenak: encontros* (Rio de Janeiro: Azougue, 2015); Eduardo Viveiros de Castro, 'No Brasil todo mundo é índio exceto quem não é', in *Povos Indígenas no Brasil 2001/2005*, ed. by C. A. Ricardo and F. Ricardo (São Paulo: Instituto Socioambiental, 2006), pp. 41–54.

[11] This movement partly resulted from the large assemblies coordinated by the Indigenous Missionary Council (CIMI) from the 1970s onwards. CIMI, which works uncompromisingly for the defence of indigenous rights, was created in 1972 following the Second Vatican Council, when the Catholic Church engaged in a process of self-criticism of its missionary practices. See Marcos P. Rufino, 'O código da cultura: o CIMI no debate da inculturação', in *Deus na aldeia: missionários, índios e mediação cultural*, ed. by P. Montero (Rio de Janeiro: Editora Globo, 2006), pp. 235–75.

[12] Mário Juruna was elected federal deputy for Rio de Janeiro in 1982. Only in 2018 would another indigenous person take a seat in Congress, when Joênia Wapichana was elected for Roraima.

[13] Sidiclei R. de Deparis, 'União das Nações Indígenas (UNI): contribuição ao movimento indígena no Brasil (1980–1988)' (unpublished Master's thesis, UFGD, 2007), pp. 81–90.

[14] Ailton Krenak, *Ideias para adiar o fim do mundo* (São Paulo: Companhia das Letras, 2019), p. 220.

This seminal political coordination marked the memory of those involved in it, such as the Yanomami shaman Davi Kopenawa:

> The first time I spoke about the forest away from home was at an assembly in the city of Manaus. However, I didn't speak to whites, but to an indigenous audience! It was the time when the gold miners were beginning to invade our lands [...]. So Ailton Krenak and Álvaro Tukano, leaders of the Union of Indigenous Nations, invited me to speak. They said: 'You must defend your people's forest with us! We need to speak out together against those who want to take over our lands! Otherwise we will all end up disappearing, like our ancestors before us!'[15]

The mobilization coordinated, alongside an expanded network of non-indigenous allies, the drafting of the 'Indians' chapter of CF-88, composed of Articles 231 and 232. Article 231 introduces three key changes related to indigenous rights: it establishes the right to land as original, recognizing its pre-existence in relation to the institution of the Brazilian state, as explained by José Afonso da Silva;[16] it creates the concept of 'Indigenous Land' (TI), which goes beyond a mere notion of territory,[17] including, as Capiberibe stresses, the human and non-human lives that comprise indigenous socio-cosmologies, in an explicit recognition of the right to difference;[18] lastly, it is a powerful legal and political tool, making it incumbent upon the federal government to demarcate and protect indigenous lands.[19]

In 1997, Bruce Albert drew attention to the way in which Article 232 changed the political game,[20] legitimizing indigenous action by bypassing the issue of tutelage,[21] and assigning to the Public Prosecution Service the institutional responsibility to act in defence of indigenous rights. As Viveiros de Castro points out, CF-88 enshrines 'the principle that indigenous communities are collective subjects with collective rights. The "Indian" gave way to the "community" and thus the individual gave way to the relational and the transindividual [...]'.[22] The destiny of indigenous peoples would no longer be assimilation and 'de-indianization', but self-determination: 'The indigenous peoples gradually

---

[15] Davi Kopenawa and Bruce Albert, *A queda do céu: palavras de um xamã yanomami* (São Paulo: Companhia das Letras, 2015), p. 385.
[16] José Afonso da Silva, 'Parecer', in *Direitos dos povos indígenas em disputa*, ed. by M. Carneiro da Cunha and S. Rodrigues Barbosa (São Paulo: Editora Unesp, 2018), pp. 17–42 (pp. 20–21).
[17] Carneiro da Cunha, 'Compartilhar a memória' p. 45.
[18] Artionka Capiberibe, 'Dos índios: em defesa da Constituição', *Publicação Oficial da Associação Juízes para a Democracia*, ano 18, nº 78 (2018), 3–5 (p. 4); available at <https://ajd.org.br/jornal-78/> [accessed 21 April 2020].
[19] *Constituição da República Federativa do Brasil: promulgada em 5 de outubro de 1988*; available at <http://www.planalto.gov.br/ccivil_03/Constituicao/Constituicao.htm> [accessed 21 April 2020].
[20] Bruce Albert, 'Territorialité, ethno-développement et développement: à propos du mouvement indien en Amazonie brésilienne', *Cahier de l'Amérique Latine*, 23 (1997), 177–210 (p. 188).
[21] The issue of tutelage is involved in constant legal disputes, as it continues being invoked to neutralize indigenous political and legal actions; see Luiz H. Eloy Terena, 'A Constituição em disputa', in *Os Índios na Constituição*, ed. by C. Loureiro Dias and Artionka Capiberibe (São Paulo: Ateliê Editorial, 2019), pp. 103–16 (p. 110).
[22] Viveiros de Castro, 'Sobre a noção de etnocídio', p. 14.

started demanding and eventually obtained the constitutional recognition of a permanent differentiated status within the so-called "national communion".[23] The consequences of those achievements would be felt in the following decade.

The 'Time of Demarcation'

The period 1990–2000 can be considered a virtuous cycle of access to the constitutionally guaranteed right to demarcation. An exemplary case is the ratification of the Yanomami Indigenous Land, driven by the work of indigenous organizations and international pressure related to environmental issues, a prominent theme at Rio 1992 (United Nations Conference on Environment and Development). Over this period, the indigenous movement achieved international recognition thanks to emblematic personalities whose speeches related indigenous and ecological issues, granting demarcation a political dimension that went beyond Brazilian borders.[24]

Going back to the Yanomami land, at the height of the civil-military dictatorship in the 1970s, when the Amazon region became the target of development and settlement policies under the National Integration Plan (PIN),[25] work was started on the North Perimeter Highway (BR-210), conceived to follow the entire borderline from Colombia to the state of Amapá, affecting lands inhabited by the Yanomami at one end and the Wajãpi at the other (see Map 1). Regarding the latter, Gallois reports:

> As a result of the contact between indigenous people and gold miners, nineteen natives died of measles in Karapanaty in 1972. There was also gold mining in the region of the Água-Preta stream between 1969 and 1970, causing the death of more than ten natives from a flu epidemic; the remaining inhabitants of that area were wiped out soon afterwards by another epidemic, *with only two survivors remaining in 1973*.[26]

Shortly afterwards, the RADAM project[27] published a survey of the region's important mineral potential, setting off what Kopenawa and Albert described as 'one of the most spectacular twentieth-century' gold rushes. Between 1985 and 1990, around one hundred clandestine airstrips were opened and 30,000 to 40,000 illegal gold miners moved into Yanomami lands, causing 'an

---

[23] Viveiros de Castro, 'No Brasil todo mundo é índio', p. 43.
[24] Highlights include the World Conference on Indigenous Peoples (Kari-Oca), a parallel event to Rio 92; the initiatives of the indigenous leader Raoni Metuktire with the singer Sting for the demarcation of the Kayapó land (from 1988) and against the Kararaô hydro power project in Pará (1989, see below); and the engagement of prominent figures of Brazilian show business, such as Milton Nascimento, who released the album *Txai* (1990). The indigenous efforts were also recognized through awards, such as the UN Global 500 Roll of Honor, granted to Paulinho Payakan (1990) and Davi Kopenawa (1991).
[25] PIN was implemented with the goal of occupying 'empty' spaces in Brazil, developing in them infrastructure works and land settlement programmes, and settling labour in the Amazon region.
[26] Dominique Gallois, 'Cap. Waiãpi — 3/Amapá, Norte do Pará', in *Povos Indígenas no Brasil*, ed. by Carlos Alberto Ricardo (São Paulo: CEDI, 1983), pp. 98–137 (p. 111, emphasis added).
[27] A project created in 1970 for radar mapping of natural resources in the Amazon region and, later, in Brazil as a whole.

From 'Flocking for Rights' to the Politics of Death

Map 1. North Perimeter Highway [design: Diogo C. dos Santos].

unprecedented epidemiological shock among the Yanomami'.[28] Evangelical missions complemented this setting.[29] The demarcation of their land was vital for the Yanomami, ensuring them a certain degree of temporary security.

The land demarcations of this virtuous cycle enabled a demographic recovery of indigenous peoples, due also to improvements in access to healthcare services and the inclusion of self-declaration in the population census. Thus, the indigenous population increased from 306,245 people in 1991 to 817,963 in 2010.[30] In addition, the responsibilities of the indigenous agency, the National Indian Foundation (FUNAI), started being redefined in this period, planning the decentralization of public policies for indigenous peoples in view of the issue of their self-determination.[31]

---

[28] Kopenawa and Albert, *A queda do céu*, pp. 561–62.
[29] The main strategy of these missions for penetrating indigenous communities is to offer basic services, especially healthcare and education, where the state is absent. These evangelical missions, known as cross-cultural missions, are the majority among indigenous peoples today. Proselytizing and guided by fundamentalist principles, they differ radically from post-Second Vatican Council (1965) Catholic missions such as CIMI and historical Protestants. See Ronaldo Almeida, 'Tradução e mediação: missões transculturais entre grupos indígenas', in *Deus na aldeia: missionários, índios e mediação cultural*, ed. by Paula Montero (Rio de Janeiro: Editora Globo, 2006), pp. 277–304 (pp. 279–84).
[30] These figures are analysed in <https://pib.socioambiental.org/pt/O_Censo_2010_e_os_Povos_Ind%C3%ADgenas> [accessed 3 June 2020].
[31] Henyo T. Barretto Filho and Adriana Ramos, 'Da luta por direitos à luta para não perdê-los: povos e terras indígenas (TIs) na guerra pela destinação de terras públicas no Brasil pós-Constituição', in *As políticas da política: desigualdades e inclusão nos governos do PSDB e do PT*, ed. by Marta Arretche, Eduardo Marques and Carlos Aurélio Pimenta de Faria (São Paulo: Editora Unesp, 2019), p. 331.

The 'Time of Projects'

The recognition of self-determination (Article 232, CF-88) led to the creation of multiple local and regional indigenous associations, helped by supporting organizations and benefiting from a government strategy to strengthen the third sector between the 1990s and 2003. One must bear in mind that this was a period marked worldwide by a policy of funding local actors that tended to reduce the state's role in promoting social well-being.[32]

Regarding indigenous peoples in Brazil, on the one hand this trend produced a harnessing of the idea of diversity-based development,[33] favouring the accommodation of the collectives and their organizations and demands to the global neoliberal agenda endorsed by multilateral agencies. The situation is similar to that described by Silvia Federici about the domestication of the feminist movement in the 1980s and 1990s by UN programs for the promotion of 'women's rights'. Under the pretext of 'emancipation' this process would undermine the autonomy of local feminist movements and depoliticize feminism 'by adapting it to the goals of global capital and the institutions that support it'.[34] Similarly, in the indigenous movement, but in the name of 'sustainable development', many associations began to focus on funding and projects (in partnership with NGOs), opening a period marked by a certain fragmentation of the indigenous movement. On the other hand, as shown by Albert[35] and Barretto Filho and Ramos,[36] this process fostered another kind of political participation, more technical and bureaucratic, which would enable indigenous action both inside and outside the state.

The 2000s also witnessed the redesigning of the public policy model influenced by the institution of legal changes related to indigenous peoples, at national and international level. Prominent among such changes were the ILO Convention 169 and the United Nations Declaration on the Rights of Indigenous Peoples (UNDRIP).[37]

In 1999 the federal government transferred the administration of indigenous health resources from FUNAI to the National Health Foundation (Funasa),[38]

---

[32] According to Albert, in 1991 there were 48 indigenous organizations, increasing to 109 by 1996 ('Territorialité, ethno-développement et développement', p. 189). Pacheco de Oliveira adds the 1999 data, totalling 290 organizations: 'Regime tutelar e globalização: um exercício de sociogênese dos atuais movimentos indígenas no Brasil', in *O nascimento do Brasil e outros ensaios: 'pacificação', regime tutelar e formação de alteridades* (Rio de Janeiro: Contra Capa, 2016), pp. 265–88 (p. 281).
[33] Oliveira, p. 299.
[34] Silvia Federici, *O ponto zero da Revolução: trabalho doméstico, reprodução e luta feminista*, trans. by Coletivo Sycorax (São Paulo: Editora Elefante, 2019), p. 238.
[35] Bruce Albert, 'Associações indígenas e desenvolvimento sustentável na Amazônia brasileira', in *Povos Indígenas no Brasil, 1996–2000*, ed. by Carlos Alberto Ricardo (São Paulo: Instituto Socioambiental, 2000), pp. 197–203 (pp. 198, 201).
[36] Barretto Filho and Ramos, 'Da luta por direitos à luta para não perdê-los', p. 323.
[37] Christian Ramos and Laís Abramo, 'Introdução', in *Convenção 169 sobre povos indígenas e tribais e Resolução referente à ação da OIT/Organização Internacional do Trabalho* (Brasília: OIT, 2011).
[38] Government body responsible for providing basic sanitation and designed to assist the implementation of SUS (Unified Health System). SUS was created by Article 196 of CF-88 and

creating thirty-four indigenous healthcare districts across the country. Thus, through agreements, local indigenous associations started playing a major role in resource management alongside local governments and civil society organizations. Decentralization brought about some improvement in healthcare delivery, but in 2004 Funasa re-centralized resource management, ending the partnership with organizations (indigenous and non-indigenous). This aggravated the already precarious financial situation of the partner institutions, which started to be defamed and 'suffer administrative interventions', in some cases having their assets seized, causing many to close down, besides damaging their image.[39]

In a similar process, acknowledgment of the specificity of indigenous education by CF-88 (Article 210, paragraph 2) led to the development of a model of public indigenous education. So far, education had been in the charge of FUNAI under rather improvised conditions, often delegated to missionary agencies.[40] In 1991, school education was transferred from FUNAI to the Ministry of Education and, in 1999, guidelines for 'indigenous schooling' were created, recognizing its specific status and transferring the responsibility for its provision to state and local governments.[41]

As stressed by Ailton Krenak, in many cases this paradigm shift from assimilationist education to an education that respects differences is not yet a reality in indigenous schooling.[42] But the movement has had important political effects, particularly in the last fifteen years. One of them related to the training of teachers, who started to play a role that went beyond schooling, either as actual leaders or by developing new leaders. In turn, this schooling system educated a critical mass of female and male students willing to claim space in the country's universities, besides affording greater visibility to the field of indigenous literatures and philosophies.[43]

implemented in 1990, following a model of universal health care (see Ana Paula do Rego Menezes, Bruno Moretti and Ademar Arthur Chioro dos Reis, 'O Futuro do SUS: impactos das reformas neoliberais na saúde pública: austeridade versus universalidade', *Saúde e Debate*, Rio de Janeiro, vol. 43, n. Especial 5 (2019), 58–70).
[39] Luiza Garnelo, 'Cap. 1. Política de Saúde Indígena no Brasil: notas sobre as tendências atuais do processo de implantação do subsistema de atenção à saúde', *Saúde Indígena: uma introdução ao tema*, ed. by Luiza Garnelo and Ana Lucia Pontes (Brasília: Secadi/UNESCO and Projeto Trilhas de Conhecimentos — LACED/Museu Nacional, 2012), pp. 18–58 (p. 48).
[40] Gersem dos Santos Luciano Baniwa, *O índio brasileiro: o que você precisa saber sobre os povos indígenas no Brasil de hoje* (Brasília: Ministério da Educação, Secretaria de Educação Continuada, Alfabetização e Diversidade; LACED/Museu Nacional, 2006), pp. 167–69; Luís Doniseti Benzi Grupioni, 'A educação escolar indígena no Brasil: a passos lentos', in *Povos Indígenas no Brasil, 1996/2000*, ed. by Carlos Alberto Ricardo (São Paulo: Instituto Socioambiental, 2000), pp. 143–47 (p. 143).
[41] Aracy Lopes da Silva, 'A educação indígena entre diálogos interculturais e multidisciplinares: introdução', in *Antropologia, história e educação*, ed. by Aracy Lopes da Silva and Mariana Kawall Leal Ferreira (São Paulo: Global: 2001), pp. 9–25 (p. 10); Grupioni, pp. 146–47.
[42] Krenak, *Encontros*, pp. 248–50.
[43] Especially prominent authors and thinkers like Daniel Munduruku, Eliane Potiguara, Cristino Wapichana, Davi Kopenawa and Ailton Krenak. More recently, a relevant indigenous artistic movement has emerged, both in visual arts with Denilson Baniwa, Jaider Esbell, Taniki and Joseca Yanomami,

From 1996, through the Integrated Project for the Protection of Indigenous Populations and Lands in the Legal Amazon (PPTAL/PPG7), international funding was provided for demarcation, especially in the Amazon region. The funding agencies encouraged 'participatory' demarcation, stimulating agreements with indigenous organizations, supporting institutions and universities.[44]

In the same period, indigenous peoples living in the country's earliest settlement regions, such as the Northeast, South, Southeast and Mato Grosso do Sul, did not benefit equally from funding, which created a gap in land demarcation and recognition of rights.[45] That contributed to an intensification of land conflicts in these regions, driving an indigenous struggle that came to be known by the term *retomada* [retaking], originally used to describe the Guarani and Kaiowá movement to recover their lands.[46] Besides exposing social and land inequalities, the drive to retake indigenous lands shows that, from an indigenous point of view, this was not a dispute over property and land use conceived as a commodity. 'Retaking' is the struggle for a way of life as a whole, which cannot be conceived outside the web of relationships woven between humans and non-humans in an inhabited space/place.[47] Retaking the land is reconnecting with the network of relationships that compose it. This is markedly personified in the cases of the Tupinambá in Bahia and the Guarani and Kaiowá in Mato Grosso do Sul,[48] and expressively stated by a prominent Kaiowá leader:

> These big woods have always been ours [...]. They [the whites] cut down all the woods to then name the place Mato Grosso do Sul [Southern Thick Woods]. So they hid from us our medicines, our meat, our game, which was the armadillo, the agouti, the tapir, the lizard: those animals were all ours. They spread them all away from us, the owners of the animals raised [to the sky] all of them. So *our food today is made by machines*.[49]

Mana and Kitxi Huni Kui, Feliciano Lana (a Desana artist, who died in May 2020 from Covid-19); and in film, with names like Ariel Ortega, Patrícia Ferreira, Alberto Álvares, Takumã Kuikuro, among others, plus the productions of indigenous collectives such as the Cultural Association of Indigenous Filmmakers (ASCURI).

[44] Cf. PPTAL guidelines, available at <https://acervo.socioambiental.org/acervo/documentos/pptal-projeto-integrado-de-protecao-populacoes-e-terras-indigenas-da-amazonia> [accessed 1 May 2020].

[45] Oliveira, pp. 299-300; Barretto Filho and Ramos, 'Da luta por direitos à luta para não perdê-los', p. 330.

[46] The retaking of land by the Guarani and Kaiowá begins in 1979 with the reoccupation of lands on the Rancho Jacaré and Guaimbé farms, in Mato Grosso do Sul (see Meire Adriana da Silva, 'O Movimento dos Guarani e Kaiowá de reocupação e recuperação de seus territórios em Mato Grosso do Sul e a participação do CIMI (Conselho Indigenista Missionário) — 1978-2001' (unpublished Master's dissertation, Universidade Federal do Mato Grosso do Sul (UFMS), 2005), pp. 122-37).

[47] Susana de Matos Viegas, *Terra Calada: Os Tupinambá na Mata Atlântica do Sul da Bahia* (Rio de Janeiro: 7Letras, 2007), pp. 270-72.

[48] Daniela Alarcon, *O retorno da terra: as retomadas na aldeia tupinambá da Serra do Padeiro, Sul da Bahia* (São Paulo: Elefante, 2019); Spensy M. Pimentel, *Elementos para uma teoria política kaiowá e guarani* (unpublished doctoral thesis, Universidade de São Paulo, 2012); Viegas, *Terra Calada*.

[49] Atanásio apud Pimentel, p. 205.

The situation in these regions increasingly exposed the unequal and violent conflict over the concept of land, its enjoyment and use. It also foreshadowed what, from 2007, would become an open war between those who struggled to ensure indigenous rights and the economic development project led by a government which, for pragmatic political reasons, forged an alliance with anti-indigenous sectors (known in Congress as the 'Beef, Bullet and Bible' block for its lobby in favour of agribusiness, the arms industry and evangelical churches). Thus, after a brief period of political and legal advances, indigenous peoples were once again facing a biased state that neglected policies for the recognition of differences, defied constitutional provisions, and privileged the hegemonic sectors of the economy. The attacks were multiple in all three branches of government (executive, legislative and judicial) and unleashed on two fronts: on the one hand in the legal sphere and, on the other, through the execution of public policies, guided by an economic development project founded on the extensive exploitation of natural and human resources,[50] and, at the same time, on a notion of social inclusion based on redistribution of income to encourage consumption.[51]

The Dark Times

One of the most significant processes in the interplay of interests surrounding indigenous lands, for its impact and multiple meanings, occurred over three of the four terms of the Workers' Party (PT, 2002–16), namely that of the Raposa Serra do Sol land in Roraima. This case would trigger the rebirth of a national pan-indigenous movement that took shape in an increasingly hostile context. It should be noted that there was a severe and progressive reduction in the demarcation of indigenous lands in this period,[52] as noted by Barretto Filho and Ramos.[53] From that moment the indigenous movement started struggling to preserve its rights.

In 2004, in the context of the struggle for the Raposa Serra do Sol TI, the 1st Free Land Camp (ATL) was organized in Brasília, attended by twenty-one indigenous peoples, with the goal of pressuring President Lula to ratify that land.[54] In 2005, ATL sparked the creation of the Coordination of

---

[50] Artionka Capiberibe and Oiara Bonilla, 'A ocupação do Congresso: contra o quê lutam os índios?', *Estudos Avançados*, 29.83 (2015), 293–313.

[51] The government implemented the *Bolsa Família* social welfare program, including for indigenous peoples, privileging such policies over land demarcation. See Ricardo Verdum, *Estudos Etnográficos sobre o Programa Bolsa Família em Povos Indígenas (Relatório Final)* (Brasília: SAGI/MDS, 2016).

[52] In the two presidential terms of Fernando Henrique Cardoso, 145 Indigenous Lands (TIs) were ratified (114 in 1994–98 and 31 in 1998–2002); in the two terms of Luiz Inácio Lula da Silva, 81 TIs were ratified (66 in 2002–06 and 21 in 2006–10); in Dilma Rousseff's two terms, 21 TIs were ratified (11 in 2010–14 and 10 in 2014–16); however, no lands were ratified in the Temer and Bolsonaro administrations. Data available at <https://pib.socioambiental.org/pt/Situação_jurídica_das_TIs_no_Brasil_hoje> [accessed 21 May 2020]. See note 3 above.

[53] Barretto Filho and Ramos, 'Da luta por direitos à luta para não perdê-los'.

[54] Gilberto Vieira dos Santos, 'O movimento indígena contemporâneo no contexto dos conflitos no campo', *Revista Terra Livre*, São Paulo, Ano 34, 1.52 (2019), 323–59 (p. 339).

Indigenous Peoples of Brazil (APIB) and was thenceforth held every year. APIB was constituted as an alliance of regional organizations,[55] becoming the main political agent and representative of indigenous demands. One of its achievements in public policy was the creation in 2011 of the Special Office for Indigenous Health (SESAI).[56]

In a 2015 article,[57] we drew attention to the large number of legal initiatives aiming to further degrade the living conditions of indigenous populations, among them the Proposed Constitutional Amendment (PEC) 215/2000, whose objective was to transfer the approval of the indigenous and *quilombola* lands, as well as of the Environmental Conservation Units, from the executive to the legislature, a proposal formulated by the Agricultural Parliamentary Front (the first B of the 'Beef, Bullet and Bible' block) in order to frustrate demarcation processes.

Such was the case of the demarcation process of the Raposa Serra do Sol Indigenous Land, which, due to the obstacles imposed by miners, cattle breeders and rice farmers, took more than three decades to be concluded. The dispute partially ended only in 2009, after several violent conflicts and a drawn-out legal battle waged in the Federal Supreme Court (STF). But the partial victory came at a price, as the STF, to guarantee the continuous demarcation of the territory, imposed nineteen conditions, many of them representing a loss of rights, such as legalizing the introduction of military bases, roads, hydro power plants and mining activities in indigenous lands without consulting their communities. Some of these conditions cater to demands by the armed forces in the so-called 'interest of national defence policy', while opening up possibilities for economic exploitation that override the indigenous peoples' original rights.

These conditions unfolded into other legal proposals, one of the most recent being Opinion 001/2017 of the General Counsel for the Federal Government (AGU). This Opinion institutes the adoption of the nineteen conditions for Raposa Serra do Sol and includes the so-called 'time reference'. Thus, one witnesses the project to dismantle indigenous rights being expanded by the incorporation of new legal instruments. The *marco temporal* [time reference], which is not provided in the Constitution, is a legal invention aiming to establish the date of the promulgation of CF-88 (10 May 1988) as a time reference point for land claims. The fallacious argument intended to support this thesis is explained by the indigenous lawyer Luiz Eloy Terena:

[55] The following are members of APIB: Coordination of Indigenous Peoples of the Northeast Region, Minas Gerais and Espírito Santo (APOINME), Council of the Terena People, Coordination of Indigenous Peoples of the Southeast Region (ARPINSUDESTE), Coordination of Indigenous Peoples of the South Region (ARPINSUL), Great Assembly of the Guarani People (ATY GUASU), Coordination of Indigenous Organizations of the Brazilian Amazon Region (COIAB) and Guarani Yvyrupa Committee. Available at <http://apib.info/apib/> [accessed 6 May 2020].
[56] Garnelo, 'Política de Saúde Indígena no Brasil', p. 25.
[57] Oiara Bonilla and Artionka Capiberibe, 'Isolados ou cadastrados: os índios na era desenvolvimentista', *Revista DR*, 1 (2015), available online as <http://revistadr.com.br/posts/isolados-ou-cadastrados-os-indios-na-era-desenvolvimentista/> [accessed 26 June 2020].

They say the following: 'Your Honour, the Constitution indeed recognized the original rights of indigenous peoples, but the Constitution used the verb in the present tense: "occupy"'. Then they point out, underline that word: 'occupy'. And they continue: 'Your Honour, the verb was in the present tense and it means that the Constitution recognized only the lands they were occupied at the exact moment the text was promulgated'. [And he concludes] [...] The grammatical interpretation of the law is the weakest interpretation in the legal world.[58]

The 'Time of Tides'

While this tsunami of legal setbacks was being set in motion, the federal government was encroaching on indigenous lands with its economic development project, notably from the PAC (*Programa de Aceleração do Crescimento* [Growth Acceleration Program]) launched in 2007 by President Lula, which included a number of major infrastructure works. The Belo Monte hydro power plant (HPP), on the Xingu River, was the most important PAC construction site and, despite opposition by social organizations, construction was initiated in 2011 and the first turbine became operational in 2016.[59]

As shown in the thesis by Sabrina Nascimento, Belo Monte is a perfect example of what, due to the recurrence of events, constitutes an 'accomplished fact'.[60] As of CF-88, a set of rules governed the performance of public administration regarding the implementation of works and business ventures, among them environmental licensing and impact studies,[61] public hearings, and consultation with affected populations. However, Belo Monte will overrule these legal precepts in the name of the country's energy security. The planning of the hydro power plant overrides legislation, prevailing over it and, in time, becoming an 'accomplished fact'. What was illegal becomes legal and irreversible.[62]

---

[58] Terena, 'A Constituição em disputa', p. 108.
[59] Belo Monte is a project first conceived by the military government (1970s) with the name of Kararaô which was repeatedly postponed due to pressure from local communities. The struggle against this project culminated in the 1st Meeting of the Indigenous Peoples of the Xingu, in Altamira in 1989, which brought together hundreds of leaders from the region, including Raoni Metuktire, Megaron Txucarramãe and Paulinho Paiakan (A. Oswaldo Sevá, 'Profanação hidrelétrica de Btyre/Xingu: fios condutores e armadilhas (até setembro de 2012)', in *Belo Monte e a questão indígena*, ed. by João Pacheco de Oliveira and Clarice Cohn (Brasília, DF: ABA, 2014), pp. 170–205 (p. 181). The group met for a second time in Altamira in 2008, and in 2011 held an occupation of the construction site attended by more than 400 indigenous people, fishermen and riverside dwellers who were removed in a military operation carried out by government forces. The struggle continues to this day.
[60] Sabrina Nascimento, 'Violência e estado de exceção na Amazônia brasileira: um estudo sobre a implantação da hidrelétrica de Belo Monte no Rio Xingu (PA)' (unpublished doctoral thesis, Núcleo de Altos Estudos Amazônicos, Belém; Universidade Federal do Pará, 2017), p. 212.
[61] The Environmental Impact Study (EIA) and the Environmental Impact Report (RIMA) are two documents of equivalent value, key to the environmental licensing processes of works and projects.
[62] In this process, a war of legal procedures was set in motion in which the local populations also made use of their bodies, as in the occupation of the construction site. For more on the idea of the body as a political weapon, see Artionka Capiberibe, 'Um interminável Brasil colônia: os povos indígenas e um outro desenvolvimento', *Maloca: Revista de Estudos Indígenas*, 1.1 (2018), 53–77.

The Juruna people (Yudjá people) of the Paquiçamba TI, who, together with the Arara people, are directly impacted by the Belo Monte HPP, denounce one of its disastrous effects, the so-called *consenso hidrográfico* [consensus hydrograph]. After the river was dammed, the rate of flow (of the rainy and dry seasons) was changed, affecting the course of the Xingu River at the point of the so-called *Volta Grande* [Big Bend].[63] Nowadays, the discharge no longer floods the surrounding vegetation, and its seasonal alternation is controlled artificially by the dam company, guided by its own interests in producing energy. This affects the flora and fauna, directly upsetting fishing activities and the Juruna people's livelihood.[64] The landscape has changed and the river has become a dangerous place, especially near the reservoir, where large waves are thrown up, posing risks to boats. One local resident stated:

> I cry when I see the 'sarobas' [riverside plants] dying on one side of the dam, the thin, half- dead turtles. [...] That makes me so scared, I'm scared of dying there in that huge lake, of dying like the trees died. *The river is now controlled by machines.* We are now living the time of tides. The Xingu River is messed up. The fish are lost and so are we.[65]

To make up for the loss of navigability in the river, a road was opened connecting the TI to the city of Altamira, creating a pathway to deforestation and land grabbing.[66] In 2018 there was an exponential increase in deforested areas around and inside the region's indigenous lands, from three hectares in May to 5000 hectares in November of the same year.[67] Besides the reduced discharge and deviation of the Xingu River, which has practically destroyed the Juruna's livelihood, the competent bodies have not regulated the demarcation of their land or cleared it of invaders, as provided for in the conditions for the construction of Belo Monte.[68]

Fifteen kilometres from the dam, impacting the same region, the Canadian company Belo Sun Mining has opened Volta Grande Gold Project, the largest open-cast gold mine in Brazil. What draws attention in the Environmental Impact Report of this project is the prospect of using electricity produced at Belo Monte. This corroborates the accusations that the power plant, which operates to its full capacity only four months a year due to the hydrological peculiarities of the Xingu River, will benefit industries rather than the population, and more precisely the so-called electro-intensive enterprises.

---

[63] Close to the city of Altamira, the Xingu River has a sharp bend which forms canals, rapids and islands that today are 'dry'. Its discharge has been restricted upstream by the Pimental dam and diverted to feed the Belo Monte reservoir. See Map 2.

[64] Juarez Pezzuti, Cristiane Carneiro, Thais Mantovanelli and Biviany Rojas Garzón, *Xingu, o rio que pulsa em nós: monitoramento independente para registro de impactos da UHE Belo Monte no território e no modo de vida do povo Juruna (Yudjá) da Volta Grande do Xingu* (São Paulo: ISA, 2018), p. 31.

[65] Dona Graça apud Pezzuti et al., p. 15, emphasis added.

[66] The term in Portuguese is *grilagem*, meaning illegal appropriation of public lands.

[67] Available at <https://www.socioambiental.org/pt-br/blog/blog-do-xingu/grandes-empreendimentos-provocam-boom-de-desmatamento-na-volta-grande-do-xingu> [accessed 15 May 2020].

[68] Nascimento, 'Violência e estado de exceção na Amazônia brasileira', pp. 219–20; 224; 285.

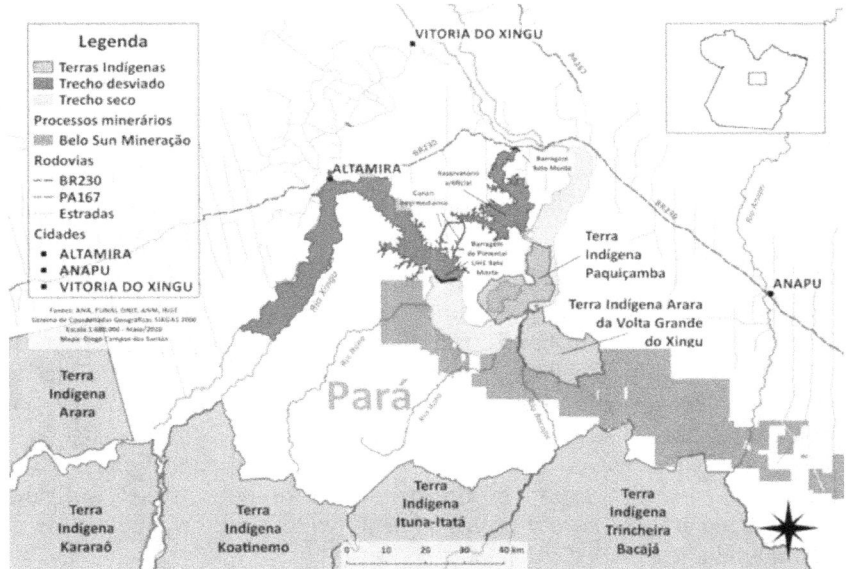

Map 2. Belo Sun Mining [design: Diogo C. dos Santos]

The effects of Belo Sun magnify those related to small-scale mining mentioned earlier. Not far from there, the Xikrin people of the Cateté River are experiencing at first hand the consequences of this type of mining. The report by the physician Vieira Filho (2020) indicates the presence of heavy metals in alarming and extremely toxic levels in local rivers close to the Onça Puma Project of the mining company Vale do Rio Doce. Added to the resulting environmental degradation is the spread of chronic degenerative diseases that genetically affect the present and future of the Xikrin:

> The Xikrin are consuming manioc, cassava, sweet potato, softening those root vegetables in the Cateté and Itacaiúnas rivers, with high levels of lead and cadmium, metals which have terrible consequences for the brain, kidneys, bones and other vital organs. The accumulation of these heavy metals in the body has been corroborated by scientific papers on DNA methylation, with alteration of gene expression transmitted across generations or to future generations by those who do not die.[69]

* * * * *

This 'Time of Tides' inaugurated a period that would engulf indigenous peoples in a politics of death focused on the destruction of the legal framework

---

[69] João Paulo B. Vieira Filho, 'A metilação do DNA (código genético) hereditariedade podendo promover doenças crônico-degenerativas para as gerações de índios Xikrin atuais e futuras, que pode ser ocasionada pelos metais pesados ou elementos químicos lançados no Rio Cateté pela Usina Onça-Puma de níquel e Rio Itacaiúnas pela Mina S11D de ferro da Cia Vale do Rio Doce', Relatório — UNIFESP (mimeograph, 2020), p. 5.

and a stated intention to physically exterminate minorities. Once again based on a militarization of the state, the strategy was now officially allied to fundamentalist religious action and rhetoric. These polluted waters always converged on the same recipe: eliminating indigenous peoples to allow the appropriation and exploitation of the land and its resources.

Jair Bolsonaro's Politics of Death

Once in power, Jair Bolsonaro put his 'genocidal verbiage' into action.[70] For indigenous people, the demolition of the democratic institutional framework began on the first day of government with the proposal to transfer the demarcation of Indigenous Lands from FUNAI to the Ministry of Agriculture, Livestock and Supply (MAPA), dominated by big landowners. The indigenous movement obstructed this attempt thanks to a widely publicized international campaign.[71] Among others initiatives in the same field, one of the most serious was FUNAI IN (*Instrução Normativa* [Normative Instruction]) 9/2020, which provided for the legalization of invaded areas in non-ratified Indigenous Lands, putting at risk 'more than 237 TIs [...], [which] can be sold, subdivided, dismembered and invaded'.[72]

The IN harmonized with Provisional Measure (MP) 910/2019, proposed by the executive and known as the '*MP da grilagem*', which, among other things, intended to provide the general legalization of illegally appropriated lands. Barred by pressure from society, the MP was revived in the Chamber of Deputies as PL (*Projeto de Lei* [Bill]) 2633/2020, once again evidencing the pact among the different branches of government against indigenous rights.[73]

To ensure the exploitation of mineral, water and hydrocarbon resources and overcome impediments to legalized mining in TIs, the Bolsonaro government presented PL 191/2020, popularly known as the *PL da devastação* [Devastation Bill], which additionally regulates existing projects and allows the production of transgenic (GM) crops in TIs.[74]

This legislation authorized all kinds of violation by introducing a politics of death that operates through increased invasions, deforestation, environmental degradation and direct physical extermination. During 2019, Bolsonaro's first

---

[70] Oiara Bonilla, 'La Vitalité des mondes possibles face à l'extrême-droite au Brésil', *Revue Terrestres*, 2 (2018). Available at <https://www.terrestres.org/2018/11/15/la-vitalite-des-mondes-possibles-face-a-lascension-de-lextreme-droite-au-bresil/> [accessed 18 May 2020].

[71] 'Nenhuma gota a mais', available at <https://www.nenhumagotamais.org/> [accessed 18 May 2020].

[72] Juliana de Paulo Batista, 'Funai edita medida que permite ocupação e até venda de áreas em Terras Indígenas', *Instituto Socioambiental* (14 April 2020). Available at <https://www.socioambiental.org/pt-br/blog/blog-do-ppds/funai-edita-medida-que-permite-ocupacao-e-ate-venda-de-areas-em-237-terras-indigenas> [accessed 19 May 2020].

[73] Capiberibe and Bonilla, 'A ocupação do Congresso'; Capiberibe, 'Um interminável Brasil colônia'.

[74] See Nurit Bensusan, 'PL da devastação ameaça alimentação dos índios ao liberar transgênicos em Terras Indígenas', *Instituto Socioambiental* (21 February 2020). Available at <https://www.socioambiental.org/pt-br/blog/blog-do-isa/pl-da-devastacao-ameaca-alimentacao-dos-indios-ao-liberar-transgenicos-em-terras-indigenas> [accessed 19 May 2020].

year in office, nine indigenous people were murdered,[75] most of them involved in surveillance of their lands. Also in 2019, record levels of destruction by forest fires were seen, with 76,720 outbreaks recorded across Brazil between January and August, up 85% from 2018.

At the same time, the government has been gradually starving FUNAI of funds, while purging the civil service to install loyalists. Qualified technicians occupying *cargos de confiança* [positions of trust][76] and leadership in the indigenous agency (as well as in two environmental bodies, IBAMA and ICMBio) are being replaced by military, evangelicals and political associates with no expertise whatsoever. An ideological war is being waged in which those professionals are intimidated and defamed in notes and official statements, with grotesque speeches and accusations.[77] An example is the replacement of the head of the Coordination Office of Isolated Indians and Recent Contact (CGIIRC), which, as a rule, should be occupied by a specialized technician and FUNAI-tenured civil servant. Bolsonaro appointed to this post a pastor from the evangelical proselytizing organization *Missão Novas Tribos do Brasil* (MNTB — New Tribes of Brazil Mission).[78]

Following the historic forest fires of 2019, the military wing of the government showed its claws by creating the National Legal Amazon Council to keep control over the region and prevent alleged international geopolitical interference, seeking to ensure its devastation project disguised as an economic project.[79] The council is composed exclusively of the military and ministers from areas deemed as strategic, headed by Vice President General Hamilton Mourão, and excludes civil society (indigenous people, traditional populations, anthropologists, environmentalists, etc.) as well as the Forum of Governors of the Legal Amazon.

* * * * *

Despite this machinery to annihilate people and their worlds, indigenous peoples have been taking a political stand. In 2013 they were the first to take to the streets, occupying Congress and foreshadowing the June demonstrations,[80]

---

[75] Available at <https://cptnacional.org.br/index.php/component/jdownloads/category/3-caderno conflitos?Itemid=-1> [accessed 5 May 2020].
[76] The Brazilian civil service includes, among other cases, positions filled by people approved in public competitions and positions filled by appointment of the government in office, the so-called positions of trust.
[77] See <https://brasil.elpais.com/brasil/2020-02-07/de-trotski-a-marx-o-discurso-ideologico-inflama-os-documentos-oficiais-da-funai-de-bolsonaro.html> [accessed 20 May 2020].
[78] On how the activities of cross-cultural evangelical missions fit into the policies of the Jair Bolsonaro government see Artionka Capiberibe, 'Reaching Souls, Liberating Lands: Cross-cultural Evangelical Missions and Bolsonaro's Government', *Brazilian Political Science Review*, 15.2 (2021), available at <https://brazilianpoliticalsciencereview.org/article/reaching-souls-liberating-lands-cross-cultural-evangelical-missions-and-bolsonaros-government/> [accessed at 11 April 2021].
[79] See the decree at <http://www.planalto.gov.br/ccivil_03/_ato2019-2022/2020/decreto/D10239.htm>.
[80] Capiberibe and Bonilla, 'A ocupação do Congresso'.

which would inaugurate a period of political turmoil that persists to this day. In January 2019, with the campaign '*Indigenous Blood. Not a single drop more*' (cf. footnote 72), they were also the first to speak out against a government that, just a few days into its term, was already trampling on their rights and equipping their executioners.[81] If for some people they seemed hasty, the situation experienced with Covid-19 confirms how correctly they predicted the size of the multidimensional catastrophe that affects them today.

As the violence of the attacks on both legal and administrative fronts increases and their consequences are felt, the indigenous struggle grows as a significant force of opposition, with the party system showing signs of wear. In recent years APIB has ensured legal representation of indigenous peoples, mobilized national campaigns, attended major international artistic events, and systematically monitored the sessions of the UN Permanent Forum on Indigenous Issues, while continuing to organize annual ATL meetings, among other activities. The indigenous movement has become a key actor on the country's political scene. Two facts evidenced this in the 2018 election: Sônia Guajajara, executive coordinator of APIB, ran for vice president for the Socialism and Freedom Party (PSOL), and Joênia Wapichana, an indigenous lawyer active in the Raposa Serra do Sol at the STF, was elected federal deputy for the Rede Sustentabilidade party (REDE).

The Covid-19 pandemic has raged as public policies and democratic institutions break down, leaving the entire country adrift. In this context, indigenous peoples have set an example of collective organization and preparation to withstand the impending cataclysm. Faced with the lack of assistance and a growing death toll, they are coordinating efforts to raise funds, procure and distribute protective equipment and food, and produce information campaigns. The deficient public services are aggravated by the perverse way in which SESAI handles the figures for indigenous victims of the disease. On the one hand, it does not account for cases occurring outside TIs, which increases underreporting, and, on the other, it does not classify deaths by indigenous groups. In view of this situation, APIB regularly publishes its own updated bulletin accounting for all cases, exposing the discrepancy with official figures.[82]

In short, Alvanei Xirixana, the first official indigenous victim of Covid-19, is the symbolic expression of the ethnocide recipe experienced by indigenous peoples for centuries and denounced incessantly by Davi Kopenawa who, observing the increasing intensity of current diseases, warns us, as if heralding what we are now experiencing, that the fate of his people is not dissociated from

---

[81] For a detailed view of the clashes between indigenous peoples and Bolsonaro, exposed during the election campaign, see Oiara Bonilla, 'La Vitalité des mondes possibles face à l'extrême-droite au Brésil' and 'Cataclysm presaged in Indigenous Land', Hot Spots, *Fieldsights*, Society for Cultural Anthropology, Series: Bolsonaro and the unmaking of Brazil, 28 January 2020. Available at <https://culanth.org/fieldsights/cataclysm-presaged-in-indigenous-lands> [accessed at 20 May 2020].

[82] Available at <http://quarentenaindigena.info/casos-indigenas/> [accessed 5 May 2020].

ours: 'There is only one and the same sky above us. There is only one sun, only one moon. We live on the same land'.[83]

This seems to be what motivates them to insist that we, non-indigenous people, realize that the earth does not exist to serve a humanity that, as Krenak explains, 'excludes all others and all other beings'. This is an awareness that can reverse the process of self-destruction in which we are engaged or, as Krenak proposes, 'postpone the end of the world'.[84]

---

[83] Kopenawa and Albert, *A queda do céu*, p. 231.
[84] Krenak, *Ideias para adiar o fim do mundo*, p. 47.

Reviews

FILOMENA SERRA (text) and FERNANDO LEMOS (photographs), *The more I desire / Quanto mais desejo*, series *Ph*, vol. 4: *Fernando Lemos* (Lisbon: Imprensa Nacional–Casa da Moeda, 2019). 136 pages. Print. Bilingual text, English and Portuguese.

Reviewed by BERNARDO PINTO DE ALMEIDA (Faculdade de Belas Artes da Universidade do Porto)

Few Portuguese artists have experienced a personal and geographic destiny as particular and erratic as that of Fernando Lemos (1926–2019), even if others, who came later, were also travellers discovering the world. Born in Lisbon, Lemos left Portugal for Brazil in 1952, having already published his first book of poems, *Teclado Universal* [Universal Keyboard]. Frustrated by Salazarism and its misery, he built a new career in this Lusophone country, where he would later be naturalized. He is part of the cultural history of both lands, not only because of his strong attachment to them, but also because of certain acts and various kinds of recognition. As he himself once stated, 'I am yet another Portuguese looking for something better'.

This intelligent, cultured and self-made man started in Portugal as a kind of jack-of-all-trades (locksmith and upholsterer; lithograph and graphic printer) that helped sustain him, and his restless talent that could not earn him a living at the time. This was before he committed himself to photography and moved towards the surrealists — the few still active — and later, in Brazil, tried his hand as a museum director, journalist, curator, competition judge and teacher, besides being an artist. He found some recognition both as a fair and set designer, as well as a photographer and even a painter.

This adventurous life made Lemos an exemplary Portuguese: an adventurer never satisfied with his lot. It also made him a daring man who adapted, wisely and good naturedly, to every circumstance, without making it a major problem or drama. Involved in so many activities and with so many desires arousing his curiosity, Lemos was able, once in Brazil, to meet other illustrious Portuguese who saw his multi-moded talent early on, and opened doors for him knowing he would never disappoint. That was how, six years after arriving there, the eminent historian Jaime Cortesão, who was preparing the Fourth Centenary Commemorations of the Foundation of São Paulo, invited him to participate and enabled Lemos to establish himself as a painter. Photography, however, had already gained him recognition in Portugal from the artistic and critical milieu. His lifelong friend, the critic and, later, historian José-Augusto França, for instance, had supported him from an early age. In Brazil, it would again bring him some attention; in particular, from the poet Manuel Bandeira, who was immediately surprised by 'the intense atmosphere of mystery, with its, one would say, fluorescent contours'.

It was also in Brazil, in the '50s, that Lemos met the poet Hilda Hilst, who was linked to the Brazilian avant-garde. Their intense year-long romance inspired one of his most beautiful series of photographs, which drew praise from René Girard and other critics and intellectuals, forming a bond between Lemos and the Brazilian intellectual milieu that lasted until the end of his days. This adventurous life, always shared between art and photography, in addition to the diverse other crafts that helped him survive, now with renewed dignity on a par with his culture and intelligence, would occupy the artist throughout the many years in which poetry continued to call him. His art was diversified into a multiplicity that suited his temperament, restless until the end, and always coherent, with a sense of experimentation (and remarkable humour) in its daring creativity.

Recognition, however, came late in Portugal, where he remained forever remembered, and deservedly so, for his significant role in the brief shining moment of the Portuguese surrealist movement, in which his career had begun with particular originality.[1] These images today are part of the history of this short but intensely lived movement, which was original despite arriving late on the scene; and in which Lemos had a prominent place. And so, after participating, in 1979, in an important exhibition *A Fotografia na Arte Moderna Portuguesa* [Photography in Portuguese Modern Art] at the Centro de Arte Contemporânea [Contemporary Art Centre], in Porto, he would be seen again in the exhibition, *Portugal, Anos Quarenta* [Portugal, the '40s] (SNBA, Lisbon). He was then invited to hold a broad retrospective at the Gulbenkian Foundation's Centre for Modern Art (CAM), organized by its then director, Jorge Molder, who definitely consecrated him as the central name in modern Portuguese photography. This led to international recognition and, shortly after, he began receiving frequent invitations to various major international photographic exhibitions.

It is to the photographer's long journey (with detours through some of his other artistic interests) that Filomena Serra, a researcher and art historian with an outstanding body of published work, recently dedicated (2019) an exhaustive essay in a new collection (Ph) dedicated to Portuguese photography, and published by the Imprensa Nacional–Casa da Moeda. In a bilingual publication

---

[1] As I wrote a few years ago, highlighting his unique place in Portuguese Surrealism, in the catalogue for the major exhibition, *Fernando Lemos e o Surrealismo* (2005), curated by Maria Nobre Franco, at the Sintra-Museu de Arte Contemporânea — Colecção Berardo: 'In fact, even if some artists have set themselves at the height of European plastic and expressive invention — and, inevitably, I will always highlight, the similarly exceptional cases of António Dacosta and Mário Cesariny — the majority of those who designed the surrealist cycle in Portuguese art, and have left indelible marks, [...] did not go beyond, that, its spirit and intentions, its enormous ethical and aesthetic significance; they did not go beyond a plan that put them at the level of merely continuing what had been done, or was still being done, in the European art that claimed to be under that banner.'

with painstaking graphic presentation, this essay, whose title, *Quanto mais desejo* [*The more I desire*], is a clear allusion to a line in a poem by Fernando Lemos, follows the trajectory of the artist and photographer's long career, with particular attention to his web of relationships with artists and intellectuals of his time. It also highlights a friendly and complicit voice: one that was able, over several years, to listen to that of the artist himself, which was often felt throughout his flowing writing.

More than a cold, analytical and detached study, Filomena Serra's text focuses only on the strict interpretation of the work. It is, in its seductive, agile construction, a living testimony, rich in details, of many other aspects, both creative and biographical, of this artist who, today, is part of the most important body of twentieth-century Portuguese artists. The reader is drawn into Fernando Lemos's long and restless journey, with Serra's fascinating text never losing its historical rigour.

Lemos is followed closely, in thought and even in humour, with defining moments or intentions underlying the work, highlighted through exactly the right quotation. In partnership with Cláudio Garrudo, the collection's director, Filomena Serra has also carefully selected images spanning several decades, which are beautifully reproduced here. Serra's book continues her in-depth historiographic approach to Lemos's long career — already the subject of a previous study by Margarida Acciaiuoli in 2005[2] — and is an important contribution to the better understanding of an artist who, despite being highly revered and cited on the cultural level, has yet to receive the greater public attention he clearly deserves: a situation that this new publication will certainly help to correct, as is only right.

ROBERT PATRICK NEWCOMB, *Iberianism and Crisis: Spain and Portugal at the Turn of the Twentieth Century* (Toronto: University of Toronto Press, 2018). 244 pages. Print and ebook.

ROBERT PATRICK NEWCOMB and RICHARD A. GORDON, eds, *Beyond Tordesillas: New Approaches to Comparative Luso-Hispanic Studies* (Columbus: Ohio University Press 2017). 261 pages. Print and ebook.

Reviewed by MANUEL VILLAVERDE CABRAL (Universidade de Lisboa)

These two books, by Robert Patrick Newcomb alone, and with his colleague Richard A. Gordon, raise a decisive question, at least to a Portuguese-speaking reader and especially one such as myself used to looking at Latin America from Portugal. If Brazil exists today basically as it stood geographically and linguistically upon independence from Portugal in September 1822, it is because of Tordesillas, i.e. the 1494 treaty signed between the crowns of Spain and Portugal in the Spanish city of Tordesillas on 2nd July of that year.

---

[2] Margarida Acciaiuoli, *Fernando Lemos: Desenho e Desígnio* (Lisbon: Caminho, 2005).

Indeed, according to the Portuguese historian Jaime Cortesão,[3] the reason why the Portuguese crown pushed so far to the west the meridian dividing what would become known as Latin America between Spain and Portugal was because it already knew of the 'Brazilian' lands, only officially discovered in 1500... True or not, this 'policy of secrecy' not only succeeded, but echoed down the ages: it was not by accident that no university was created in Brazil before independence and that the first press was only allowed into Brazil after the Portuguese royal family moved there in 1808, while most Brazilian politicians and high administrators were trained in the Portuguese university of Coimbra until long after independence: this, essentially, was how the unity of the country was maintained, according to the Brazilian historian, Murilo de Carvalho![4]

Exchanges between Brazilian writers and artists and those from other Latin American countries are nowadays possibly as frequent and perhaps more influential than specific cultural contacts with Portugal or even Spain. Nevertheless, it seems unlikely to me that many Portuguese intellectuals will wholeheartedly agree with the replacement of Portuguese- and Spanish-language university departments by a single branch of Luso-Hispanic studies, let alone 'Hispanic studies' *tout court*. The financial and organizational reasons put forward in the US for moving in such a direction appear to me understandable but insufficient to counterbalance the risk of obscuring the cultural specificity of both Spanish- and Portuguese-speaking geographical areas on both sides of the Atlantic. In other words, at least from the European viewpoint, I believe that going beyond Tordesillas is a difficult proposition.

Along with Professor Joan Ramon Resina of the University of Stanford, the author of *Iberianism and Crisis*, R. P. Newcomb of the University of California, Davis, is one of the main figures theorizing North American universities' current movement away from 'Hispanism' or 'Luso-Hispanic Studies' towards 'Iberian Studies' as a comparative approach to literary and wider cultural activities covering the whole range of countries speaking Spanish, Portuguese, Catalan, Galician and possibly other idioms of Iberian or Latin-American origin, not excluding African countries where Spanish and Portuguese are official languages and other regions where these languages are spoken. Newcomb approaches this 'ongoing debate', to use his words, in the conclusion of *Iberianism and Crisis*, after several chapters comparing Spanish and Portuguese authors who at different historical moments examined the crises at the turn of the twentieth century, driven by colonial defeats suffered by Spain and Portugal in order to ponder which dimension — 'peninsular' or 'national' — ultimately prevailed in each country and their remaining colonies.

In my understanding, Newcomb identifies a broadly common situation affecting Spain and Portugal, both then and at other historical occasions,

---

[3] J. Cortesão, *A Política de Sigilo nos Descobrimentos nos Tempos do Infante D. Henrique e de D. João II* (Lisbon: IN-CM, 1997).
[4] J. M. de Carvalho, *A construção da ordem: a elite política imperial* (Rio de Janeiro: Campus, 1980).

irrespective of their centuries-long independent status and that of their colonies, namely in Africa and Latin America, though the author is definitely less concerned with the so-called Spanish and Portuguese 'colonial empires' than with the 'ethnic Iberian groups' speaking different languages in 'Iberia' or 'Hispania'. He discerns a predicament common to Spain and Portugal in the 1890s when he compares the inability of both countries to resist the political and territorial pressures placed respectively by the United States and Britain on segments of their colonies.

Newcomb does not mention in this context the inauguration of the Republic in Brazil (1889) and he is right not to do so, although it had an enormous financial impact on Portugal. This event was only of economic concern, as opposed to the serious political repercussions of Britain's ultimatum (1890) regarding the African territories, which was indeed equivalent to the US interventions in former Spanish colonies (1898 and 1899). Thus, his approach to both 'crises' is more concerned with the political effects they had ten years apart in Portugal and Spain than with the crises of confidence in both countries and the supposed impact on relations between them. In fact, they ultimately had none outside the intellectual elites, despite a wave of Catalan separatism due to the weakening of the central Spanish government.

Much more serious were the frequent criticisms voiced by Spanish authors concerned not just with political relations between Spain and Portugal, but indeed with the alleged 'ethnic ties' between the peoples of 'Hispania', authors such as Unamuno, Maragall and Madariaga, none of whom, oddly enough, were Castilians. Drawing on two key Portuguese writers, namely Antero de Quental and Oliveira Martins, both of whom belonged to the critical Generation of 1870 and were highly critical of Portuguese parliamentarianism in that period, the author of *Iberianism and Crisis* — a title that refers to a very specific moment — has shown that, as had already occurred at the beginning of the nineteenth century under the pressure of the Napoleonic Wars and later during the Republican movements across Europe in the late 1860s and early 1870s, Liberal and Socialist Portuguese intellectuals were attracted by events and ideas coming from Spain.

With the early exception of Henriques Nogueira (1823–1858) quoted by our author, Portuguese federalism was a rather short-lived affair and only reappeared momentarily under the banner of Anarchism during the Spanish Civil War; on the other hand, all the Spanish pro-federalists mentioned by Newcomb tended to think that Portugal should join an 'Iberian Federation' instead of surrendering political independence to its long-term British ally (an alliance going back perhaps to the seizure of Lisbon from the 'Arabs' in 1147). The pros and cons of such a trade-off have been a topic of discussion in Portugal ever since, though perhaps Britain's recent decision to exit the European Union has brought it to a conclusion. Today, most left-wing intellectuals in Portugal support Catalonia's current call for independence from the Spanish state in order — one supposes — to weaken the Spanish central government! It seems to me that the true relationship between Portugal and Spain is more a matter of geography than 'ethnicity'. 'Portugal is Europe's visage facing the Ocean', as Fernando Pessoa once wrote, and the approach of the historian Jaime Cortesão about the role of maritime factors in the country's formation remain of interest.[5]

Whatever the undeniable burden of Portuguese dependence on Britain until very recently, the country's engagement in Atlantic exploration and the colonization of large tracts of land in Africa, India and America, including the transportation of African slaves to Brazil over several centuries, led to a model of colonization quite different from the Spanish ways of dealing with similar processes, especially in today's Latin America. In particular, indigenous civilizations such as the Aztecs, Mayas and Incas were entirely different from the indigenous populations in Brazil and North America. In reality, there was no more an overarching unity of [Iberian] civilization before the so-called Discoveries and the Age of Colonization than afterwards, either in geographic, demographic, linguistic or cultural terms. All in all, dependence on Britain and Portuguese models of colonization seem to have been much more important factors than any 'Iberian roots' that would have suited the predominance of Castile over Portugal.

* * * * *

In a slightly earlier book edited by Robert Patrick Newcomb and his colleague Richard A. Gordon entitled *Beyond Tordesillas* (2017), the notion of 'Iberian Studies' had already been assayed in a number of comparative essays on cultural forms of expression in various countries speaking the so-called 'Iberian' languages. In their introduction to the volume, the editors describe their general intention as 'Against Luso-Hispanic Disjunction: Correcting the scholarly record', or in other words, in defence of the same programme I criticized earlier, of going as it were 'Beyond Tordesillas'. Nevertheless, the volume contains excellent comparative studies on works and cultural activities carried out at similar periods in the languages initiated in the Iberian Peninsula and later spread through Latin America, namely Portuguese in Brazil and Spanish in the other countries of the region.

In the case of this collection of essays, one realizes that, depending on the countries involved and the periods under study, there were obviously a lot more meaningful intellectual and even linguistic comparisons to be made than featured in the debates between *fin-de-siècle* Spanish and Portuguese authors about 'Iberian culture' and the political union of Spain and Portugal. Simultaneously, according to the specific moment compared as well as the countries and languages involved, one realizes that the convergence between

[5] Jaime Cortesão, 'Os Factores Democráticos na Formação de Portugal', introduction to *História do Regímen Republicano em Portugal*, ed. by Luís de Montalvor, 2 vols (Lisbon: Ática, 1930).

the languages concerned is much meaningful than among different countries at other periods. In other words, for the reasons I outlined earlier, there seems to be times and countries more amenable than others to a meaningful 'Iberian approach'.

As I mentioned at the outset, it seems likely that — depending on languages, countries, themes and given moments in time — Latin American studies has converged due to the impact of globalization over the past half-century, especially in fields such as music, cinema and visual culture. However, a comparative approach taking in Spain, including its 'linguistic nations', Hispanophone America, and Portugal, as well as Brazil and Portuguese-speaking African countries, may be at many moments quite misleading, especially when national governments get involved in political, economic and cultural matters, as happens when the political associations of Portuguese- and Spanish-speaking countries step in, as they do so often. A very ambiguous example mentioned in Newcomb's single-authored work is Nobel Prize winner José Saramago's *The Stone Raft* (1986), published just after Spain and Portugal joined the European Union as a piece of party propaganda against the so-called 'Europeanization of the Iberian Peninsula'. So, it remains difficult to surrender entirely to J. R. Resina's aforementioned notion of 'Iberian Studies' as though there has been no clear state demarcations strengthening linguistic ones for so many centuries.

MARCOS FLAMÍNIO PERES, *As minas e a agulheta: romance e história em 'As minas de prata', de José de Alencar* (Belo Horizonte: Editora UFMG, 2015). 124 pages. Print and ebook.

Reviewed by RODRIGO CERQUEIRA (Universidade Federal de São Paulo)

Marcos Flamínio Peres's *As minas e a agulheta* is not only a new and fresh reading of José de Alencar's novel, *As minas de prata*, but also has another merit that soon becomes clear. He seeks to follow up a lead given in João Luiz Lafetá's review of Roberto Schwarz's book on Machado de Assis, *Ao vencedor as batatas*, concerning Schwarz's analytical perspective in his interpretation of *Senhora*.[6] Overly fixated on the paradigm of the realist novel, according to Lafetá, Schwarz ignored the conventions of the romance, which were used by Alencar to write *Senhora*. Although it has a different subject, namely the historical novel, *As minas e a agulheta* is a direct heir to this still barely explored legacy. If we use only Georg Lukács's theoretical perspective, perhaps the most important one on the genre within which Alencar's narrative is to a large extent written, we would be left with the everlasting feeling that the Brazilian novel falls short compared with the European model. Peres, however, avoids this trap. He explores a very specific combination of genres made by Alencar (analogous

---

[6] João Luiz Lafetá, 'Batatas e desejos', in *A dimensão da noite e outros ensaios* (São Paulo: Duas Cidades, Editora 34, 2004), pp. 103–13.

to that highlighted by Lafetá between realism and romance in *Senhora*). The result is a composite, and therefore particular, work, which owes nothing to the model from which it departs.

As minas e a agulheta is a very good example of how recent studies on the novel as a form have reshaped the field. Instead of the old distinction between novel and romance, in which all the prestige accrues to the former, the more serious for its realist pretensions, as identified by Ian Watt and Georg Lukács, what stands out in Peres's reading is a somewhat more complex process. The two concepts of the novel and the romance are not opposed as they were once thought to be; they overlap. With this new understanding, the Brazilian novel, which always depended on many different sources, assumes a new and distinctive place in the field, because here, unlike in Europe, we lacked a tradition that limited the development of the genres. Hence, this persistence of the old, of the romance, is no longer a mark of our backwardness; it is rather a structuring feature of the novel itself.

It is worth mentioning other aspects of Marcos Flamínio Peres's book. The 'Introduction' and the 'Conclusion' have a more theoretical approach, to which I will return at the end of this review. Two chapters in particular are dedicated to a more rigorous reading of the novel. In the second chapter, 'A lei e a espada', Peres painstakingly presents the tense relationship between the historiography of our colonial past, which was appearing in the pages of the *Revista do IHGB*, and its fictional use by Alencar. Let's take the description of Salvador, that opens the novel, as an example. The city that emerges from the narrative is not the centre of the colony's 'administration, finance and judiciary', divided between the upper and lower city, as described by travellers and historians. Modified by Alencar's fictional gaze, the city is swept away from its 'historical contingencies' (p. 37), which does not mean a naïve detachment from reality. His description uses elements from an 'imaginário cortês' (p. 36), that is not new in itself. Yet, this 'unrealistic' approach, so to speak, is based on a certain interpretation of Brazil's historical reality. The fact that the city is situated between the sea and the backlands puts it in a position to symbolize an important issue lying at the heart of Empire: the relationship between civilization, Europe beyond the sea, and the wildness of a country that is yet to be built. This same type of procedure is replicated several times, such as the deformation of a historical festivity ('cavalhada') in order to account for the conflict between the State and the Society of Jesus. However, the key to this chapter lies beyond these comparisons. Peres tries to demonstrate that 'essa opção pela força da imaginação em Alencar — algo que poderia ser considerado um retrocesso ou um passadismo no momento em que o romance europeu começava a se avizinhar do realismo — não exclui, antes reforça, a capacidade de síntese do momento histórico' [the preference in Alencar's writing for the power of imagination — something which could be considered regressive or unfashionable at a time when the European novel was approaching Realism

— does not exclude, but rather reinforces, the capacity for synthesis of this historical moment] (p. 34). In other words, what Peres highlights is Alencar's fidelity to the nation, which is greater than his fidelity to literary conventions, that is, fidelity to the presuppositions of the genres he was using. And instead of yielding to that old feeling of inferiority, according to which the national writer would not be capable of correctly using the imported genre, it is worth mentioning that for Peres this must be understood differently: Alencar knew perfectly well that if he had committed to the individualistic dimension of the adventure novel ('romance de capa e espada'), the nation-building project, with which he was imbued, would lose its prominence. It is important to emphasize here how much this represents an important reassessment of Alencar's political and literary capacities.

In the third chapter, 'O capítulo enxertado', Peres shows how Father Molina, one of the most important characters in the novel, changes between the first and the definitive version of the book. In the first, whose initial chapters appeared in Coleção Biblioteca Brasileira, conceived by Quintino Bocaiúva, Father Molina was an important secondary character, but without the investment he would later have. When the novel reaches its final version, three years later, five new chapters have been inserted, with the function of deepening this character's origins. Peres's reading shows how this change modifies the structure of the novel, which then abandons its 'busca do factual, cujo horizonte é a verdade histórica [...] para a validação do romanesco como verdade *possível*' [search for the factual, whose horizon is historical truth [...] in favour of the validation of the novelistic as *possible* truth] (p. 65).

And with the appearance of Father Molina, we return to the central question of *As minas e a agulheta*, which, besides its innovative reading of *As minas de prata*, has a theoretical framework worth exploring further. The capacity of Alencar to sew together different genres in the same narrative structure is at first, according to a more orthodox conception of literature, bound to fail. The historical novel and the *feuilleton* do not mix. Ingeniously, Peres notes that, in the chapters inserted between the first and the final version of the novel, there is one of special interest, 'Da malga que se bebia na taberna do judengo', in which the reprise of the trope of the Wandering Jew, common in the *feuilleton*, opens new political and spatial dimensions within the historical novel genre. Counter-intuitively, the political and economic dimensions of world history are emphasized in Alencar, since the plans of the Dutch West India Company have a narrative function, something that does not happen in the European model. With regard to the spatial dimension of the narrative, Alencar's novel, like those of its counterparts Alexandre Dumas's *Three Musketeers*, and Eugène Sue's *The Wandering Jew*, explores other countries. However, and here is the key point of Peres's reading, unlike those, which remain attached to the picturesque, without major contributions to the plot, 'em Alencar, tal deslocamento responde a uma dinâmica político-histórica legítima, que exerce função significativa para o entrecho do romance' [in Alencar, such a displacement responds to a legitimate political and historical dynamic, which exercises a significant function in the plot of the novel] (p. 66). This theoretical insight is full of implications, because it reverses the direction of dependency: it is the fact of being a copy, i.e. not limited by genre boundaries, that brings forth the qualitative leap of the peripheral novel. In other words, by misappropriating the European literary repertoire, Alencar takes the lead in a race that otherwise he would always lose.

In short, the structure of Alencar's novel is constructed in a very particular way, because it does not adhere to either of the two great literary genres at his disposal, the historical novel and the *feuilleton*. This is the cornerstone the argument, because for Peres the result is far from being absurd:

> o narrador de *As minas de prata* não abre mão das possibilidades totalizantes que lhe oferecem os gêneros-matrizes com que trabalha — o Romance e a História. Além disso, não deixa de lançar mão das fissuras que a ênfase folhetinesca na fragmentação inflige nesses dois amplos edifícios discursivos, num esforço para mimetiza a matéria histórica difusa e volátil de que trata.

> [The narrator of *As minas de prata* does not let go of the all-encompassing possibilities offered to him by the genres he is working with — the Novel and History. Furthermore, he reaches for those interstices that the emphasis on the feuilleton imposes upon those two ample discursive edifices, in an effort to represent the historical subject matter that he is drawing on, which is diffuse and versatile.] (p. 98)

The combination, which for purists may seem odd, would rather be something to praise, because it ends up formalizing a particular dimension of Brazilian reality — its loose, solvent social structure, to use the words of Capistrano de Abreu quoted by the author himself — that cannot be captured by the Realistic novel, since our historical background is a different one.

If I am not entirely mistaken, the theoretical scope of the book is the already mentioned criticism of Schwarz by Lafetá,[7] that the former did not take into account the genre chosen by Alencar (or rather, developed by Alencar, since he ends up mixing a couple of them). Lafetá's criticism is valid and should be developed in all its potentiality, of which the book by Peres is a good example. However, it is worth asking one question: by departing from Schwarz's theoretical perspective as he does, does Peres not miss a more critical dimension of importing the novel to Brazil? In *As minas e a agulheta*, the historical specificity of Alencar's work is the nation, which leads him to use, without any inferiority complex, the prestigious genres of Europe, although not according to their own logic, but as a way to fulfil his commitment to his own endeavour. Is there not a contradiction in this very same process? Thus, the class-ridden, authoritarian, and slave-owning features of the consolidating nation, emphasized by Schwarz, are left aside, leaving only the somewhat positive and

---

[7] See also Lafetá's 'Imagens do desejo', in the same volume as previously, pp. 423–31.

progressive view that we find in Antonio Candido's *Formação da literatura brasileira*, an important but historically outdated study, since it responded to the yearning to overcoming the national backwardness that characterized the democratic interregnum in which it was written (1945 to 1959). The Schwarzian perspective, post-1964, with all its problems, is a criticism made from the point of view of the dissolution of that hope. Thus, the question remains: what does it mean — in 2015, the year *As minas e a agulheta* was published — to argue for the originality of this peripheral writer, who, aligned with a national-building project (one that we must not forget was aristocratic and slave-owning) was capable of using, without guilt or reverence, in a very particular way, all that the contact with the European literary repertoire put at his disposal?

More than four decades after the release of *Ao vencedor as batatas*, where we can find the aforementioned essay on Alencar, a critique of Schwarz's perspective is still necessary. New research has opened up fresh possibilities for rethinking the relationship between literary genres and the social reality of a peripheral country. But it is also important not to lose sight of Schwarz's critical insights, especially in a historical period in which the national elite, always imbued with its 'constructive' effort, is showing its true colours.

VINCENZO RUSSO, *La Resistenza continua: il colonialismo portoghese, le lotte di liberazione e gli intellettuali italiani* (Milan: Meltemi editore, 2020). 190 pages. Print and ebook.

Reviewed by NICOLA GAVIOLI (Florida International University)

The second volume of the series *Pensiero Atlantico* [Atlantic Thought] curated by Roberto Vecchi and Vincenzo Russo, *La Resistenza continua* is a clear and well-documented study of the international dimension of the debates originated by the fight for independence within African colonies under Portuguese domination. Special emphasis is given to the role that Italy and the Vatican played on the geopolitical stage in the struggles for liberation. A historical introduction, three chapters, and a final section with selected iconographic and written documents, structure the volume. In a 'methodological note' (pp. 28–29), Russo explains how the project was carried out as an attempt to shed light on 'aspetti marginali o dimenticati' [marginal or forgotten aspects] of cultural history, following Said's lesson in 'contrapuntal reading' (p. 29). Eduardo Lourenço's attempts to contrast the various forms of 'silence' throughout colonial history and its representation also comes to mind as an immediate reference (on 'silence' in Lourenço, see the introduction, co-written by the two curators of the series, to the first volume *Del colonialismo come impensato: il caso del Portogallo* by Eduardo Lourenço). Following the numerous paths that anticolonialist discourse took in Italy, Russo reconstitutes an as-of-yet unexplored cultural landscape. Readers get to know the 'heterogeneous constellation of movements' (p. 12) and organizations born in Italy in which

African anticolonialist theories and acts of resistance were followed, discussed, and admired. We are made aware of the synergetic bond established between African leaders, thinkers, and poets and their Italian cultural mediators. Russo re-evokes a period in history (the 1960s and '70s specifically) in which an emotional and pragmatic political participation was second nature for many Italian activists. The atmosphere in those years — the meetings, the rush to exchange information, the collective sensation of participating in historical revolutionary changes — is strongly depicted in the book; the nostalgia for a more participative society ('ciò che eravamo come italiani' [what we were as Italians], p. 140) is also widespread within the pages of the volume.

Clearly and vividly written, *La Resistenza continua* is rigorous in the analysis of its sources and epistemologically ambitious in gathering the vast array of voices and counter-voices within the Italian anticolonial debate during the '60s and '70s. Dismantling commonplaces is also a strong quality of the volume. The author clarifies the fallacy of a binary association that often became commonplace: antifascist and anticolonial thought did not necessarily overlap. No 'blocco monolitico' [monolithic block] (p. 21) of Italian anticolonialism or general 'epistemological' convergence (p. 21) among participants really existed. Russo explains the reasons for this difference and asks readers to think outside the boxes of overgeneralized and undifferentiated categories.

In Chapter 1, the fascinating figures of Giovanni Pirelli and Joyce Lussu — key cultural agents of numerous material and symbolic exchanges between African and Italian activists — are presented through selected paradigmatic episodes of their intellectual and emotional *Bildung*. But even if some biographical digressions are vivid and memorable, the book is far from being anecdotal. Each personal 'snapshot' serves to recreate the history and the atmosphere of a time in which engagement and cross-fecundation of ideas were widespread. From belligerent zones of Africa, a corpus of theoretical and poetic writings and speeches (by Agostinho Neto, José Craveirinha and Amílcar Cabral, among others) reached Italian circles and organizations through the intermediary work of Giovanni Pirelli and Joyce Lussu; the latter is of particular interest for her belief in the political act of translation (which she defined 'eticopoliticopoetica,' p. 73). In Chapter 2, Russo describes the activities of the Centro Franz Fanon and the holding of the 'Treviglio Seminar' (1964) as turning points for the growth of an Italian anti-imperial and anticolonial consciousness. The critical words of Amílcar Cabral are put centre-stage in this chapter as reminders of the ambiguities of Italy. While supporters of the anticolonial cause were numerous in the country, the Italian government continued to provide Portugal with weapons to be deployed in the so-called African 'overseas territories'. Chapter 3 offers the most memorable and surprising section in the book, in its chronicling of a true *coup de théâtre*: the encounter of the African leaders Agostinho Neto, Amílcar Cabral, and Marcelino dos Santos with Pope Paul VI on 1 July 1970. The event, which took place at the Vatican in the guise of a private audience, surprised the international community, scandalized the Portuguese government and its Catholic authorities, and was interpreted as a symbolic gesture in favour of the African freedom fighters. What was the significance of this event? How did it happen? How did the media portray it? Russo contextualizes the facts, registers public reactions, antagonisms, and nuances of interpretation, and shows hermeneutical dispute at work over a short, unprecedented event. The attention to prismatic and contradictory readings of the same event makes this volume particularly timely and resonant with our contemporary cultural climate. The volume ends with the transcription of a pressing Q&A with journalists given by Amílcar Cabral and Marcelino dos Santos the day after their meeting with the Pope in the Vatican.

For clarity of style, rich historiographical research, and narrative precision, *La Resistenza continua* stands out as a fresh and significant contribution to Lusophone cultural history and its refractions beyond Portugal and its African colonies. A translation of the volume into Portuguese and other languages is therefore desirable to foster its international reception and its inclusion in the bibliography of colonial and postcolonial studies.

PATRÍCIA I. VIEIRA, *States of Grace: Utopia in Brazilian Culture* (Albany: State University of New York, 2018). xix + 214 pages. Print and ebook.

Reviewed by ALESSANDRA SANTOS (University of British Columbia)

Utopia is a complex word which, in the Western tradition, is attributed to Thomas More's homonymous satirical novel published in England in 1516. Since then, the term has been transformed, and has been used innumerable times to signify a variety of meanings to multiple people, in multiple contexts. As a literary genre and as a social theory, utopia has developed globally, usually to portray and discuss ideal communities. As a concept, utopia has been associated with the desire for equality, and with a positive impulse of hope, which would allow for concrete social change (Ernest Bloch). Ruth Levitas defined it simply as 'dreams of a better life'. *States of Grace* links utopia to a specific nation and proposes a new reading of the concept, thus contributing to the ongoing discussion of utopia as a contextually based notion.

Patrícia Vieira suggests that the 'utopian drive is particularly salient in the case of Brazil' (p. x). The author proposes that Brazil's unique historical position, during and after Portuguese colonization, offered an idealized potential manifest in her culture. Utopia is defined as being related to 'three distinct domains, namely utopian thought, utopian literature [...] and practical attempts to found better societies' (p. xiii). The goals of the book are to examine 'key moments in the development of utopia in Brazil' (p. xiii), and 'to trace the evolution of utopian thought as it has been configured in Brazil, rather than analyzing specific literary portrayals of fictional utopias set on Brazilian soil or concrete attempts to found perfect communities in the area' (p. xiii).

The author claims to 'espouse a broad understanding of utopian thought' (p. xiii), and connects utopia to a 'state of grace'. This state, as mentioned in the book's introduction, 'understood not only as a fleeting condition but also as a political configuration, is therefore transformed by grace, which allows us to imagine a better sociopolitical arrangement' (p. xv). The author acknowledges that 'state of grace evokes [...] a theological paradigm', but claims 'that utopias have inherited and secularized some of these religious undertones' (p. xv). In order to identify the state of grace as utopian thought in Brazil, the author has chosen specific case studies which allude to 'a view of Brazil as a sociopolitical alternative to the ruling global order' (p. 155).

In addition to a brief introduction and an epilogue, the book is divided into four chapters. The first chapter, 'The Theologico-Political Utopia of Father Antônio Vieira', examines the writings of the Jesuit priest Antônio Vieira (1608–1697). Vieira was born in Portugal and lived in Brazil, moving to the northern region of the country to work as a missionary. Vieira is portrayed as a defender of the indigenous populations, and as someone who developed a prophecy called 'the Fifth Empire,' which attributes a messianic role to Portugal. This chapter discusses Vieira's ideas as a sign of a shift in perspective, whereby 'the world looks radically different when viewed from the Americas, as opposed to Europe' (p. 28). The chapter provides close readings of passages, while examining Vieira's utopian messianic propositions. The author also claims that 'Vieira's vision of a just, felicitous, and peaceful realm will resonate throughout Brazil's subsequent utopian thought' (p. 29).

The second chapter, 'Amazons in the Amazon: Communitarian Matriarchy in the Jungle', concerns narratives that draw on particular myths of the Amazonian region, specifically matriarchy and the naming of the region after mythological Greek women warriors. The chapter introduces literature pertaining to the Amazon, and works that 'feminize' the region. The main textual analyses in the chapter include three works: Gastão Cruls's novel *A Amazônia misteriosa* (1925), Abguar Bastos's novel *Terra de Icamiaba: romance da Amazônia* (1934), and Oswald de Andrade's *Manifesto antropófago* (1928). The chapter examines how the first novel, inspired by H. G. Wells, sets a 'jungle utopia in a matriarchal tribe composed only of women', 'adhering to a series of stereotypes about gender while, at the same time, reconfiguring the usual valuation of these characteristics' (p. 49). The second novel presents a nationalistic story which 'links the Amazons to a utopia that stands in contrast to the rest of Brazilian society' (p. 53). Finally, Oswald de Andrade's manifesto is discussed in relation to matriarchy and primitivism. Mário de Andrade's novel *Macunaíma* (1928) is also mentioned. The chapter combines an unusual set of works, particularly in the study of jingoist nationalist literature paired with Andrade's manifesto, which, in addition, is not normally studied as literature of the Amazon. Oswald de Andrade's anti-messianic thought is examined as a creative counterpoint to a state of grace.

The third chapter, 'Zoophytographia: Interspecies Literature and the Writings of Clarice Lispector', examines links between literature and nature. The goal of the chapter is to 'analyze the work of Brazilian authors whose encounter with other living beings has been at the core of their texts' (p. 69). The author coins the term that titles the chapter, explaining: 'I define the imbrication of plants and animals in literature as *zoophytographia*, or interspecies writing' (p. 70). The chapter offers analyses of texts by authors Guimarães Rosa and Clarice Lispector, with a theoretical framework based on anthropologist Eduardo Viveiros de Castro's ideas of perspectivism. The chapter approaches utopia as 'coexistence among human and nonhuman lives' (p. 73). The proposed approach is innovative, offering a well-researched contribution to the field of animal and plant studies in the Humanities.

The fourth chapter, 'Idling in the Tropics: Utopias of Leisure', discusses texts in which a leisurely society is presented as utopian. The chapter examines several authors, such as the historian Sérgio Buarque de Holanda, modernist writers Mário de Andrade and Oswald de Andrade, as well as the literary critic Antonio Cândido. The author elaborates on notions of leisure, particularly in relation to the Brazilian urban folk-trickster figure of the *malandro*, and to carnival. The main theoretical argument addresses Giorgio Agamben and Herbert Marcuse. The chapter offers a productive discussion of leisure as utopia, navigating a variety of ideas partly based on main archetypes and stereotypes of Brazil.

The book concludes with an epilogue in which the author reviews the multiple perspectives proposed as utopian thought in Brazil. The linking of utopia with states of grace, and the proposition that a state of grace may be political, are curious and inquisitive. Overall, *States of Grace* offers an erudite collection of essays, and discusses works that would not normally be examined together in Brazilianist literary and cultural criticism. The book is an ambitious effort to identify certain utopian moments in Brazilian literature, and it will be of interest to those in the fields of Brazilian Studies and Latin American Studies, and to anyone interested in utopias.

Abstracts

Overcoming the Legacy of the Military Dictatorship through the National Truth Commission in Brazil: An Ongoing Debate
JANAÍNA DE ALMEIDA TELES

ABSTRACT. Over thirty years into the (re)democratization process, significant gaps can be observed between Brazil's past and present. Although the political transition has brought about some changes, it occurred under the tutelage of the army, meaning that there was no visible break with the past, which, in turn, has made it difficult for the country to establish deep and long-lasting transformations, as well as to face the legacy of dictatorship. The crimes committed by the dictatorial State, such as torture, murder, and forced disappearance, among other violations of human rights, remain unresolved. This study aims at tracing an outline of the creation process of the Brazilian Truth Commission (2012–14), and to accompany its course as it unfolded. In addition, we seek to develop a balance sheet regarding the contradictory National Truth Commission report, so as to contribute with analyses on its repercussions and how it relates to the current political setbacks. To this end, this text has taken advantage of unpublished or virtually unexplored documents and a comprehensive review of the existing bibliography on the subject, in order to present a critical balance of the National Truth Commission's operation and the report it resulted in.

KEYWORDS. Military dictatorship, repressive apparatus, memory, human rights, National Truth Commission.

RESUMO. Transcorridos mais de trinta anos desde a (re)democratização no Brasil, observam-se importantes lacunas nas articulações entre o passado e o presente, no que tange ao legado da ditadura militar. A transição política tutelada possibilitou algumas mudanças, mas sem ruturas aparentes, foi insuficiente para estabelecer transformações amplas e duradouras, adiando o enfrentamento do legado da ditadura. Os crimes cometidos pelo Estado ditatorial, tais como a tortura, os assassinatos e desaparecimentos forçados, entre outras graves violações de direitos humanos, permanecem sem resolução. Este estudo pretende delinear o processo de criação da Comissão Nacional da Verdade (2012–14), seus desdobramentos, bem como estabelecer um balanço acerca do relatório da CNV, a fim de contribuir com as análises sobre suas repercussões e os retrocessos políticos da atualidade. Para tanto, este texto beneficiou-se de documentos inéditos ou pouco explorados e de uma revisão da bibliografia existente sobre o assunto, a fim de apresentar um balanço crítico sobre a atuação da CNV e seu relatório.

PALAVRAS-CHAVE. Ditadura militar, aparato repressivo, memória, direitos humanos, Comissão Nacional da Verdade.

Challenges to Democracy in the Twenty-first Century: The Current Situation of Brazil — New Variations of the Same Dilemmas
EDUARDO C. B. BITTAR

ABSTRACT. This article discusses the challenges to democracy in the twenty-first century, with emphasis on the situation of Brazil, but within the context of the rise of authoritarian regimes throughout the world. In particular, this article is dedicated to understanding the rise of an extreme right-wing government in Brazil, in the 2018 elections, and its consequences for Brazilian democracy, still young and fragile. Throughout this text, these consequences are analysed historically, economically, politically and socially, in the knowledge that they pose more challenges for the consolidation of Brazilian democracy. In a context of incomplete modernity, the country is living with an excessive number of evils that prevent it from entering a cycle of maturation of its institutions and democracy.

KEYWORDS. Democracy, authoritarian regimes, Brazilian democracy, incomplete modernity.

RESUMO. Este artigo discute os desafios da democracia no século XXI, com ênfase na situação do Brasil, no contexto de aparição de regimes autoritários em todo o mundo. Em particular, este artigo se dedica a compreender o surgimento do governo de extrema-direita no Brasil, no ano eleitoral de 2018, e as suas consequências para a democracia brasileira, jovem e fragilizada. Através deste texto, estas consequências são analisadas nas perspetivas histórica, econômica, política e social, sabendo-se que acabam por impor ainda maiores desafios para a consolidação da democracia brasileira. Num contexto de modernidade incompleta, o país está vivendo com um excessivo número de males que acabam por impedi-lo de entrar num ciclo de maturidade de suas instituições e de sua democracia.

PALAVRAS-CHAVE. Democracia, regimes autoritários, democracia brasileira, modernidade incompleta.

Torture: Notes and Perspectives in a Context of Governmental Support for Gross Violations of Human Rights in Brazil
PAULO ENDO

ABSTRACT. This article seeks to examine the possibility of torture being adopted as a government practice in Brazil, from 2019, due to the fact, unprecedented in the country's history, that a candidate widely known to be in favour of torture was elected to the presidency of the Republic. This event poses unparalleled challenges to political research and action in Brazil from 2019 on. I will briefly examine the context of a naturalization of torture in the democratic period in Brazil and some hypotheses about the consequences of this practice in the coming years, considering the Latin American context and the influence of the practices of the French army during the independence process of its former colonies.

KEYWORDS. Torture, democracy, human rights, psychoanalysis.

RESUMO. O artigo procura examinar as possibilidades de adoção da tortura como prática governamental no Brasil a partir de 2019, diante do fato inédito na história do país em que um candidato, sabidamente favorável à prática da tortura, foi eleito à presidência da República. Tal evento político propõe desafios inéditos à pesquisa e à ação políticas no Brasil a partir do início desse governo. Examinarei brevemente o contexto de naturalização da tortura no período democrático no Brasil e algumas hipóteses sobre os desdobramentos dessa prática nos próximos anos, considerando o contexto Latino-americano e a influência das práticas do exército francês durante o processo de independência de suas ex-colônias.

PALAVRAS-CHAVE. Tortura, democracia, direitos humanos, psicanálise.

Millennium Starts: Morphological and Seminal Embryos of Contemporary Brazilian Literature
ROBERTO VECCHI

ABSTRACT. It is always challenging to approach Brazilian literature — for its vitality and richness — through any simplistic scheme, which may make quite difficult a critic's gesture of cutting and selecting of some condition in order to make it represent complex and partially indecipherable movements. At the same time, it is worth recalling that Brazilian literature and arts are among the most powerful archives of the country's functioning, capable of grasping some deep figures of a plural, inexhaustible and metamorphic society such as the Brazilian one, constantly criss-crossed by violent historical turbulences, as in the last two decades. With the aim of avoiding what could be simply a long list or a mapping of works, the present article, inspired by the principle of Foucauldian genealogy, tackles a couple of embryonic authors at the threshold of the present millennium. Their legacy, in a certain way, has been drafting the porous horizons of contemporary literary tendencies, creating also strong echoes not only limited within the literary field, but also in the strict, internal dialogue of a structural hendiadys for the Brazilian culture, that is, literature and society. In this perspective, authors such as Luiz Ruffato and Rubens Figueiredo have been forging through their works a peculiar literary space, which is turning their aesthetical engagement in significant and exemplary beginnings of a new millennium's literary season. It is an alternative way in order to rethink a different ontology of Brazilian literature, in harsh, controversial times.

KEYWORDS. Public space in Brazilian literature, common, public means, contemporary Brazilian literature, literary topographies.

RESUMO. É sempre um desafio aproximar-se da literatura brasileira — pelo seu vitalismo e pela sua riqueza — através de um esquema único, que torna problemático o gesto crítico de cortar e selecionar algumas condições para fazer com que representem os movimentos complexos e parcialmente indecifráveis dessa literatura. Ao mesmo tempo, vale a pena lembrar que a literatura e as artes brasileiras representam arquivos fundamentais do Brasil, capazes de fixar algumas figuras profundas de uma sociedade plural, inexaurível e metamórfica como a brasileira, sempre atravessada por violentas turbulências históricas, como foi nas últimas duas décadas. Evitando um elenco ou um mapeamento esquemáticos de obras, o artigo, inspirado na ideia de genealogia, analisa dois romances embrionários no limiar do novo milênio. Seu legado de certo modo contribuiu para criar o horizonte poroso das tendências literárias contemporâneas cujo eco não se limita ao campo literário, mas também ao diálogo interno de uma hendíadis ontológica para a cultura brasileira, literatura e sociedade. Nesta perspetiva, autores como Luiz Ruffato e Rubens Figueiredo configuraram através da obra um espaço literário peculiar, que transforma o engajamento estético em inícios significativos e exemplares de uma nova estação literária do novo milênio. Um modo alternativo para repensar as diferentes ontologias da literatura brasileira, em tempos difíceis e controversos.

PALAVRAS-CHAVE. Espaço público na literatura brasileira, comum, meios públicos, literatura brasileira contemporânea, topografias literárias.

The Predicament of Contemporary Brazilian Fiction and its Spatiotemporal Modalities
KARL ERIK SCHØLLHAMMER

ABSTRACT. This article will argue that the irruption of the present economic and political crises reveals a challenge to a certain optimism that enveloped the discourse of the contemporary since the beginning of the century. Through the readings of a small selection of novels from 2018 and 2019, by the writers Joca Reiners Terron, Chico Buarque de Holanda, Ana Paula Maia, Itamar Vieira Junior, Luiz Ruffato and Milton Hatoum, we will analyse divergent historical perspectives revealed by these narratives as implicit or explicit intervention into the present authoritarian brutalization of the national self-fashioning. In *Essa Gente*, the author's ambition aims to dive into the 'presence of the present' in a hallucinatory simultaneity with political occurrences; *Torto Arado* by Itamar Vieira Junior offers another dimension of the anachronical actuality of the traumatic past of slavery; while *Verão Tardio* by Luiz Ruffato dives into the melancholic return of the main character to a past he cannot get rid of. In Joca Reiners Terron's *A Morte e o Meteoro* and in *Enterrem seus Mortos* by Ana Paula Maia the retrofuturistic narratives expose the ongoing extermination of indigenous cultures in the Amazon region and the latency of the anthropocene through human interaction with animal nature.

KEYWORDS. The contemporary closure, historical perspectives in present fiction, spatial challenges to national literature.

RESUMO. Este artigo argumentará que a irrupção da atual crise econômica e política revela um desafio de certo otimismo que vem envolvendo o discurso do contemporâneo desde o início do século. Por meio das leituras de uma pequena seleção de romances de 2018 e 2019, dos escritores Joca Reiners Terron, Chico Buarque de Holanda, Ana Paula Maia, Itamar Vieira Junior, Luiz Ruffato e Milton Hatoum, analisará perspetivas históricas divergentes reveladas por essas narrativas como intervenção implícita ou explícita na presente brutalização autoritária da imagem de si nacional. Em *Essa Gente*, a ambição do autor visa mergulhar na 'presença do presente' em uma simultaneidade alucinatória com acontecimentos políticos; *Torto Arado* de Itamar Vieira Junior oferece outra dimensão da contemporaneidade anacrônica do passado traumático da escravidão; enquanto *Verão Tardio* de Luiz Ruffato mergulha no retorno melancólico do protagonista a um passado do qual não consegue se livrar. Em *A Morte e o Meteoro* de Joca Reiners Terron e em *Enterrem seus Mortos* de Ana Paula Maia, as narrativas retrofuturísticas expõem o extermínio em curso de culturas indígenas na região amazônica e a latência do antropoceno por meio da interação do homem com a natureza animal.

PALAVRAS-CHAVE. O fechamento contemporâneo, perspetivas históricas na ficção atual, desafios espaciais para a literatura nacional.

The Arts as a Space of Memory and Resistance to Denialist Policies in Brazil Today
MÁRCIO SELIGMANN-SILVA

ABSTRACT. This article proposes a study of the gradual transformation of the artistic field over the last decade. This field at the beginning of the century was divided into two large groups. On the one hand, we had a production still predominantly linked to Modernity, to its abstract developments and that was contained within the scope of 'art for art's sake'. On the other hand, more and more active artists have emerged in the building of a resilient cultural memory including the agendas of gender and racial minorities. From the middle of the last decade, there has been also a new urgency in this field: the need to revise the history of Brazil, either to show continuities between the colonial past and our authoritarian present, or to retrieve the memory of the 1964–85 dictatorship, which until then was practically not thematized by post-dictatorial artists. The text discusses to what extent this artistic movement that proposes a historical revision can link a history of violence against minorities with the denial of the arbitrariness that characterized the dictatorial period. Politicians currently in power create educational programmes aimed at presenting the dictatorial period as the pinnacle of the country's history. In response to this revisionist and denialist movement, artists and academics are developing ways to record and present a counter-history that must underpin new political struggles that are now being articulated.

KEYWORDS. Art and dictatorship in Brazil, counter-memory, art and resistance, censorship.

RESUMO. O artigo propõe um estudo sobre a transformação gradual do campo artístico na última década. Este campo no início do século estava dividido em dois grandes grupos. Por um lado, tínhamos uma produção ainda predominantemente ligada à Modernidade, aos seus desdobramentos abstratos e que se inseria no âmbito da 'arte pela arte'. Por outro lado, mais e mais artistas ativos surgiram na construção de uma memória cultural resiliente, incluindo as agendas de gênero e minorias raciais. A partir de meados da última década, surgiu também uma nova urgência nesse campo: a necessidade de revisar a história do Brasil, seja para mostrar continuidades entre o passado colonial e nosso presente autoritário, seja para resgatar a memória dos anos 1964–85, que até então praticamente não era tematizada por artistas pós-ditatoriais. O texto discute em que medida esse movimento artístico que propõe uma revisão histórica pode vincular uma história de violência contra as minorias com a negação da arbitrariedade que caracterizou o período ditatorial. Políticos atualmente no poder criam programas educacionais com o objetivo de apresentar o período ditatorial como o auge da história do país. Em resposta a esse movimento revisionista e negador, artistas e acadêmicos estão desenvolvendo maneiras de registrar e apresentar uma contra-história que deve sustentar novas lutas políticas que agora estão sendo articuladas.

PALAVRAS-CHAVE. Arte e ditadura no Brasil, contra-memória, arte e resistência, censura.

From 'Flocking for Rights' to the Politics of Death: Indigenous Struggle and Indigenous Policy in Brazil (1980–2020)
OIARA BONILLA and ARTIONKA CAPIBERIBE

ABSTRACT. This article presents an overview of the recent history of the relations between indigenous peoples and the Brazilian state. While also looking back to the 1980s, the central focus of the article is on the public policies on development adopted by different governments over the last twenty years. It shows how these policies increasingly affected the lives of the indigenous peoples, taking strategic advantage of a weakening of the existing legislation in the country and a disregard for international guarantees, won over several decades of political struggle. The article analyses the harmful effects of these public policies, which have reached their apex in the present policy of death claimed and applied by the government of Jair Bolsonaro. Finally, the article demonstrates how the indigenous movement not only confronts, but reinvents forms of resistance to this catastrophic scenario.

KEYWORDS. Indigenous peoples of Brazil, violation of human rights, politics of development, land appropriation, deforestation, indigenous movement.

RESUMO. Este artigo apresenta um panorama sobre a história recente da relação entre povos indígenas e Estado brasileiro. Apesar de haver um recuo aos anos 1980, o foco central do artigo são as políticas públicas de desenvolvimento estabelecidas por diferentes governos, nos últimos vinte anos. O artigo mostra como tais políticas vêm crescentemente afetando a vida dos povos indígenas, valendo-se, estrategicamente, do enfraquecimento da legislação vigente no país e do desrespeito a garantias internacionais, conquistadas ao longo de várias décadas de luta política. O artigo analisa os efeitos deletérios dessas políticas públicas, que atingem seu ápice na atual política de morte reivindicada e aplicada pelo governo de Jair Bolsonaro. Por fim, o artigo demonstra como o movimento indígena não apenas enfrenta, mas reinventa formas de resistência neste cenário catastrófico.

PALAVRAS-CHAVE. Povos indígenas no Brasil, violação de direitos humanos, políticas de desenvolvimento, expropriação de terras, desmatamento, movimento indígena.

www.ingramcontent.com/pod-product-compliance
Lightning Source LLC
Chambersburg PA
CBHW071404290426
44108CB00014B/1673